JURISPRUDENCE SOURCEBOOK

Dennis Paling
BA, BCL, MLitt, PhD

HLT Publications

HLT PUBLICATIONS
200 Greyhound Road, London W14 9RY

First published 1992

ISBN 0 7510 0234 8

ACKNOWLEDGEMENT
The publishers and author would like to thank The Incorporated Council of Law Reporting for England and Wales for kind permission to reproduce extracts from the Weekly Law Reports.

British Library Cataloguing-in-Publication Data

Jurisprudence. – Sourcebook. – (Bachelor of Laws (LLB) Series)

I. Paling, Dennis II. Series
340

ISBN 0–7510–0234–8

Printed and bound in Great Britain

CONTENTS

Legal and Social Theory

PREFACE

This *Jurisprudence Sourcebook* is intended as a companion to the *Jurisprudence Textbook* published by HLT Publications. It endeavours to include key extracts from the principal sources referred to in the Textbook, and to follow the same sequence of chapter headings. As such it is not aimed at any particular syllabus, and some of the material included in both the Textbook and the Sourcebook may fall outside the scope of a particular examining body's requirements.

Having extracted passages from some of the leading authorities on Natural Law and Positivism, the Sourcebook proceeds to consider some of the minor schools of jurisprudence - Realism, Marxism, and Sociological, Historical Jurisprudence etc. Any student must, of course, have an understanding of the positions of such contemporary supporters of the theory of Natural Law as Dworkin, Rawls, Finnis and Fuller; and of the contrasting positions of Hart, Kelsen, Austin, Bentham and the positivists. But jurisprudence is not simply a Natural Law/Positivism debate. Others such as Holmes, Frank, Pound, Marx, Mill, Savigny, Maine or Olivecrona have something important to say.

This *Jurisprudence Sourcebook* is intended to be an aid in studying the Textbook, and therefore does not present a continuous narrative. However, it will assist the student who does not have ready access to a library.

ACKNOWLEDGEMENTS

We would like to thank the authors and publishers for their kind permission to reproduce extracts from the following:

Roger Cotterrell (1984) *The Sociology of Law: An Introduction*, Butterworths, London.

Roger Cotterrell (1989) *The Politics of Jurisprudence*, Butterworths, London.

Lord Denning (1981) *The Family Story*. Butterworths, London.

R W M Dias (1972) *Jurisprudence*, 5th edn. Butterworths, London.

Ronald Dworkin (1977) *Taking Rights Seriously*. Duckworth, London. By permission of Duckworth.

J Frank (1949) *Courts on Trial*. Sweet & Maxwell, London.

J Frank (1949) *Law and the Modern Mind*, English edition. Sweet & Maxwell, London.

Robert Freedman (1969) *Marx on Economics*. Pelican Books, London

L L Fuller (1949) 'The Case of the Speluncean Explorers'. *Harvard Law Review*, Massachusetts

L L Fuller (1969) 'Human Interaction and the Law'. 14 *American Journal of Jurisprudence* 1.

Gerald Gardiner (1958) 'The Purpose of Criminal Punishment'. 21 *Modern Law Review* 117 at 122-125.

Sir Ernest Gowers (1954) *The Complete Plain Words*. HMSO, London. Reproduced with the permission of the Controller of HMSO

H L A Hart (1958) 'Positivism and the Separation of Law and Morals'. 71 *Harvard Law Review*, Massachusetts.

H L A Hart (1954) 'Definition and Theory in Jurisprudence'. 70 *Law Quarterly Review* 37. Sweet & Maxwell, London

R F V Heuston (1986) 'Judicial Prospography'. 102 *Law Quarterly Review* 90. Sweet & Maxwell, London.

Hans Kelsen 'The Pure Theory of Law'. (1934) 50 *Law Quarterly Review;* (1935) 51 *Law Quarterly Review*. Sweet & Maxwell, London.

Lee Loevinger (1949) 'Jurimetrics - The Next Step Forward'. *Minnesota Law Review*. © University of Minnesota Law School, Minneapolis.

P Milton (1984) 'Review of H L A Hart "Essays in Jurisprudence and Philosophy" and Neil MacCormick "H L Hart" '. 47 *Modern Law Review* 751.

Karl Olivecrona (1971) *Law as Fact,* 2nd edition. Sweet & Maxwell, London.

D Pannick (1980) 'A Note on Dworkin and Precedent.' 43 *Modern Law Review* 36.

J Stone (1966) *Law and the Social Sciences.* University of Minnesota Press, Minneapolis. © Minnesota Press

E P Thompson (Allen Lane, 1975) *Whigs and Hunters.* Penguin Books, London. © E P Thompson, 1975.

Nigel West (Robert Allason MP) *MI5: British Security Service Operations 1909-1945.* The Bodley Head, London

A Wilson (1981) 'The Imperative Fallacy in Kelsen's Theory.' 44 *Modern Law Review* 751.

The Method and Point of Jurisprudence

1. THE NATURE OF JURISPRUDENCE

R W M DIAS
Jurisprudence [1]
(1972)

Jurisprudence was the first of the social sciences to be born', said Wurzel[2] ...

The Latin expression, *juris prudentia*, means either 'knowledge of' or 'skill in law'. The Roman jurists, however, never developed any such subject as *'jurisprudentia'*[3]. In the sense of 'knowledge of law', the word sometimes describes expositions of particular branches of the law, eg the name 'Equity Jurisprudence' was once given to a textbook on Equity[4]. This use of the word, current on the Continent, is no longer fashionable in common law countries. In a wide sense 'jurisprudence' is used also to describe the legal connections of any body of knowledge: so 'Dental Jurisprudence', 'Architectural Jurisprudence' or 'Medical Jurisprudence' would be titles for expositions of such aspects of dentistry, architecture or medicine as may be important in law. Some criticisms of this use of the term are somewhat misconceived. There has been a tendency to suppose that the word 'jurisprudence' has, or should have, some 'proper' meaning, which makes it inapplicable to this kind of study[5]. As will appear, no word, least of all 'jurisprudence', has a 'proper' meaning. There is also the argument that such studies as these are not 'scientific'[6], which presupposes some special meaning of the word 'science'. The reason for avoiding a term like 'medical jurisprudence' is that this kind of expression is no longer current in English-speaking countries, although occasional instances may still be found[7]. It may be noted that in French law *la jurisprudence* is the term applied to the body of law built up by the decisions of particular courts'[8].

In England it was not until the time of Bentham and his disciple Austin in the

---

[1] Dias, RWM (1985) *Jurisprudence*, 5th edn Butterworths, London, p3.

[2] Wurzel 'Methods of Juridical Thinking' in *Science of Legal Method: Select Essays*, p289

[3] Ulpian's remark in the *Digest*, quoted in the opening of Justinian's *Institutes*, *'Juris prudentia est divinarum atque humanarum rerum notitia, justia atque injusti scientia'* (D 1.1.10.2; *Inst* 1.1.1: jurisprudence is the concept of things divine and human, knowledge of the just and the unjust), was only a piece of rhetoric not pursued by the Romans.

[4] Ames *Equity Jurisprudence.* See the comments of Stone *The Province and Function of Law*, p26.

[5] Holand *Jurisprudence* p4, n4.

[6] Gray *The Nature and Sources of the Law*, pp134, 147.

[7] The term 'medico–legal jurisprudence' has largely been superseded by 'forensic medicine'.

[8] The equivalent of 'jurisprudence' in its Anglo-American sense is *Théorie Générale de Droit*.

early part of the nineteenth century that the word began to acquire a technical significance among English lawyers[9]. The former distinguished between examination of the law as it is and as it ought to be ('expositorial' and 'censorial' jurisprudence), and he was also much concerned with law reform ('deontology'). The latter, who was the first Professor of Jurisprudence in the University of London, occupied himself with 'expository' jurisprudence, and his work consisted mainly of a formal analysis of the structure of English law. Analytical exposition of the type which Bentham pioneered, and Austin developed, has dominated English legal thought almost to the present. It was therefore inevitable that the word 'jurisprudence' came to mean in this country almost exclusively the analysis of the formal structure of law and its concepts. This was the nearest that the word came to bearing a precise meaning.

Towards the end of the nineteenth century changing human affairs had brought about an ever-increasing preoccupation with conflicting ideologies and troubled social conditions, which resulted in a decisive shift in outlook with the result that jurisprudence came to be envisaged in a broader sense than in Austin's day. Buckland described the change vividly. 'The analysis of legal concepts', he said[10], 'is what jurisprudence meant for the student in the days of my youth. In fact it meant Austin. He was a religion; today he seems to be regarded rather as a disease'. The breadth of the modern attitude is well summed up by Julius Stone who described jurisprudence as:

> 'The lawyers extraversion. It is the lawyer's examination of the precepts, ideals, and techniques of the law in the light derived from present knowledge in disciplines other than the law'[11].

So vast a coverage may be summed up in the proposition that jurisprudential study nowadays concerns thought about law, its nature, function and functioning, on the broadest possible basis, and about its adaptation, improvement and reform.

THOUGHT ABOUT LAW

Writings on jurisprudence are not concerned with expositions *of* law, but with disquisitions *about* law[12]. Various branches of substantive law[12], for example, teach how rights and duties are acquired, whereas jurisprudence would investigate such questions as What are rights and duties? How are they used? How do they work? It also improves the use of law by drawing together insights from different branches, criminal, constitutional etc, in the solution of problems. Thought about law is also a story of movements in outlook and ever-changing ideas, and developments are taking place in contemporary physical, moral and other sciences, which make it difficult to decide once and for all how, if at all, these should be taken into account.

---

[9] For their work, see chs 6 and 8 post.
[10] Buckland *Some Reflections on Jurisprudence*, p2.
[11] Stone *Legal System and Lawyers' Reasonings*, p16.
[12] King 'Propositions about Law' (1951) 11 *Criminal Law Journal* 31.

2. LANGUAGE AND THE LAW: THE PROBLEM OF DEFINITION

H L A HART

Definition and Theory in Jurisprudence [1]

(1954)

Long ago Bentham issued a warning that legal words demanded a special method of elucidation, and he enunciated a principle that is the beginning of wisdom in this matter, though it is not the end. He said we must never take these words alone, but consider whole sentences in which they play their characteristic role. We must take not the *word* 'right' but the sentence 'You have a right', not the *word* 'State' but the sentence 'He is a member of an official of the State'[2]. His warning has largely been disregarded and jurists have continued to hammer away at single words.

. . .

1. First, let us take words like 'right' or 'duty' or the names of corporations, not alone but in examples of typical contexts where these words are at work. Consider them when used in statements made on a particular occasion by a judge or an ordinary lawyer. They will be statements such as 'A has a right to be paid £10 by B.'; 'A is under a duty to fence off his machinery.'; 'A & Company Ltd have a contract with B.'. It is obvious that the use of these sentences silently assumes a special and very complicated setting, namely the existence of a legal system with all that this implies by way of general obedience, the operation of the sanctions of the system, and the general likelihood that this will continue. But though this complex situation is assumed in the use of these statements of rights or duties they do not *state* that it exists. There is a parallel situation in a game. 'He is out' said in the course of a game of cricket has as its proper context the playing of the game, with all that this implies by way of general compliance by both the players and the officials of the game in the past, present, and future. Yet one who says 'He is out'

---

[1] Hart, H L A 'Definition and Theory in Jurisprudence' (1954) 70 *Law Quarterly Review* 37.

[2] See *A Fragment on Government*, ch. V, notes to section v: § (5) 'For expounding the words duty, right, title, and those other terms of the same stamp that abound so much in ethics and jurisprudence either I am much deceived or the only method by which any instruction can be conveyed is that which is here exemplified. An exposition framed after this method I would term paraphrase. § (6) A word may be said to be expounded by paraphrases when not that word alone is translated into other words but some whole sentence of which it forms part is translated into another sentence. § (7) The common method of defining – the method *per genus et differentiam* as logicians calls it, will in many cases not at all answer the purpose.'

does not *state* that a game is being played or that the players and officials will comply with the rules. 'He is out' is an expression used to appeal to rules, to make claims, or give decisions under them; it is not a statement *about* the rules to the effect that they will be enforced or acted on in a given case, nor any other kind of statement *about* them. The analysis of statements of rights and duties as predictions ignores this distinction, yet it is just as erroneous to say that 'A has a right' is a prediction that a court or official will treat A in a certain way as to say that 'He is out' is a prediction that the umpire is likely to order the batsman off the field or the scorer to mark him out. No doubt, when someone has a legal right a corresponding prediction will normally be justified, but this should not lead us to identify two quite different forms of statement.

2. If we take 'A has a right to be paid £10 by B' as an example, we can see what the distinctive function of this form of statement is. For it is clear that as well as presupposing the existence of a legal system, the use of this statement has also a special connection with a particular rule of the system. This would be made explicit if we asked 'Why has A this right?' For the appropriate answer could only consist of two things: first, the statement of some rule or rules of law (say those of Contract), under which given certain facts certain legal consequences follow; and secondly, a statement that these facts were here the case. But again it is important to see that one who says that 'A has a right' does not *state* the relevant rule of law; and that though, given certain facts, it is correct to say 'A has a right', one who says this does not state or describe those facts. He has done something different from either of these two things: he has drawn a conclusion from the relevant but unstated rule, and from the relevant but unstated facts of the case. 'A has a right', like 'He is out', is therefore the tail-end of a simple legal calculation: it records a result and may be well called a conclusion of law. It is not therefore used to predict the future, as the American Realists say; it refers to the present, as their opponents claim, but unlike ordinary statements does not do this by describing present or continuing facts. This it is – this matter of principle – and not the existence of stray exceptions for lunatics or infants – that frustrates the definition of a right in factual terms such as expectations or powers. A paralysed man watching the thief's hand close over his gold watch is properly said to have a right to retain it as against the thief, though he has neither expectation nor power in any ordinary sense of these words. This is possible just because the expression 'a right' in this case does not describe or stand for any expectation, or power, or indeed anything else, but has meaning only as part of a sentence the function of which as a whole is to draw a conclusion of law from a specific kind of legal rule.

3. A third peculiarity is this: the assertion 'Smith has a right to be paid £10' said by a judge in deciding the case has a different status from the utterance of it out of court, where it may be used to make a claim, or an admission and in many other ways. The judge's utterance is official, authoritative, and, let us assume, final; the other is none of these things, yet in spite of these differences the sentences are of the same sort: they are both conclusions of law. We can compare this similarity in

spite of differences with 'He is out' said by the umpire in giving his decision and said by a player to make a claim. Now of course the unofficial utterance may have to be withdrawn in the light of a later official utterance, but this is not a sufficient reason for treating the first as a prophecy of the last, for plainly not all mistakes are mistaken predictions. Nor surely need the finality of a judge's decision either be confused with infallibility or tempt us to *define* laws in terms of what courts do, even though there are many laws which the courts must first interpret before they can apply them. We can acknowledge that what the scorer says is final; yet we can still abstain from defining the notion of a score as what the scorer says. And we can admit that the umpire may be wrong in his decision though the rules give us no remedy if he is and though there may be doubtful cases which he has to decide with but little help from the rules.

4. In any system, legal or not, rules may for excellent practical reasons attach identical consequences to any one of a set of very different facts. The rule of cricket attaches the same consequence to the batsman's being bowled, stumped, or caught. And the word 'out' is used in giving decisions or making claims under the rule, and in other verbal applications of it. It is easy to see here that no one of these different ways of being out is more essentially what the word means than the others, and that there need be nothing common to all these ways of being out other than their falling under the same rule, though there *may* be some similarity or analogy between them.[3] But it is less easy to see this in those important cases where rules treat a *sequence* of different actions or states of affairs in a way which unifies them. In a game a rule may simply attach a single consequence to the successive actions of a set of different men – as when a team is said to have won a game. A more complex rule may prescribe that what is to be done at one point in a sequence shall depend on what was done or occurred earlier; and it may be indifferent to the identity of the persons concerned in the sequence so long as they fall under certain defining conditions. An example of this is when a team permitted by the rules of a tournament to have a varying membership is penalised only in the third round – when the membership has changed – for what was done in the first round. In all such cases a sequence of action or states of affairs is unified simply by falling under certain rules; they *may* be

[3] Yet neglect of just these features of the language of rules has complicated the exposition of the concept of possession. Here the word is, of course, ambiguous as between (i) certain legal consequences attached to certain kinds of fact and (ii) those kinds of fact. But when we come to define the word in the second of these uses we are liable to assume that there is something which really or essentially is 'possession in fact' independent of any legal system, and that there is something *illogical* in the terminology of a legal system if it does not confine its use of the word 'possession' to this (see Paton *Jurisprudence*, 2nd edn, p461). But the only meaning of 'possession' which is independent of the rules of a legal system is the vague meaning in common non-legal usage, and there is no logical vice in disregarding this. Or again we may assume that there *must* be some single factor common to all the diverse cases which are treated alike by the rules. This will lead us either, as the classical theories do, to select one predominant case as a paradigm and to degrade the rest to the level of 'exceptions', or to obscure the real diversity of the facts with expository devices ('constructive' or 'fictitious' possession). Preoccupation with the search for some common feature is apt in either case to divert us from the important inquiries, which are (1) what for any given legal system are the conditions under which possessory rights are acquired and lost; (2) what general features of the given system and what practical reasons lead to diverse cases being treated alike in this respect. Cf Kocourek (1927) *Jural Relations*. Indianapolis, ch. XX, passim, on 'continuing possession' and 'legal possession'.

otherwise as different as you please. Here can be seen the essential elements of the language of legal corporations. For in law, the lives of ten men that overlap but do not coincide may fall under separate rules under which they have separate rights and duties, and then they are a collection of individuals for the law; but their actions may fall under rules of a different kind which make what is to be done by any one or more of them depend in complex ways on what was done or occurred earlier. And then we may speak in appropriately unified ways of the sequence so unified, using a terminology like that of corporation law which will show that it is *this* sort of rule we are applying to the facts. But here the unity of the rule may mislead us when we come to define this terminology. It may cast a shadow: we may look for an identical continuing thing or person or quality *in* the sequence. We may find it – in 'corporate spirit'. This is real enough; but it is a secret of success not a criterion of identity.

These four general characteristics of legal language explain both why definition of words like 'right', 'duty' and 'corporation' is baffled by the absence of some counterpart to 'correspond' to these words, and also why the unobvious counterparts which have been so ingeniously contrived – the future facts, the complex facts, or the psychological facts – turn out not to be something in terms of which we can define these words, although to be connected with them in complex or indirect ways. The fundamental point is that the primary function of these words[4] is not to stand for or describe anything but a distinct function; this makes it vital to attend to Bentham's warning that we should not, as does the traditional method of definition, abstract words like 'right' and 'duty', 'State' or 'corporation' from the sentences in which alone their full function can be seen, and then demand of them so abstracted their genus and differentia.

Let us see what the use of this traditional method of definition presupposes and what the limits of its efficacy are, and why it may be misleading. It is of course the simplest form of definition, and also a peculiarly satisfying form because it gives us a set of words which can always be substituted for the word defined whenever it is used; it gives us a comprehensible synonym or translation for the word which puzzles us. It is peculiarly appropriate where the words have the straightforward function of standing for some kind of thing, or quality, person, process, or event, for here we are not mystified or puzzled about the general characteristics of our subject-matter, but we ask for a definition simply to locate within this familiar general kind or class some special subordinate kind or class.[5] Thus since we are not puzzled about the general notions of furniture or animal we can take a word like 'chair' or 'cat' and

---

[4] Lawyers might best understand the distinctive function of such expressions as 'He has a right' and others which I discuss here, by comparing them to the *operative* words of a conveyance as distinct from the *descriptive* words of the recitals. The point of similarity is that 'He has a right', like 'X hereby conveys', is used to *operate with* legal rules and not to state or describe facts. Of course there are great differences: one who says 'He has a right' operates with a rule by drawing a conclusion from it, whereas one who uses operative words in a conveyance does something to which the rule attaches legal consequences.

[5] Bentham's reason for rejecting the common method of defining legal words was that 'among such abstract terms we soon come to such as have no superior genus. A definition *per genus et differentiam* when applied to these it is manifest can make no advance ... As well in short were it to define in this manner a proposition or a conjunction ... a *through* is a ... a *because* is is a ... and so go on defining them? *A Fragment on Government, ubi sup.*

give the principle of its use by first specifying the general class to which what it is used to describe belongs, and then going on to define the specific differences that mark it off from other species of the same general kind. And of course if we are *not* puzzled about the general notion of a corporate body but only wish to know how one species (say a college) differs form another (say a limited company) we can use this form of definition of single words perfectly well. But just because the method is appropriate at this level of inquiry, it cannot help us when our perplexities are deeper. For if our question arises, as it does with fundamental legal notions because we are puzzled about the general category to which something belongs and how some general type of expression relates to fact, and not merely about the place within that category, then until the puzzle is cleared up this form of definition is at the best unilluminating and at the worst profoundly misleading. It is unilluminating because a mode of definition designed to locate some subordinate species within some familiar category cannot elucidate the characteristics of some anomalous category; and it is misleading because it will suggest that what is in fact an anomalous category is after all some species of the familiar. Hence if applied to legal words like 'right', 'duty', 'State', or 'corporation' the common mode of definition suggests that these words like ordinary words stand for or describe some thing, person, quality, process, or event; when the difficulty of finding these becomes apparent, different contrivances varying with tastes are used to explain or explain away the anomaly. Some say the difference is that the things for which these legal words stand are real but not sensory, others that they are fictitious entities, others that these words stand for plain fact but of a complex, future, or psychological variety. So this standard mode of definition forces our familiar triad of theories into existence as a confused way of accounting for the anomalous character of legal words.

How then shall we define such words? If definition is the provision of a synonym which will not equally puzzle us these words cannot be defined. But I think there is a method of elucidation of quite general application and which we can call definition, if we wish. Bentham and others practised it, though they did not preach it. But before applying it to the highly complex legal cases, I shall illustrate it from the simple case of a game. Take the notion of a trick in a game of cards. Somebody says 'What is a trick?' and you reply 'I will explain: when you have a game and among its rules is one providing that when each of our players has played a card then the player who has put down the highest card scores a point, in these circumstances that play is said to have "taken a trick".' This natural explanation has not taken the form of a definition of the single word 'trick': no synonym has been offered for it. Instead we have taken a sentence in which the word 'trick' plays its characteristic role and explained it first by specifying the conditions under which the whole sentence is true, and secondly by showing how it is used in drawing a conclusion from the rules in a particular case. Suppose now that after such an explanation your questioner presses on: 'That is all very well, that explains "taking a trick"; but I still want to know what the word "trick" means just by itself. I want a definition of "trick"; I want some thing which can be substituted for it whenever it is used.' If we yield to this demand for a single word definition we might reply: 'The trick is just a collective name for the four cards.' But someone may object: 'The trick is not just a name for the four cards because these four cards will not always constitute a trick. It must therefore be some entity to which the four cards belong.' A third might say: 'No, the trick is a fictitious entity which the players pretend exists and to which by fiction which is part of the game they ascribe the cards.' But in so simple a case we would not tolerate these theories, fraught as they are with mystery and empty of any guidance as to the use made of the word within the game: we would stand by the original two-fold explanation; for this surely gave us all we needed when it explained the conditions under which the statement 'He has taken a trick' is true and showed us how it was used in drawing a conclusion from the rules in a particular case.

If we turn back to Bentham we shall find that when his explanation of legal notions is illuminating, as it very often is, it conforms to this method, though only loosely. Yet curiously what he tells us to do is something different: it is to take a word like 'right' or 'duty' or 'State'; to embody it in a sentence such as 'you have a right' where it plays a characteristic role, and then to find a *translation* of it into what we should call factual terms. This he called the method of paraphrase - giving phrase for phrase, not word for word. Now this method is applicable to many cases and has shed much light; but it distorts many legal words like 'right' or 'duty' whose characteristic role is not played in statements of fact but in conclusions of law. A paraphrase of these in factual terms is not possible, and when Bentham proffers such a paraphrase it turns out not to be one at all.

But more often and much to our profit he does not claim to paraphrase: but he makes a different kind of remark, in order to elucidate these words ... They are not paraphrases but they specify some of the conditions necessary for the truth of a sentence of the form 'You have a right'. Bentham shows us how these conditions include the existence of a law imposing a duty on some other person; and moreover, that it must be a law which provides that the breach of the duty shall be visited with a sanction if you or someone on your behalf so choose. This has many virtues. By refusing to identify the meaning of the word 'right' with any psychological or physical fact it correctly leaves open the question whether on any given occasion a person who has a right has in fact any expectation or power; and so it leaves us free to treat men's expectations or powers as what in general men will have if there is a system of rights, and as part of what a system of rights is generally intended to secure. Some of the improvements which should be made on Bentham's efforts are obvious. Instead of characterising a right in terms of punishment many would do so in terms of the remedy. But I would prefer to show the special position of one who has a right by mentioning not the remedy but the choice which is open to one who has a right as to whether the corresponding duty shall be performed or not. For it is, I think, characteristic of those laws that confer rights (as distinguished from those that only impose obligations) that the obligation to perform the corresponding duty is made by law to depend on the choice of the individual who is said to have the right or the choice of some person authorised to act on his behalf.

I would, therefore, tender the following as an elucidation of the expression 'a legal right': (1) A statement of the form 'X has a right' is true if the following conditions are satisfied:

(a)   There is in existence a legal system.

(b)   Under a rule or rules of the system some other person Y is, in the events which have happened, obliged to do or abstain from some action.

(c)   This obligation is made by law dependent on the choice either of X or some other person authorised to act on his behalf so that either Y is bound to do or abstain from some action only if X (or some authorised person) so chooses or alternatively only until X (or such person) chooses otherwise.

(1) A statement of the form 'X has a right' is used to draw a conclusion of law in a particular case which falls under such rules.[6]

SIR ERNEST GOWERS
The Complete Plain Words [7]
(1954)

A DIGRESSION ON LEGAL ENGLISH

> Even where the Counsel in chambers is merely 'advising on a case' or drawing up a conveyance of property, he is really thinking of what view the court and the judges will take of his advice or his draftsmanship if any dispute arises on them. ... The supreme test in every case is: "Will this stand the scrutiny of the Court?"

> Stephens *Commentaries on the Laws of England*

The peculiarities of legal English are often used as a stick to beat the official with. They are cited (to quote a typical comment) to show that 'it would be a herculean task to teach the Civil Service to write its own language creditably'. The style in which Acts of Parliament are written is contemptuously called 'official jargon'. That the style has peculiarities cannot be denied, but if it is jargon – an arguable question – its species is the legal not the official. It is written by lawyers, not by civil servants (in the sense in which the critics use the term), and its peculiarities arise from causes exactly opposite to those of the peculiarities alleged against officials. Those of the one come from a desire to convey a precise meaning; those of the other – so it is said – come too often from a reluctance to convey any meaning at all. The only

---

[6] This deals only with a right in the first sense (correlative to duty) distinguished by Hohfeld. But the same form of elucidation can be used for the cases of 'liberty', 'power', and 'immunity', and will I think show what is usually left unexplained, viz why these four varieties in spite of differences are referred to as 'rights'. The unifying element seems to be this: in all four cases the law specifically recognises the *choice* of an individual either negatively by not impeding or obstructing it (liberty and immunity) or affirmatively by giving legal effect to it (claim and power). In the negative cases there is no law to interfere if the individual chooses to do or abstain from some action (liberty) or to retain his legal position unchanged (immunity); in the affirmative cases the law gives legal effect to the choice of an individual that some other person shall do or shall abstain from some action.

[7] Gowers, E *The Complete Plain Words* (1954), HMSO, London, pp8-10, 12.

difference between the language of Acts of Parliament and that of private legal documents is that in the skilled and experienced hands of Parliamentary Counsel its inevitable peculiarities are less obtrusive and ungraceful than they are in the hands of the ordinary private practitioner. Such as they are, they are caused by the necessity of being unambiguous. That is by no means the same as being readily intelligible; on the contrary, the nearer you get to the one the further you are likely to get from the other.

The reason why certainty of meaning must be the paramount aim is clear enough. These documents impose obligations and confer rights, and neither the parties to them nor the draftsmen of them have the last word in deciding exactly what those rights and obligations are. That can only be settled in a Court of Law on the words of the document. If anyone is to be held irrevocably to meaning what he says, he must be very careful to say what he means. And words are an imperfect instrument for expressing complicated concepts with certainty; only mathematics can be sure of doing that. As Dr Glanville Williams has pointed out in this connexion, 'words have a penumbra of uncertainty'. He writes:

The ordinary man is not usually troubled with these perplexities. It does not matter to the seaman whether an anchor is or is not called part of a vessel. A chemist does not need to answer the question, yes or no, does a rolled-gold watch come within the description gold. Biologists may find difficulty with their classification, but nothing turns on the question whether they classify a creature under one head or another: it is simply a question of verbal expediency. With the lawyer it is different. The lawyer, like the theologian, is faced with a number of texts that he regards as authoritative and that are supposed to settle any question that can conceivably arise. Each text was once drawn up by someone who presumably meant something by it; but once the document has left its author's hands it is the document that matters, not any unexpressed meaning that still remains in the author's mind. For the lawyer the words of the document are authoritative as words and there is no possibility of obtaining further information from the author, either because the author is dead or because of the rules of evidence precluding reference to him.[8]

It is accordingly the duty of a draftsman of these authoritative texts to try to imagine every possible combination of circumstances to which his words might apply and every conceivable misinterpretation that might be put on them, and to take precautions accordingly. He must avoid all graces, not be afraid of repetitions, or even of identifying them by *aforesaids*; he must limit by definition words with a penumbra dangerously large, and amplify with a string of near-synonyms words with a penumbra dangerously small; he must eschew all pronouns when their antecedents might possibly be open to dispute, and generally avoid every potential grammatical ambiguity. (An application for quashing a New Towns Order turned on the true antecedent of a *thereto*.) All the time he must keep his eye on the rules of legal interpretation and the case-law on the meaning of particular words, and choose his

---

[8] 'Language and the Law' (1945) *Law Quarterly Review*.

phraseology to fit them. (Previous judicial interpretations of the word *money* compelled the beneficiaries under a will to take a case to the House of Lords in order to establish that *money* meant what everyone knew the testatrix had intended it to mean.) No one can expect pretty writing from anyone thus burdened. A well-meant attempt was made by the Minister in charge of the Bill that became the Workmen's Compensation Act 1906 to make perfectly clear to ordinary people what sort of accidents gave rise to a right to compensation; he insisted on using the simple words 'arising out of and in the course of' the employment. Simplicity proved to have been bought at such cost in precision that those words must have caused more litigation than any other eight words on the Statute Book. *Halsbury's Laws of England* takes more than 38 pages to explain the phrase and cite the cases on it.

. . .

[Consider] this extract from the Shops (Sunday Trading Restriction) Act 1936:

> '... the following provisions of this Act shall extend only to shops, that is to say, those provisions of section six and section eight which relate to the approval by occupiers of shops of orders made under those sections, the provisions of paragraph (e) of subsection (1) of section seven and the provisions of paragraph (a) of section twelve.'

If example were needed to prove that legal language cannot be elegant or luminous, this would serve well enough. But that needs no proof; everyone knows it. To a reader with the Act before him (and he cannot expect to understand it unless he has) the meaning that this subsection conveys is precise: it says unambiguously that certain provisions of the Act apply to trading only in shops and that all the others apply to trading not only in shops, but also in any place that is not a shop. The trouble in this case arose not from any obscurity in the words quoted, but from the penumbra round the word *place* used in another section. The Court held that it was not as large as the draftsman had thought. He had naturally assumed that, when he had covered both sales in shops and sales in places that are not shops, he had left nothing outside. But he was wrong. He forgot the stop-me-and-buy-one man. The Court held that the ice-cream vendor's tricycle is neither a shop nor a place; and the bit of ground on which it happened to be standing is not a place either. His sales are therefore outside both categories, and he escapes the meshes of the Act. This curious instance of the waywardness of words shows how hard it is for the draftsman to foresee every possible path down which the judicial mind may be led by what he writes, and also provides another illustration of the truth that legal ambiguities are caused more often by over-simplicity of dictation than by over-elaboration.

3. LAW AS AN
ARGUMENTATIVE ATTITUDE

R v Dudley and Stephens (1884) 14 QBD 273

A man who, in order to escape death from hunger, kills another for the purpose of eating his flesh, is guilty of murder although, at the time of the act, he is in such circumstances that he believes, and has reasonable grounds for believing, that it affords the only chance of saving his life.

Dudley and Stephens were charged at the Devon Assizes with the murder of a boy.

The prisoners, the deceased and a fourth person were shipwrecked, and cast adrift in an open boat a thousand miles from land. After eighteen days, by which time they had been without food for seven days, and without water for five days, the prisoners decided to kill the deceased in order that they might eat his body. On the 20th day, Dudley, with the assent of Stephens (the fourth man refusing to assent), knifed the deceased who, on account of his youth, was in a weaker state than any other member of the party, and who in no way assented to his death. The three survivors lived on the flesh of the deceased for a further four days, after which they were picked up by a passing ship. At the time the boy was killed, there was no reasonable prospect of relief, and there was every probability that, unless the prisoners ate the deceased, or one of the other members of the party, they would have died of starvation.

On these findings, Huddleston B adjourned the case for argument before five judges in the Queen's Bench Divisional Court where the accused were held guilty of murder.

LORD COLERIDGE, CJ: '... it appears sufficiently that the prisoners were subject to terrible temptation, to sufferings which might break down the bodily power of the strongest man, and try the conscience of the best. Other details yet more harrowing, facts still more loathsome and appalling, were presented to the jury, and are to be found recorded in my learned Brother's notes. But nevertheless this is clear, that the prisoners put to death a weak and unoffending boy upon the chance of preserving their own lives by feeding upon his flesh and blood after he was killed, and with the certainty of depriving him of any possible chance of survival ...

There remains to be considered the real question in the case - whether killing under the circumstances set forth in the verdict be or be not murder. The contention that it could be anything else was, to the minds of us all, both new and strange, and we stopped the Attorney-General in his negative argument in order that we might hear what could be said in support of a proposition which appeared to us to be at once dangerous, immoral, and opposed to all legal principle and analogy. All, no doubt, that can be said has been urged before us, and we are now to consider and determine what it amounts to. First it is said that it follows from various definitions of murder in books of authority, which definitions imply, if they do not state, the doctrine, that in order to save your own life you may lawfully take away the life of another, when that other is neither attempting nor threatening yours, nor is guilty of any illegal act whatever towards you or anyone else. But if these definitions be looked at they will not be found to sustain this contention.

... Decided cases there are none ... The American case cited by my brother Stephen in his Digest, from Wharton on Homicide, in which it was decided, correctly indeed, that sailors had no right to throw passengers overboard to save themselves, but on the somewhat strange ground that the proper mode of determining who was to be sacrificed was to vote upon the subject by ballot, can hardly, as my brother Stephen says, be an authority satisfactory to a court in this country ...

Now, except for the purpose of testing how far the conservation of a man's own life is in all cases and under all circumstances, an absolute, unqualified, and paramount duty, we exclude from our consideration all the incidents of war. We are dealing with a case of private homicide, not one imposed upon young men in the service of their Sovereign and in the defence of their country. Now it is admitted that the deliberate killing of this unoffending and unresisting boy was clearly murder, unless the killing can be justified by some well-recognised excuse admitted by law. It is further admitted that there was in this case no such excuse, unless the killing was justified by what has been called "necessity". But the temptation to the act which existed here was not what the law has ever called necessity. Nor is this to be regretted. Though law and morality are not the same, and many things may be immoral which are not necessarily illegal, yet the absolute divorce of law from morality would be of fatal consequence; and such divorce would follow if the temptation to murder in this case were to be held by law an absolute defence of it. It is not so. To preserve one's life is generally speaking a duty, but it may be the plainest and the highest duty to sacrifice it. War is full of instances in which it is a man's duty not to live, but to die. The duty, in case of shipwreck, of a captain to his crew, of the crew to the passengers, of soldiers to women and children, as in the noble case of *The Birkenhead*; these duties impose on men the moral necessity, not of the preservation, but of the sacrifice of their lives for others, from which in no country, least of all, it is to be hoped, in England, will men ever shrink, as indeed, they have not shrunk ... It would be a very easy and cheap display of common place learning to quote from Greek and Latin authors, from Horace, from Juvenal, from Cicero, from Euripides, passage after passage, in which the duty of dying for others has been laid down in glowing and emphatic language as resulting from the principles of heathen ethics; it is enough in a Christian country to remind ourselves of the Great Example whom we profess to follow ...

It must not be supposed that in refusing to admit temptation to be an excuse for crime it is forgotten how terrible the temptation was; how awful the suffering; how hard in such trials to keep the judgement straight and the conduct pure. We are often compelled to set up standards we cannot reach ourselves, and to lay down rules which we could not ourselves satisfy. But a man has no right to declare temptation to be an excuse, though he might himself have yielded to it, nor allow compassion for the criminal to change or weaken in any manner the legal definition of the crime. It is therefore our duty to declare that the prisoner's act in this case was wilful murder, that the facts as stated in the verdict are no legal justification of the homicide; and to say that in our unanimous opinion the prisoners are upon this special verdict guilty of murder.'

The prisoners were sentenced to death but their sentence was commuted on the advice of the Home Secretary to six months' imprisonment.

L L FULLER
The Case of the Speluncean Explorers [1]
(1949)

IN THE SUPREME COURT OF NEWGARTH, 4300

The defendants, having been indicted for the crime of murder, were convicted and sentenced to be hanged by the Court of General Instances of the County of Stowfield. They bring a petition of error before this Court. The facts sufficiently appear in the opinion of the Chief Justice.

TRUEPENNY, CJ: 'The four defendants are members of the Speluncean Society, an organization of amateurs interested in the exploration of caves. Early in May 4299, they, in the company of Roger Whetmore, then also a member of the Society, penetrated into the interior of a limestone cavern ... While they were in a position remote from the entrance to the case, a landslide occurred. Heavy boulders fell in such a manner as to block completely the only known opening to the case. When the men discovered their predicament they settled themselves near the obstructed entrance to wait ... a rescue party. When the imprisoned men were finally released it was learned that on the twenty-third day after their entrance into the case Whetmore had been killed and eaten by his companions.

From the testimony of the defendants, which was accepted by the jury, it appears that it was Whetmore who first proposed that they might find the nutriment without which survival was impossible in the flesh of one of their own number. It was also Whetmore who first proposed the use of some method of casting lot, calling the attention of the defendants to a pair of dice he happened to have with him ...

[1] From 62 *Harvard Law Review* 616. Copyright © 1949 The Harvard Law Review Association.

Before the dice were cast, however, Whetmore declared that he withdrew from the arrangement, as he had decided on reflection to wait for another week before embracing an expedient so frightful and odious. The others charged him with a breach of faith and proceeded to cast the dice. When it came Whetmore's turn, the dice were cast for him by one of the defendants, and he was asked to declare any objections he might have to the fairness of the throw. He stated that he had no such objections. The throw went against him, and he was then put to death and eaten by his companions.

After the rescue of the defendants ... they were indicted for the murder of Roger Whetmore ... [T]he trial judge ruled that the defendants were guilty of murdering Roger Whetmore. The judge then sentenced them to be hanged, the law of our Commonwealth permitting him no discretion with respect to the penalty to be imposed. After the release of the jury, its members joined in a communication to the Chief Executive asking that the sentence be commuted to an imprisonment of six months. The trial judge addressed a similar communication to the Chief Executive ...

It seems to me that in dealing with this extraordinary case the jury and the trial judge followed a course that was not only fair and wise, but the only course that was open to them under the law ... This statute permits of no exception applicable to this case, however our sympathies may incline us to make allowance for the tragic situation in which these men found themselves.

In a case like this the principle of executive clemency seems admirably suited to mitigate the rigours of the law, and I propose to my colleagues that we follow the example of the jury and the trial judge by joining in the communications they have addressed to the Chief Executive. There is every reason to believe that these requests for clemency will be heeded. ... It is highly improbable that the Chief Executive would deny these requests ... If this is done, then justice will be accomplished without impairing either the letter or spirit of our statutes and without offering any encouragement for the disregard of law.'

FOSTER, J: 'I am shocked that the Chief Justice, in an effort to escape the embarrassments of this tragic case, should have adopted, and should have proposed to his colleagues, an expedient at once so sordid and so obvious. I believe something more is on trial in this case than the fate of these unfortunate explorers; that is the law of our Commonwealth. If this Court declares that under our law these men have committed a crime, then our law is itself convicted in the tribunal of common sense, no matter what happens to the individuals involved in this petition of error. For us to assert that the law we uphold and expound compels us to a conclusion we are ashamed of, and from which we can only escape by appealing to a dispensation resting within the personal whim of the Executive, seems to me to amount to an admission that the law of this Commonwealth no longer pretends to incorporate justice.

For myself, I do not believe that our law compels the monstrous conclusion that these men are murderers. I believe, on the contrary, that it declares them to be innocent of any crime. I rest this conclusion on two independent grounds, either of which is of itself sufficient to justify the acquittal of these defendants.

The first of these grounds rests on a premise that may arouse opposition until it has been examined candidly. I take the view that the enacted or positive law of this Commonwealth, including all of its statutes and precedents, is inapplicable to this case, and that the case is governed instead by what ancient writers in Europe and America called "the law of nature."

This conclusion rests on the proposition that our positive law is predicated on the possibility of men's coexistence in society. When a situation arises in which the coexistence of men becomes impossible, then a condition that underlies all of our precedents and statutes has ceased to exist. When that condition disappears, then it is my opinion that the force of our positive law disappears with it. We are not accustomed to applying the maxim *cesante ratione legis, cessat et ipsa lex* to the whole of our enacted law, but I believe that this is a case where the maxim should be so applied.

The proposition that all positive law is based on the possibility of men's coexistence has a strange sound, not because the truth it contains is strange, but simply because it is a truth so obvious and pervasive that we seldom have occasion to give words to it. Like the air we breathe, it so pervades our environment that we forget that it exists until we are suddenly deprived of it. Whatever particular objects may be sought by the various branches of our law, it is apparent on reflection that all of them are directed toward facilitating and improving men's coexistence and regulating with fairness and equity the relations of their life in common. When the assumption that men may live together loses its truth, as it obviously did in this extraordinary situation where life only became possible by the taking of life, then the basic premises underlying our whole legal order have lost their meaning and force.

Had the tragic events of this case taken place a mile beyond the territorial limits of our Commonwealth, no one would pretend that our law was applicable to them. We recognize that jurisdiction rests on a territorial basis ... Now I contend that a case may be removed morally from the force of a legal order, as well as geographically. If we look to the purposes of law and government, and to the premises underlying our positive law, these men when they made their fateful decision were as remote from our legal order as if they had been a thousand miles beyond our boundaries. Even in a physical sense, their underground prison was separated from our courts and writ-servers by a solid curtain of rock that could be removed only after the most extraordinary expenditures of time and effort.

I conclude, therefore, that at the time Roger Whetmore's life was ended by these defendants, they were, to use the quaint language of nineteenth-century writers, not in a "state of civil society" but in a "state of nature." This has the consequence that the law applicable to them is not the enacted and established law of this Commonwealth, but the law derived from those principles that were appropriate to their condition. I have no hesitancy in saying that under those principles they were guiltless of any crime.

What these men did was done in pursuance of an agreement accepted by all of them and first proposed by Whetmore himself. Since it was apparent that their extraordinary predicament made inapplicable the usual principles that regulate men's relations with one another, it was necessary for them to draw, as it were, a new charter of government appropriate to the situation in which they found themselves.

It has from antiquity been recognized that the most basic principle of law or government is to be found in the notion of contract or agreement. Ancient thinkers, especially during the period from 1600 to 1900, used to base government itself on a supposed original social compact. Skeptics pointed out that this theory contradicted the known facts of history, and that there was no scientific evidence to support the notion that any government was ever founded in the manner supposed by the theory. Moralists replied that, if the compact was a fiction from a historical point of view, the notion of a compact or agreement furnished the only ethical justification on which the powers of government, which include that of taking life, could be rested. The powers of government can only be justified morally on the ground that these are powers that reasonable men would agree upon and accept if they were faced with the necessity of constructing anew some order to make their life in common possible.

Fortunately, our Commonwealth is not bothered by the perplexities that beset the ancients. We know as a matter of historical truth that our government was founded upon a contract or free accord of men. The archeological proof is conclusive that in the first period following the Great Spiral the survivors of that holocaust voluntarily came together and drew up a charter of government. Solphistical writers have raised questions as to the power of those remote contractors to bind future generations, but the fact remains that our government traces itself back in an unbroken line to that original charter ...

This concludes the exposition of the first ground of my decision. My second ground proceeds by rejecting hypothetically all the premises on which I have so far proceeded. I concede for purposes of argument that I am wrong in saying that the situation of these men removed them from the effect of our positive law, and I assume that the Consolidated Statutes have the power to penetrate five hundred feet of rock and to impose themselves upon these starving men huddled in their underground prison.

Now it is, of course, perfectly clear that these men did an act that violates the literal wording of the statute which declares that he who 'shall willfully take the life of another' is a murderer. But one of the most ancient bits of legal wisdom is the saying that a man may break the letter of the law without breaking the law itself. Every proposition of positive law, whether contained in a statute or a judicial precedent, is to be interpreted reasonably, in the light of its evident purpose. This is a truth so elementary that it is hardly necessary to expatiate on it. Illustrations of its application are numberless and are to be found in every branch of the law. In *Commonwealth* v *Staymore* the defendant was convicted under a statute making it a crime to leave one's car parked in certain areas for a period longer than two hours. The defendant had attempted to remove his car, but was prevented from doing so because the streets were obstructed by a political demonstration in which he took no part and which he had no reason to anticipate. His conviction was set aside by this Court, although his case fell squarely within the wording of the statute ...

The statute before us for interpretation has never been applied literally. Centuries ago it was established that a killing in self-defense is excused. There is nothing in the wording of the statute that suggests this exception. Various attempts have been made to reconcile the legal treatment of self-defense with the words of the statute, but in my opinion these are all merely ingenious sophistries. The truth is that the exception in favour of self-defense cannot be reconciled with the *words* of the statute, but only with its *purpose*.

The true reconciliation of the excuse of self-defense with the statute making it a crime to kill another is to be found in the following line of reasoning. One of the principal objects underlying any criminal legislation is that of deterring men from crime. Now it is apparent that if it were declared to be the law that a killing in self-defense is murder such a rule could not operate in a deterrent manner. A man whose life is threatened will repel his aggressor, whatever the law may say. Looking therefore to the broad purpose of criminal legislation, we may safely declare that this statute was not intended to apply to cases of self-defense.

When the rationale of the excuse of self-defense is thus explained, it becomes apparent that precisely the same reasoning is applicable to the case at bar. If in the future any group of men ever find themselves in the tragic predicament of these defendants, we may be sure that their decision whether to live or die will not be controlled by the contents of our criminal code. Accordingly, if we read this statute intelligently it is apparent that it does not apply to this case. The withdrawal of this situation from the effect of the statute is justified by precisely the same considerations that were applied by our predecessors in office centuries ago to the case of self-defense ...

I therefore conclude that on any aspect under which this case may be viewed these defendants are innocent of the crime of murdering Roger Whetmore, and that the conviction should be set aside.'

TATTING, J: '... As I analyze the opinion just tendered by my brother Foster, I find that it is shot through with contradictions and fallacies. Let us begin with his first proposition: these men were not subject to our law because they were not in a "state of civil society" but in a "state of nature." I am not clear why this is so, whether it is because of the thickness of the rock that imprisoned them, or because they were hungry, or because they had set up a "new charter of government" by which the usual rules of law were to be supplanted by a throw of the dice. Other difficulties intrude themselves. If these men passed from the jurisdiction of our law to that of the "law of nature," at what moment did this occur? Was it when the entrance to the cave was blocked, or when the threat of starvation reached a certain undefined degree of intensity, or when the agreement for the throwing of the dice was made? These uncertainties in the doctrine proposed by my brother are capable of producing real difficulties. Suppose, for example, one of these men had had his twenty-first birthday while he was imprisoned within the mountain. On what date would we have to consider that he had attained his majority – when he reached the age of twenty-one, at which time he was, by hypothesis, removed from the effects of our law, or only when he was released from the case and became again subject to what my brother calls our "positive law"? These difficulties may seem fanciful, yet they only serve to reveal the fanciful nature of the doctrine that is capable of giving rise to them.

But it is not necessary to explore these niceties further to demonstrate the absurdity of my brother's position. Mr Justice Foster and I are the appointed judges of a court of the Commonwealth of Newgarth, sworn and empowered to administer the laws of that Commonwealth. By what authority do we resolve ourselves into a Court of Nature? If these men were indeed under the law of nature, whence comes out authority to expound and apply that law? Certainly *we* are not in a state of nature.

Let us look at the contents of this code of nature that my brother proposes we adopt as our own and apply to this case. What a topsy-turvy and odious code it is! It is a code in which the law of contracts is more fundamental than the law of murder. It is a code under which a man may make a valid agreement empowering his fellows to eat his own body. Under the provisions of this code, furthermore, such an agreement once made is irrevocable, and if one of the parties attempts to withdraw, the others may take the law into their own hands and enforce the contract by violence – for though my brother passes over in convenient silence the effect of Whetmore's withdrawal, this is the necessary implication of his argument.

The principles my brother expounds contain other implications that cannot be tolerated. He argues that when the defendants set upon Whetmore and killed him … they were only exercising the rights conferred upon them by their bargain. Suppose, however, that Whetmore had had concealed upon his person a revolver, and that when he saw the defendants about to slaughter him he had shot them to death in order to save his own life. My brother's reasoning applied to these facts would make Whetmore out to be a murderer, since the excuse of self-defense would have to be denied to him. If his assailants were acting rightfully in seeking to bring about his death, then of course he could no more plead the excuse that he was defending his own life than could a condemned prisoner who struck down the executioner lawfully attempting to place the noose about his neck.

All of these considerations make it impossible for me to accept the first part of my brother's argument. I can neither accept his notion that these men were under a code of nature which this Court was bound to apply to them, nor can I accept the odious and perverted rules that he would read into that code. I come now to the second part of my brother's opinion …

The gist of my brother's argument may be stated in the following terms: No statute, whatever its language, should be applied in a way that contradicts its purpose. One of the purposes of any criminal statute is to deter. The application of the statute making it a crime to kill another to the peculiar facts of this case would contradict this purpose, for it is impossible to believe that the contents of the criminal code could operate in a deterrent manner on men faced with the alternative of life or death. The reasoning by which this exception is read into the statute is, my brother observes, the same as that which is applied in order to provide the excuse of self-defense ...

Now let me outline briefly, however, the perplexities that assail me when I examine my brother's demonstration more closely. It is true that a statute should be applied in the light of its purpose, and that *one of* the purposes of criminal legislation is recognized to be deterrence. The difficulty is that other purposes are also ascribed to the law of crimes. It has been said that one of its objects is to provide an orderly outlet for the instinctive human demand for retribution ... It has also been said that its object is the rehabilitation of the wrongdoer ... Other theories have been propounded. Assuming that we must interpret a statute in the light of its purpose, what are we to do when it has many purposes or when its purposes are disputed?

A similar difficulty is presented by the fact that although there is authority for my brother's interpretation of the excuse of self-defense, there is other authority which assigns to that excuse a different rationale ... The taught doctrine of our law schools, ... runs in the following terms: The statute concerning murder requires a "willful" act. The man who acts to repel an aggressive threat to this own life does not act "willfully," but in response to an impulse deeply ingrained in human nature. I suspect that there is hardly a lawyer in this Commonwealth who is not familiar with this line of reasoning ...

Now the familiar explanation of the excuse of self-defense just expounded obviously cannot be applied by analogy to the facts of this case. These men acted not only 'willfully' but with great deliberation and after hours of discussing what they should do. Again we encounter a forked path, with one line of reasoning leading us in one direction and another in a direction that is exactly the opposite. This perplexity is in this case compounded, as it were, for we have to set off one explanation, incorporated in a virtually unknown precedent of this Court, against another explanation, which forms a part of the taught legal tradition of our law schools, but which, so far as I know, has never been adopted in any judicial decision ...

I have difficulty in saying that no deterrent effect whatever could be attributed to a decision that these men were guilty of murder. The stigma of the word "murderer" is such that it is quite likely, I believe, that if these men had known that their act was deemed by the law to be murder they would have waited for a few days at least before carrying out their plan. During that time some unexpected relief might have come. I realize that this observation only reduces the distinction to a matter of degree, and does not destroy it altogether. It is certainly true that the element of deterrence would be less in this case than is normally involved in the application of the criminal law.

There is still a further difficulty in my brother Foster's proposal to read an exception into the statute to favour this case, though again a difficulty not even intimated in his opinion. What shall be the scope of this exception? Here the men cast lots and the victim was himself originally a party to the agreement. What would we have to decide if Whetmore had refused from the beginning to participate in the plan? Would a majority be permitted to overrule him? Or, suppose that no plan were adopted at all and the others simply conspired to bring about Whetmore's death, justifying their act by saying that he was in the weakest condition. Or again, that a plan of selection was followed by one based on a different justification on the one adopted here, as if the others were atheists and insisted that Whetmore should die because he was the only one who believed in afterlife. These illustrations could be multiplied, but enough have been suggested to reveal what the quagmire of hidden difficulties my brother's reasoning contains ...

The more I examine this case and think about it, the more deeply I become involved. My mind becomes entangled in the meshes of the very nets I throw out for my own rescue. I find that almost every consideration that bears on the decision of the case is counterbalanced by an opposing consideration leading in the opposite direction. My brother Foster has not furnished to me, nor can I discover for myself, any formula capable of resolving the equivocations that beset me on all sides.

I have given this case the best thought of which I am capable. I have scarcely slept since it was argued before us. When I feel myself inclined to accept the view of my brother Foster, I am repelled by a feeling that his arguments are intellectually unsound and approach mere rationalization. On the other hand, when I incline toward upholding the conviction, I am struck by the absurdity of directing that these men be put to death when their lives have been saved at the cost of the lives of ten heroic workmen. It is to me a matter of regret that the Prosecutor saw fit to ask for an indictment for murder. If we had a provision in our statutes making it a crime to eat human flesh, that would have been a more appropriate charge. If no other charge suited to the facts of this case could be brought against the defendants, it would have been wiser, I think, not to have indicted them at all. Unfortunately, however, the men have be indicted and tried, and we have therefore been drawn into this unfortunate affair.

Since I have been wholly unable to resolve the doubts that beset me about the law of this case, I am with regret announcing a step that is, I believe, unprecedented in the history of this tribunal. I declare my withdrawal from the decision of this case.'

KEEN, J.: 'I should like to begin by setting to one side two questions which are not before this Court.

The first of these is whether executive clemency should be extended to these defendants if the conviction is affirmed. Under our system of government, that is a question for the Chief Executive, not for us. I therefore disapprove of that passage in the opinion of the Chief Justice in which he in effect gives instructions to the Chief Executive as to what he should do in this case and suggests that some impropriety will attach if these instructions are not heeded ... In the discharge of my duties as a judge, it is neither my function to address directions to the Chief Executive, nor to take into account what he may or may not do, in reaching my own decision, which must be controlled entirely by the law of this Commonwealth.

The second question that I wish to put to one side is that of deciding whether what these men did was "right" or "wrong," "wicked" or "good." That is also a question that is irrelevant to the discharge of my office as a judge sworn to apply, not my conceptions of morality, but the law of the land. In putting this question to one side I think I can also safely dismiss without comment the first and more poetic portion of my brother Foster's opinion. The element of fantasy contained in the arguments developed there has been sufficiently revealed in my brother Tatting's somewhat solemn attempt to take those arguments seriously ...

Whence arise all the difficulties of the case, then, and the necessity for so many pages of discussion about what ought to be so obvious. The difficulties, in whatever tortured form they may present themselves, all trace back to a single source, and that is a failure to distinguish the legal from the moral aspects of this case. To put it bluntly, my brothers do not like the fact that the written law requires the conviction of these defendants. Neither do I, but unlike my brothers I respect the obligations of an office that requires me to put my personal predilections out of my mind when I come to interpret and apply the law of this Commonwealth.

Now, of course, my brother Foster does not admit that he actuated by a personal dislike of the written law. Instead he develops a familiar line of argument according to which the court may disregard the express language of a statute when something not contained in the statute itself, called its "purpose," can be employed to justify the result the court considers proper. Because this is an old issue between myself and my colleague, I should like, before discussing his particular application of the argument to the facts of this case, to say something about the historical background of this issue and its implications for law and government generally ...

We now have a clear-cut principle, which is the supremacy of the legislative branch of our government. From that principle flows the obligation of the judiciary to enforce faithfully the written law, and to interpret that law in accordance with its plain meaning without reference to our personal desires or our individual conceptions of justice. I am not concerned with the question whether the principle that forbids the judicial revision of statutes is right or wrong, desirable or undesirable; I observe merely that this principle has become a tacit premise underlying the whole of the legal and governmental order I am sworn to administer ...

We are all familiar with the process by which the judicial reform of disfavored legislative enactments is accomplished ...

The process of judicial reform requires three steps. The first of these is to divine some single "purpose" which the statute serves. This is done although not one statute in a hundred has any such single purpose, and although the objectives of nearly every statute are differently interpreted by the different classes of its sponsors. The second step is to discover that a mythical being called "the legislator," in the pursuit of this imagined "purpose," overlooked something or left some gap or imperfection in his work. Then comes the final and most refreshing part of the task, which is, of course, to fill in the blank thus created. *Quod erat faciendum* ...

One could not wish for a better case to illustrate the specious nature of this gap-filling process than the one before us. My brother thinks he knows exactly what was sought when men made murder a crime, and that was something he calls "deterrence," My brother Tatting has already shown how much is passed over in that interpretation. But I think the trouble goes deeper, I doubt very much whether our statute making murder a crime really has a "purpose" in my ordinary sense of the term. Primarily, such a statute reflects a deeply felt human conviction that murder is wrong and that something should be done to the man who commits it. If we were forced to be more articulate about the matter, we would probably take refuge in the more sophisticated theories of the criminologists, which, of course, were certainly not in the minds of those who drafted our statute. We might also observe that men will do their own work more effectively and live happier lives if they are protected against the threat of violent assault ...

If we do not know the purpose of (the law), how can we possibly say there is a "gap" in it? How can we know what its draftsmen thought about the question of killing men in order to eat them? ... [I]t remains abundantly clear that neither I nor my brother Foster knows what the "purpose" of (the law) is.

Considerations similar to those I have just outlined are also applicable to the exception in favor of self-defense, which plays so large a role in the reasoning of my brothers Foster and Tatting. As in dealing with the statute, so in dealing with the exception, the question is not the conjectural *purpose of* the rule, but its *scope*. Now the scope of the exception in favor of self-defense as it has been applied by this Court is plain: it applies to cases of resisting an aggressive threat to the party's own life. It is therefore too clear for argument that this case does not fall within the scope of the exception, since it is plain that Whetmore made no threat against the lives of these defendants.

... You simply cannot apply a statute as it is written and remake it to meet your own wishes at the same time.

Now I know that the line of reasoning I have developed in this opinion will not be acceptable to those who look only to the immediate effects of a decision and ignore the long-run implications of an assumption by the judiciary of a power of dispensation. A hard decision is never a popular decision. Judges have been celebrated in literature for their sly prowess in devising some quibble by which a litigant could be deprived of his rights where the public thought it was wrong for him to assert those rights. But I believe that judicial dispensation does more harm in the long run than hard decisions. Hard cases may even have a certain moral value by bringing home to the people their own responsibilities toward the law that is ultimately their creation, and by reminding them that there is no principle of personal grace that can relieve the mistakes of their representatives ...

I conclude that the conviction should be affirmed.'

HANDY, J: 'I have listened with amazement to the tortured ratiocinations to which this simple case has given rise. I never cease to wonder at my colleagues' ability to throw an obscuring curtain of legalisms about every issue presented to them for decision. We have heard this afternoon learned disquisitions on the distinction between positive law and the law of nature, the language of the statute and the purpose of the statute, judicial functions and executive functions, judicial legislation and legislative legislation ...

What have all these things to do with the case? The problem before us is what we, as officers of the government, ought to do with these defendants. That is a question of practical wisdom, to be exercised in a context, not of abstract theory, but of human realities. When the case is approached in this light, it becomes, I think, one of the easiest to decide that has ever been argued before this Court.

Before stating my own conclusions about the merits of the case, I should like to discuss briefly some of the more fundamental issues involved – issues on which my colleagues and I have been divided ever since I have been on the bench.

I have never been able to make my brothers see that government is a human affair, and that men are rules, not by words on paper or by abstract theories, but by other men. They are rules well when their rulers understand the feelings and conceptions of the masses. They are rules badly when that understanding is lacking.

Of all branches of the government, the judiciary is the most likely to lose its contact with the common man. The reasons for this are, of course, fairly obvious. Where the masses react to a situation in terms of a few salient features, we pick into little pieces every situation presented to us. Lawyers are hired by both sides to analyze and dissect. Judges and attorneys vie with one another to see who can discover the greatest number of difficulties and distinctions in a single set of facts. Each side tries to find cases, real or imagined, that will embarrass the demonstrations of the other side. To escape this embarrassment, still further distinctions are invented and imported into the situation. When a set of facts has been subjected to this kind of treatment for a sufficient time, all the life and juice have gone out of it and we have left a handful of dust.

Now I realize that wherever you have rules and abstract principles lawyers are going to be able to make distinctions. To some extent the sort of thing I have been describing is a necessary evil attaching to any formal regulation of human affairs. But I think that the area which really stands in need of such regulation is greatly overestimated. There are, of course, a few fundamental rules of the game that must be accepted if the game is to go on at all. I would include among these the rules relating to the conduct of elections, the appointment of public officials, and the term during which an office is held. Here are some restraint on discretion and dispensation, some adherence to form, some scruple for what does and what does not fall within the rule, is, I concede, essential. Perhaps the area of basic principle should be expanded to include certain other rules, such as those designed to preserve the free civilmoign system.

But outside of these fields I believe that all government officials, including judges, will do their jobs best if they treat forms and abstract concepts as instruments. We should take as our model, I think, the good administrator, who accommodates procedures and principles to the case at hand, selecting from among the available forms those most suited to reach a result.

The most obvious advantage of this method of government is that it permits us to go about our daily tasks with efficiency and common sense. My adherence to this philosophy has, however, deeper roots. I believe that it is only with the insight this philosophy gives that we can preserve the flexibility essential if we are to keep our actions in reasonable accord with the sentiments of those subject to our rule. More governments have been wrecked, and more human misery caused, by the lack of this accord between rules and ruled than by any other factor of people and those who direct their legal, political, and economic life, and our society is ruined. Then neither Foster's law of nature nor Keen's fidelity to written law will avail us anything.

Now when these conceptions are applied to the case before us, its decision becomes, as I have said, perfectly easy. In order to demonstrate this I shall have to introduce certain realities that my brothers in their coy decorum have been seen fit to pass over in silence, although they are just as acutely aware of them as I am.

The first of these is that this case has aroused an enormous public interest, both here and abroad. Almost every newspaper and magazine has carried articles about it: columnists have shared with their readers confidential information as to the next governmental move: hundreds of letters-to-the-editor have been printed. One of the great newspaper chains made a poll of public opinion on the question, "What do you think the Supreme Court should do with the Speluncean explorers?" About ninety per cent expressed a belief that the defendants should be pardoned or let off with a kind of token punishment. It is perfectly clear, then, how the public feels about the case. We could have known this without the poll, of course, on the basis of common sense, or even by observing that on this Court there are apparently four-and-a-half men, or ninety per cent, who share the common opinion.

This makes it obvious, not only what we should do, but what we must do if we are to preserve between ourselves and public opinion a reasonable and decent accord. Declaring these men innocent need not involve us in any undignified quibble or trick. No principle of statutory construction is required that is not consistent with the past practices of this Court. Certainly no layman would think that in letting these men off we had stretched the statute any more than our ancestors did when they created the excuse of self-defense. If a more detailed demonstration of the method of reconciling our decision with the statute is required, I should be content to rest on the arguments developed in the second and less visionary part of my brother Foster's opinion.

Now I know that my brothers will be horrified by my suggestion that this Court should take account of public opinion. They will tell you that public opinion is emotional and capricious, that is based on half-truths and listens to witnesses who are not subject to cross-examination. They will tell you that the law surrounds the trial of a case like this with elaborate safeguards, designed to insure that the truth will be known and that every rational consideration bearing on the issues of the case has been taken into account. They will warn you that all of these safeguards go for naught if a mass opinion formed outside this framework is allowed to have any influence on our decision.

But let us look candidly at some of the realities of the administration of our criminal law. When a man is accused of crime, there are, speaking generally, four ways in which he may escape punishment. One of these is a determination by a judge that under the applicable law he has committed no crime. This is, of course, a determination that takes place in a rather formal and abstract atmosphere. But look at the other three ways in which he may escape punishment. These are: (1) a decision by the Prosecutor not to ask for an indictment: (2) an acquittal by the jury: (3) a pardon or commutation of sentence by the executive. Can anyone pretend that these decisions are held within a rigid and formal framework of rules that prevents factual error, excludes emotional and personal factors, and guarantees that all the forms of the law will be observed?

In the case of the jury we do, to be sure, attempt to cabin their deliberations within the area of the legally relevant, but there is no need to deceive ourselves into believing that this attempt is really successful. In the normal course of events the case now before us would have gone on all of its issues directly to the jury. Had this occurred we can be confident that there would have been an acquittal or at least a division that would have prevented a conviction. If the jury had been instructed that the men's hunger and their agreement were no defense to the charge of murder, their verdict would in all likelihood have ignored this instruction and would have involved a good deal more twisting of the letter of the law than any that is likely to tempt us. Of course the only reason that didn't occur in this case was the fortuitous circumstance that the foreman of the jury happened to be a lawyer. His learning enabled him to devise a form of words that would allow the jury to dodge its usual responsibilities.

My brother Tatting expresses annoyance that the Prosecutor did not, in effect, decide the case for him by not asking for an indictment. Strict as he is himself in complying with the demands of legal theory, he is quite content to have the fate of these men decided out of court by the Prosecutor on the basis of common sense. The Chief Justice, on the other hand, wants the application of common sense postponed to the very end, though like Tatting, he wants no personal part in it.

This brings me to the concluding portion of my remarks, which has to do with executive clemency. Before discussing that topic directly, I want to make a related observation about the poll of public opinion. As I have said, ninety per cent of the people wanted the Supreme Court to let the men off entirely or with a more or less nominal punishment. The ten per cent constituted a very oddly assorted group, with the most curious and divergent opinions ... [A]lthough almost every conceivable variety and shade of opinion was represented in this group, there was, so far as I know, not one of them, nor a single member of the majority of ninety per cent, who said, "I think it would be a fine thing to have the courts sentence these men to be hanged, and then to have another branch of the government come along and pardon them." Yet this is a solution that has more or less dominated our discussions and which our Chief Justice proposes as a way by which we can avoid doing an injustice and at the same time preserve respect for law. He can be assured that if he is preserving anybody's morale, it is his own, and not the public's, which knows nothing of his distinctions. I mention this matter because I wish to emphasize once more the danger that we may get lost in the patterns of our own thought and forget that these patterns often cast not the slightest shadow on the outside world.

I come now to the most crucial fact in this case, a fact known to all of us on this Court, though one that my brothers have seen fit to keep under the cover of their judicial robes. This is the frightening likelihood that if the issue is left to him, the Chief Executive will refuse to pardon these men or commute their sentences. As we all know, our Chief Executive is a man now well advanced in years, of very stiff notions. Public clamor usually operates on him with the reverse of the effect intended ...

Their sample about acquiring accurate information directly does not prevent them from being very perturbed about what they have learned indirectly. Their acquaintance with the facts I have just related explains why the Chief Justice, ordinarily a model of decorum, saw fit in his opinion to flap his judicial robes in the face of the Executive and threaten him with excommunication if he failed to commute the sentence. It explains, I suspect, my brother Foster's feat of levitation by which a whole library of law books was lifted from the shoulders of these defendants. It explains also why even my legalistic brother Keen emulated Pooh-Bah in the ancient comedy by stepping to the other side of the stage to address a few remarks to the Executive "in my capacity as a private citizen", ...

I must confess that as I grow older I become more and more perplexed at men's refusal to apply their common sense to problems of law and government, and this truly tragic case has deepened my sense of discouragement and dismay. I only wish that I could convince my brothers of the wisdom of the principles I have applied to the judicial office since I first assumed it ...

I conclude that the defendants are innocent of the crime charged, and that the conviction and sentence should be set aside.'

TATTING, J: 'I have been asked by the Chief Justice whether, after listening to the two opinions just rendered, I desire to re-examine the position previously taken by me. I wish to state that after hearing these opinions I am greatly strengthened in my conviction that I ought not to participate in the decision of this case.

The Supreme Court being evenly divided, the conviction and sentence of the Court of General Instances is *affirmed*. It is ordered that the execution of the sentence shall occur at 6 am, Friday, April 2, 4300, at which time the Public Executioner is directed to proceed with all convenient dispatch to hang each of the defendants by the neck until he is dead.'

Are Moral Judgments Part of Law?

4. THE NATURE OF MORALITY

H L A HART
The Concept of Law [1]
(1961)

THE MINIMUM CONTENT OF NATURAL LAW

In considering the simple truisms which we set forth here, and their connexion with law and morals, it is important to observe that in each case the facts mentioned afforded a *reason* why, given survival as an aim, law and morals should include a specific content. The general form of the argument is simply that without such a content laws and morals could not forward the minimum purpose of survival which men have in associating with each other. In the absence of this content men, as they are, would have no reason for obeying voluntarily any rules; and without a minimum of co-operation given voluntarily by those who find that it is in their interest to submit to and maintain the rules, coercion of others who would not voluntarily conform would be impossible. It is important to stress the distinctively rational connexion between natural facts and the content of legal and moral rules in this approach, because it is both possible and important to inquire into quite different forms of connexion between natural facts and legal or moral rules. Thus, the still young sciences of psychology and sociology may discover or may even have discovered that, unless certain physical, psychological, or economic conditions are satisfied, eg unless young children are fed and nurtured in certain ways within the family, no system of laws or code of morals can be established, or that only those laws can function successfully which conform to a certain type. Connexions of this sort between natural conditions and systems of rules are not mediated by *reasons*; for they do not relate the existence of certain rules to the conscious aims or purpose of those whose rules they are. Being fed in infancy in a certain way may well be shown to be a necessary condition or even a *cause* of a population developing or maintaining a moral or legal code, but it is not a *reason* for their doing so. Such causal connexions do not of course conflict with the connexions which rest on purposes or conscious aims; they may indeed be considered more important or fundamental that the latter, since they may actually explain why human beings have those conscious

---

[1] Hart, H L A (1961) *The Concept of Law*. Oxford University Press, Oxford, pp189–193.

aims or purposes which Natural Law takes as its starting-points. Causal explanations of this type do not rest on truisms nor are they mediated by conscious aims or purposes: they are for sociology or psychology like other sciences to establish by the methods of generalization and theory, resting on observation and, where possible, on experiment. Such connexions therefore are of a different kind from those which relate the content of certain legal and moral rules to the facts stated in the following truisms.

Human vulnerability

The common requirements of law and morality consist for the most part not of active services to be rendered but of forbearances, which are usually formulated in negative form as prohibitions. Of these the most important for social life are those that restrict the use of violence in killing or inflicting bodily harm. The basic character of such rules may be brought out in a question: If there were not these rules what point could there be for beings such as ourselves in having rules of *any* other kind? The force of this rhetorical question rests on the fact that men are both occasionally prone to, and normally vulnerable to, bodily attack. Yet though this is a truism it is not a necessary truth; for things might have been, and might one day be, otherwise. There are species of animals whose physical structure (including exoskeletons or a carapace) renders them virtually immune from attack by other members of their species and animals who have no organs enabling them to attack. If men were to lose their vulnerability to each other there would vanish one obvious reason for the most characteristic provision of law and morals: *Thou shalt not kill.*

Approximate equality

Men differ from each other in physical strength, agility, and even more in intellectual capacity. Nonetheless it is a fact of quite major importance for the understanding of different forms of law and morality, that no individual is so much more powerful than others, that he is able, without co-operation, to dominate or subdue them for more than a short period. Even the strongest must sleep at times and, when asleep, loses temporarily his superiority. This fact of approximate equality, more than any other, makes obvious the necessity for a system of mutual forbearance and compromise which is the base of both legal and moral obligation. Social life with its rules requiring such forbearances is irksome at times; but it is at any rate less nasty, less brutish, and less short than unrestrained aggression for beings thus approximately equal. It is, of course, entirely consistent with this and an equal truism that when such a system of forbearance is established there will always be some who will wish to exploit it, by simultaneously living within its shelter and breaking its restrictions. This indeed is, as we later show, one of the natural facts which makes the step from merely moral to organized, legal forms of control a necessary one. Again, things might have been otherwise. Instead of being approximately equal there might have been some men immensely stronger than others and better able to dispense with rest, either because some were in these ways far above the present average, or because most were far below it. Such exceptional men might have much to gain by aggression and little to gain from mutual forbearance or compromise with others. But we need not have recourse to the fantasy of giants among pygmies to see the cardinal importance of the fact of approximate equality: for it is illustrated better by the facts of international life, where there are (or were) vast disparities in strength and vulnerability between the states. This inequality, as we shall later see, between the units of international law is one of the things that has imparted to it a character so different from municipal law and limited the extent to which it is capable of operating as an organized coercive system.

Limited altruism

Men are not devils dominated by a wish to exterminate each other, and the demonstration that, given only the modest aim of survival, the basic rules of law and morals are necessities, must not be identified with the false view that men are predominantly selfish and have no disinterested interest in the survival and welfare of their fellows. But if men are not devils, neither are they angels; and the fact that they are a mean between these two extremes is something which makes a system of mutual forbearances both necessary and possible. With angels, never tempted to harm others, rules requiring forbearances would not be necessary. With devils prepared to destroy, reckless of the cost to themselves, they would be impossible. As things are, human altruism is limited in range and intermittent, and the tendencies to aggression are frequent enough to be fatal to social life if not controlled.

Limited resources

It is a merely contingent fact that human beings need food, clothes, and shelter; that these do not exist at hand in limitless abundance; but are scarce, have to be grown or won from nature, or have to be constructed by human toil. These facts alone make indispensable some minimal form of the institution of property (though not necessarily individual property), and the distinctive kind of rule which requires respect for it. The simplest forms of property are to be seen in rules excluding persons generally other than the 'owner' from entry on, or the use of land, or from taking or using material things. If crops are to grow, land must be secure from indiscriminate entry, and food must, in the intervals between its growth or capture and consumption, be secure from being taken by others. At all times and places life itself depends on these minimal forbearances. Again, in this respect, things might have been otherwise than they are. The human organism might have been constructed like plants, capable of extracting food from air, or what it needs might have grown without cultivation in limitless abundance.

The rules which we have so far discussed are *static* rules, in the sense that the obligations they impose and the incidence of these obligations are not variable by individuals. But the division of labour, which all but the smallest groups must develop to obtain adequate supplies, brings with it the need for rules which are *dynamic* in the sense that they enable individuals to create obligations and to vary their incidence. Among these are rules enabling men to transfer, exchange, or sell their products; for these transactions involve the capacity to alter the incidence of those initial rights and obligations which define the simplest form of property. The same inescapable division of labour, and perennial need for co-operation, are also factors which make other forms of dynamic or obligation-creating rule necessary in social life. These secure the recognition of promises as a source of obligation. By this device individuals are enabled by words, spoken or written, to make themselves liable to blame or punishment for failure to act in certain stipulated ways. Where altruism is not unlimited, a standing procedure providing for such self-binding operations is required in order to create a minimum form of confidence in the future behaviour of others, and to ensure the predictability necessary for co-operation. This is most obviously needed where what is to be exchanged or jointly planned are mutual services, or wherever goods which are to be exchanged or sold are not simultaneously or immediately available.

Limited understanding and strength of will

The facts that make rules respecting persons, property, and promises necessary in social life are simple and their mutual benefits are obvious. Most men are capable of seeing them and of sacrificing the immediate short-term interests which conformity to such rules demands. They may indeed obey, from a variety of motives: some from prudential calculation that the sacrifices are worth the gains, some from a disinterested interest in the welfare of others, and some because they look upon the rules as worthy of respect in themselves and find their ideals in devotion to them. On the other hand, neither understanding of long-term interest, nor the strength or goodness of will, upon which the efficacy of these different motives towards obedience depends, are shared by all men alike. All are tempted at times to prefer their own immediate interests and, in the absence of a special organization for their detection and punishment, many would succumb to the temptation. No doubt the advantages of mutual forbearance are so palpable that the number and strength of those who would co-operate voluntarily in a coercive system will normally be greater than any likely combination of malefactors. Yet, except in very small closely-knit societies, submission to the system of restraints would be folly if there were no organization for the coercion of those who would then try to obtain the advantages of the system without submitting to its obligations. 'Sanctions' are therefore required not as the normal motive for obedience, but as a *guarantee* that those who would voluntarily obey shall not be sacrificed to those who would not. To obey, without this, would be to risk going to the wall. Given this standing danger, what reason demands is *voluntary* co-operation in a *coercive* system.

H L A HART
Positivism and the Separation of Law and Morals [2]
(1958)

One criticism of the separation of law and morals is of a very distinct character; it is less an intellectual argument against the Utilitarian distinction than a passionate appeal supported not only by detailed reasoning but also by reminders of a terrible experience. ...

This appeal comes from those German thinkers who lived through the Nazi regime and reflected upon its evil manifestations in the legal system. One of these thinks, Gustav Radbruch, had himself shared the 'positivist' doctrine until the Nazi tyranny, but he was converted by this experience and so his appeal to other men to discard the doctrine of the separation of law and morals has the special poignancy of a recantation. What is important about this criticism is that it really does confront the particular point which Bentham and Austin had in mind in urging the separation of law as it is and as it ought to be. These German thinkers put their insistence on the need to join together what the Utilitarians separated just where this separation was of most importance in the eyes of the Utilitarians; for they were concerned with the problem posed by the existence of morally evil laws.

Before his conversion Radbruch held that resistance to law was a matter for the personal conscience, to be thought out by the individual as a moral problem, and the validity of a law could not be disproved by showing that its requirements were morally evil or even by showing that the effect of compliance with the law would be more evil than the effect of disobedience. Austin, it may be recalled, was emphatic in condemning those who said that if human laws conflicted with the fundamental principles of morality then they cease to be laws, as talking 'stark nonsense'.

> 'The most pernicious laws, and therefore those which are most opposed to the will of God, have been and are continually enforced as laws by judicial tribunals. Suppose an act innocuous, or positively beneficial, be prohibited by the sovereign under the penalty of death; if I commit this act, I shall be tried and condemned, and if I object to the sentence, that it is contrary to the law of God ... the court of justice will demonstrate the inconclusiveness of my reasoning by hanging me up, in pursuance of the law of which I have impugned the validity. An exception, demurrer, or plea, founded on the law of God was never heard in a Court of Justice, from the creation of the world down to the present moment.'[3]

These are strong, indeed brutal words, but we must remember that they went along – in the case of Austin and, of course, Bentham – with the conviction that if laws reached a certain degree of iniquity then there would be a plain moral obligation to

[2] From 71 *Harvard Law Review* 593. © 1958 The Harvard Law Review Association.
[3] Austin (1945) *The Province of Jurisprudence Determined*. Library of Ideas edn, p185.

resist them and to withhold obedience. We shall see, when we consider the alternatives, that this simple presentation of the human dilemma which may arise has much to be said for it.

Radbruch, however, had concluded from the ease with which the Nazi regime had exploited subservience to mere law – or expressed, as he thought, in the 'positivist' slogan 'law as law' (*Gesetz als Gesetz*) – and from the failure of the German legal profession to protect against the enormities which they were required to perpetrate in the name of law, that 'positivism' (meaning here the insistence on the separation of law as it is from law as it ought to be) had powerfully contributed to the horrors. His considered reflections led him to the doctrine that the fundamental principles of humanitarian morality were part of the very concept of *Recht* or Legality and that no positive enactment or statute, however clearly it was expressed and however clearly it conformed with the formal criteria of validity of a given legal system, could be valid if it contravened basic principles of morality. This doctrine can be appreciated fully only if the nuances imported by the German word *Recht* are grasped. But it is clear that the doctrine meant that every lawyer and judge should denounce statutes that transgressed the fundamental principles not as merely immoral or wrong but as having no legal character. ...

It is impossible to read without sympathy Radbruch's passionate demand that the German legal conscience should be open to the demands of morality and his complaint that this has been too little the case in the German tradition. On the other hand there is an extraordinary naïvité in the view that insensitiveness to the demands of morality and subservience to state power in a people like the Germans should have arisen from the belief that law might be law though it failed to conform with the minimum requirements of morality. Rather this terrible history prompts inquiry into why emphasis on the slogan 'law is law', and the distinction between law and morals, acquired a sinister character in Germany, but elsewhere, as with the Utilitarians themselves, went along with the most enlightened liberal attitudes. But something more disturbing than naïveté is latent in Radbruch's whole presentation of the issues to which the existence of morally iniquitous laws give rise. It is not, I think, uncharitable to say that we can see in his argument that he has only half digested the spiritual message of liberalism which he is seeking to convey to the legal profession. For everything that he says is really dependent upon an enormous overvaluation of the importance of the bare fact that a rule may be said to be a valid rule of law, as if this, once declared, was conclusive of the final moral question: 'Ought this rule of law to be obeyed?' Surely the truly liberal answer to any sinister use of the slogan 'law is law' or of the distinction between law and morals is, 'Very well, but that does not conclude the question. Law is not morality; do not let it supplant morality.'

However, we are not left to a mere academic discussion in order to evaluate the plea which Radbruch made for the revision of the distinction between law and morals. After the war Radbruch's conception of law as containing in itself the essential moral principle of humanitarianism was applied in practice by German courts in certain cases in which local war criminals, spies, and informers under the Nazi regime were published. The special importance of these cases is that the persons accused of these crimes claimed that what they had done was not illegal under the laws of the regime in force at the time these actions were performed. This plea was met with the reply that the laws upon which they relied were invalid as contravening the fundamental principles of morality. Let me cite briefly one of these cases.[4]

In 1944 a woman, wishing to be rid of her husband, denounced him to the authorities for insulting remarks he had made about Hitler while home on leave from the German army. The wife was under no legal duty to report his acts, though what he had said was apparently in violation of statutes making it illegal to make statements detrimental to the government of the Third Reich or to impair by any means the military defence of the German people. The husband was arrested and sentenced to death, apparently pursuant to these statutes, though he was not executed but was sent to the front. In 1949 the wife was prosecuted in a West German court for an offence which we would describe as illegally depriving a person of his freedom (*rechtswidrige Freiheitsberaubung*). This was punishable as a crime under the German Criminal Code of 1871 which had remained in force continuously since its enactment. The wife pleaded that her husband's imprisonment was pursuant to the Nazi statutes and hence that she had committed no crime. The court of appeal to which the case ultimately came held that the wife was guilty of procuring the deprivation of her husband's liberty by denouncing him to the German courts, even though he had been sentenced by a court for having violated a statute, since, to quote the words of the court, the statute 'was contrary to the sound conscience and sense of justice of all decent human beings'. This reasoning was followed in many cases which have been hailed as a triumph of the doctrines of natural law and as signalling the overthrow of positivism. The unqualified satisfaction with this result seems to me to be hysteria. Many of us might applaud the objective – that of punishing a woman for an outrageously immoral act – but this was secured only be declaring a statute established since 1934 not to have the force of law, and at least the wisdom of this course must be doubted. There were, of course, two other choices. One was to let the woman go unpunished; one can sympathise with and endorse the view that this might have been a bad thing to do. The other was to face the fact that if the woman were to be punished it must be pursuant to the introduction of a frankly retrospective law and with a full consciousness of what was sacrificed in securing her punishment in this way. Odious as retrospective criminal legislation and punishment may be, to have pursued it openly in this case would at least have had the merits of candour. It would have made plain that in punishing the woman a choice had to be made between two evils, that of leaving her unpunished and that of sacrificing a very precious principle of morality endorsed by most legal systems. Surely if we have learned anything from

---

[4] Judgment of 27 July 1949, Oberlandsgericht, Bamberg, 5 Süddeutsche Juristen-Zeitung 207 (Germany, 1950), 64 *Harvard Law Review* 1005 (1951); see Friedmann (1953) *Legal Theory*, 3rd edn p457.

the history of morals it is that the thing to do with a moral quandary is not to hide it. Like nettles, the occasions when life forces us to choose between the lesser of two evils must be grasped with the consciousness that they are what they are. The vice of this use of the principle that, at certain limiting points, what is utterly immoral cannot be law or lawful is that it will serve to cloak the true nature of the problems with which we are faced ...

It may seem perhaps to make too much of forms, even perhaps of words, to emphasize one way of disposing of this difficult case as compared with another which might have led, so far as the woman was concerned, to exactly the same result. Why should we dramatize the difference between them? We might punish the woman under a new retrospective law and declare overtly that we are doing something inconsistent with our principles as the lesser of two evils; or we might allow the case to pass as one in which we do not point out precisely where we sacrifice such a principle. But candour is not just one among many minor virtues of the administration of law, just as it is not merely a minor virtue of morality. For if we adopt Radbruch's view, and with him and the German courts make our protest against evil law in the form of an assertion that certain rules cannot be law because of their moral iniquity, we confuse one of the most powerful, because it is the simplest, forms of moral criticism. If with the Utilitarians we speak plainly, we say that laws may be law but too evil to be obeyed. This is a moral condemnation which everyone can understand and it makes an immediate and obvious claim to moral attention. If, on the other hand, we formulate our objections as an assertion that these evil things are not law, here is an assertion which many people do not believe, and if they are disposed to consider it at all, it would seem to raise a whole host of philosophical issues before it can be accepted. So perhaps the most important single lesson to be learned from this form of the denial of the Utilitarian distinction is the one that the Utilitarians are most concerned to teach: when we have the ample resources of plain speech we must not present the moral criticism of institutions as propositions of a disputable philosophy.

. . .

This line of argument, found (at least in embryo form) in Austin, where he draws attention to the fact that every developed legal system contains certain fundamental notions which are 'necessary' and 'bottomed in the common nature of man',[5] is worth pursuing – up to a point – and I shall say briefly why and how far this is so.

... There is a wish, which may be understandable, to cut straight through the question whether a legal system, to be a legal system, must measure up to some moral or other standard with simple statements of fact: for example, that no system which utterly failed in this respect has ever existed or could endure; that the normally fulfilled assumption that a legal system aims at some form of justice

---

[5] Austin 'Uses of the Study of Jurisprudence' in (1954) *The Province of Jurisprudence Determined*. Library of Ideas edn, pp365, 373, 367–8.

colours the whole way in which we interpret specific rules in particular cases, and if this normally fulfilled assumption were not fulfilled no one would have any reason to obey except fear (and probably not that) and still less, of course, any moral obligation to obey. The connection between law and moral standards and principles of justice is therefore as little arbitrary and as 'necessary' as the connection between law and sanctions, and the pursuit of the question whether this necessity is logical (part of the 'meaning' of law) or merely factual or causal can safely be left as an innocent pastime for philosophers.

Yet in two respects I should wish to go further (even though this involves the use of a philosophical fantasy) and show what could intelligibly be meant by the claim that certain provisions in a legal system are 'necessary'. ... suppose that men were to become invulnerable to attack by each other, were clad perhaps like giant land crabs with an impenetrable carapace, and could extract the food they needed from the air by some internal chemical process. In such circumstances (the details of which can be left to science fiction) rules forbidding the free use of violence and rules constituting the minimum form of property – with its rights and duties sufficient to enable food to grow and be retained until eaten – would not have the necessary nonarbitrary status which they have for us, constituted as we are in a world like ours. At present, and until such radical changes supervene, such rules are so fundamental that if a legal system did not have them there would be no point in having any other rules at all. Such rules overlap with basic moral principles vetoing murder, violence, and theft; and so we can add to the factual statement that all legal systems in fact coincide with morality at such vital points, the statement that this is, in this sense, necessarily so. And why not call it a 'natural' necessity?

... Natural-law theory, however, in all its protean guises, attempts to push the argument much further and to assert that human beings are equally devoted to and united in their conception of aims (the pursuit of knowledge, justice to their fellow men) other than that of survival, and these dictate a further necessary content to a legal system (over and above my humble minimum) without which it would be pointless. Of course we must be careful not to exaggerate the differences among human beings, but it seems to me that above this minimum the purposes men have for living in society are too conflicting and varying to make possible much extension of the argument that some fuller overlap of legal rules and moral standards is 'necessary' in this sense.

Another aspect of the matter deserves attention. If we attach to a legal system the minimum meaning that it must consist of general rules – general both in the sense that they refer to courses of action, not single actions, and to multiplicities of men, not single individuals – this meaning connotes the principle of treating like cases alike, though the criteria of when cases are alike will be, so far, only the general elements specified in the rules. It is, however, true that *one* essential element of the concept of justice is the principle of treating like cases alike. This is justice in the administration of the law, not justice of the law. So there is, in the very notion of law consisting of general rules, something which prevents us from treating it as if morally it is utterly neutral, without any necessary contact with moral principles. Natural procedural justice consists therefore of those principles of objectivity and impartiality in the administration of the law which implement just this aspect of law and which are designed to ensure that rules are applied only to what are genuinely cases of the rule or at least to minimise the risks of inequalities in this sense.

These two reasons (or excuses) for talking of a certain overlap between legal and moral standards as necessary and natural, of course, should not satisfy anyone who is really disturbed by the Utilitarian or 'positivist' insistence that law and morality are distinct. This is so because a legal system that satisfied these minimum requirements might apply, with the most pedantic impartiality as between the persons affected, laws which were hideously oppressive, and might deny to a vast rightless slave population the minimum benefits of protection from violence and theft. The stink of such societies is, after all, still in our nostrils and to argue that they have (or had) no legal system would only involve the repetition of the argument. Only if the rules failed to provide these essential benefits and protection for anyone – even for a slave-owning group – would the minimum be unsatisfied and the system sink to the status of a set of meaningless taboos. Of course no one denied those benefits would have any reason to obey except fear and would have every moral reason to revolt.

NIGEL WEST
MI5: British Security Service Operations 1909–1945 [6]

Throughout the summer of 1940 MI5 concentrated their efforts on the second-echelon internments and the business of investigating the reports of Fifth Column activity that poured into Wormwood Scrubs via the War Office's Room 055. Hundreds of hours were spent following up tip-offs but not one resulted in the conviction of an enemy agent. When H L A Hart joined MI5 his first job was to make an inspection of the telegraph poles in the southern counties and submit a security report on each of them. Someone had written to the War Office claiming that coded messages had been left on the poles to guide invading parachutists! The public were constantly warned about the dangers of careless talk and several prosecutions were publicised. An aerodrome labourer, William Jackson, was sent to prison for a month when his indiscreet conversation in a Welsh pub was overheard by a group of security-conscious soldiers in May 1940. The following month a mother and daughter were spotted on the banks of the Tyne discussing the passing ships. They were denounced by some schoolboys and fined £5 each.

. . .

[6] Nigel West (Robert Allason MP) (1980) *MI5: British Security Service Operations 1909–1945*. Bodley Head, London, pp122, 170

The first meeting of the Twenty Committee included representatives from MI5, MI6, NID, HDE, War Office, Air Ministry Intelligence, Air Ministry Deception and GHQ Home Forces and took place on 2 January 1941. The actual membership changed later during the war to reflect intelligence development.

The establishment of the Twenty Committee allowed the 'positive counter-intelligence' lobby to demonstrate the extent of their newly-acquired expertise. BI(a) continued to manage the agents on a day-to-day basis but their efforts were now combined with BI(b), a hybrid unit devoted to the art of assessment of the enemy. BI(b) was headed by Helenus ('Buster') Milmo. He gathered around him an extraordinary galaxy of brain-power, drawn from the law and from the universities. They included Anthony Blunt a transfer from 'D' Division, Herbert Hart the left-wing barrister, Patrick Day the philosopher from New College, Oxford, and E B Stamp.

BI(b) were given overall responsibility for combining all the available sources of intelligence concerning the Abwehr and SD and developing a strategy for the double cross agents. Herbert Hart was granted unlimited access to the intercepts concerning the German intelligence services (code-named ISOS) and analysed them for material pertinent to MI5's operations. Other staff examined captured documents while Milmo prepared questionnaires for the Latchmere House 020 people and Royal Victoria Patriotic School refugee processing centre interrogators. Meanwhile John Gwyer and Patrick Day, who transferred to MI5 from the Gunners, began composing a picture of the various different branches of the German intelligence system.

As BI(a) and BI(b) got down to work they were joined by Victor Rothschild, another Trinity, Cambridge, graduate, whose anti-sabotage unit was designated BI(c).

The potentially combustible mixture of regular officers, academics and lawyers worked and the BI sections quickly became the hub of MI5's counter-intelligence activities. Information gleaned from the ULTRA decrypts (courtesy of MI6), the interrogators at 020 and 001, and the double agents proved its worth without delay and the terrible gamble of providing the enemy with deceptive intelligence was won.

Oppenheimer v Cattermole (Inspector of Taxes): Notham v Cooper (Inspector of Taxes) [1975] 2 WLR 347

The taxpayer O, a German Jew, emigrated to England in 1939 as a result of Nazi persecution. In 1948 he became a naturalised British subject. From 1953 onwards he was paid an annual pension by the Federal German Republic. He was assessed to income tax in respect of that pension for the years 1953-54 to 1967-68 and appealed to the special commissioners claiming exemption from income tax under article IX(1) of the Double Taxation Relief (Taxes on Income) (Federal Republic of Germany) Order 1955 and article IX(2) of the Order of 1967 on the ground that he had dual British and German nationality. Two German laws were proved before the commissioners: a law of 1913 under which a German who was neither domiciled nor permanently resident in Germany lost his nationality on acquisition of a foreign nationality, and a decree of November 1941 by which a German Jew lost his nationality if he was ordinarily resident abroad at the date of the decree. The commissioners held that O was not entitled to relief under the double taxation relief orders because he had ceased to be a German national not later than 1948 when he became a naturalised British subject. Goulding J allowed an appeal by O, holding, inter alia, that the decree of 1941 should be disregarded. On appeal by the Crown, the Court of Appeal allowed the appeal.

O appealed. After the conclusion of submissions, it appeared that there were grounds for thinking that the findings of the special commissioners as to the relevant German law might have been based on inadequate material, and in particular that article 116(2) of the Basic Law of the Federal German Republic, enacted in 1949, might be relevant. The case was subsequently remitted to the special commissioners for further consideration, and the appeal was then restored for further argument. At the same time, an appeal by the taxpayer N was heard which raised, inter alia, the same point as to nationality as that in O's case:

Held, dismissing the appeals, that on the true construction of article 116(2) of the Basic Law the appellants had on the enactment of the Basic Law ceased to be German nationals unless and until they applied to be such, which they had not done and that there was no reason to attribute German nationality to them for the purposes of the double taxation legislation.

Per curiam. The doctrine that in time of war English law will for certain purposes disregard changes of status made by the enemy state no longer applies after the end of hostilities (per Lord Pearson, at latest when the war was officially declared to be at an end).

Naturalisation of a person as a British subject, whether in peace time or in war time, does not affect a person's foreign nationality as determined by the municipal law of the foreign state concerned.

PER LORD HAILSHAM OF ST MARYLEBONE, LORD HODSON, LORD CROSS OF CHELSEA AND LORD SALMON: The 1941 decree would, having regard to its nature, not have been recognised by the courts of this country as effective to deprive the appellants of their German nationality.

LORD PEARSON: 'My Lords, I have had the advantage of reading the opinion prepared by my noble and learned friend, Lord Cross of Chelsea, and I agree that these two appeals should be dismissed for the reasons given by him.

On the other hand, I am not able to agree with my noble and learned friend as to the conclusion which should have been reached if the relevant German law had consisted, as we thought it did, simply and solely of the 1941 decree and the 1913 law. When a government, however wicked, has been holding and exercising full and exclusive sovereign power in a foreign country for a number of years, and has been recognised throughout by our government as the government of that country, and some legislative or executive act of that government, however unjust and discriminatory and unfair, has changed the status of an individual by depriving him of his nationality of that country, he does in my opinion effectively cease to be a national of that country and becomes a stateless person unless and until he has acquired some other nationality (as the appellant Oppenheimer did in this case). Suppose then that the wicked government is overthrown. I do not think it would be right for the courts of this country on their own initiative to disregard that person's change of status which in fact had occurred and deem that it never had occurred. A decision on that fictitious basis might be no kindness to the person concerned, who might be quite content with his new status and unwilling to have his former status artificially restored to him. The problem of effecting any necessary rectification of the position created by the unjust decree of the wicked government is a problem for the successor government of the foreign country, and we know that in the present case the problem was dealt with by the successor government of West Germany by its Basic Law of 1949. But if the successor government had not dealt with the problem, I do not see that the courts of this country would have had any jurisdiction to restore to the person concerned his lost nationality of the foreign country. There is the rule of public policy that our courts may refuse to recognise in war time a change of the nationality of an enemy alien, but that rule would cease to apply at the end of the war, which would be at latest when the war was officially declared to be at an end.

   I would dismiss the appeals.'

LORD CROSS OF CHELSEA: 'My Lords, the question at issue in the appeal *Oppenheimer* v *Cattermole* is whether the appellant, Mr Oppenheimer, is liable to pay United Kingdom income tax for the tax years 1953–54 to 1967–68 inclusive on certain pension payments which he received during those years from German public funds. Mr Oppenheimer, who is a Jew, was born in Germany in 1896. From 1919 to 1939 he taught at a Jewish orphanage in Bavaria but in 1939, after having been detained for a short period in a concentration camp, he succeeded in leaving Germany and coming to this country where he has lived ever since. On June 4, 1948, he was granted a certificate of naturalisation and became a British subject. As a former employee of a Jewish religious community he has been since 1953 in receipt of a pension payable out of the revenues of the German Federal Republic. Conventions with regard to double taxation relief were made between the United Kingdom and the Federal Republic in 1954 and 1964 and made law in this country by the Double Taxation Relief (Taxes on Income) (Federal Republic of Germany) Orders 1955 and 1967.

· · ·

The point at issue is whether the appellant was in the years of assessment not only a British subject but also a German national.

   … Neither convention contains any definition of the term "a national". Accordingly the question whether the appellant was a German national during the years of assessment has to be determined by English law. But, as Russell J pointed out in *Stoeck* v *Public Trustee* [1921] 2 Ch 67, 82, English law refers the question whether a person is a national of another state to the municipal law of that state – though it may in certain circumstances "deem" a person to be a national of that state although he is not in fact a national of it. The special commissioners to whom the appellant appealed against the assessments made on him by the respondent inspector of taxes heard evidence from Dr Cohn, an expert in German law called by the respondent, and in the light of it found that under German law the appellant ceased to be a German national not later than June 4, 1948, when he became a national of the United Kingdom. At the request of the appellant, the special commissioners stated a case for the opinion of the court and in view of the subsequent history of this case it is important to set out what was the material to which, according to the case stated, Dr Cohn referred them and what was their understanding of the effect of his evidence in relation to it. First, they had before them and exhibited to the case parts of a decree made on November 25, 1941, by the National Socialist Government providing that a Jew of German nationality who had his usual place of abode abroad when the decree came into force should lose his nationality forthwith. Secondly, they had before them and exhibited to the case part of the German nationality law of July 22, 1913, which provides that a German who has neither his natural residence or permanent abode in Germany loses his nationality on acquiring a foreign nationality unless he had the previous written permission of the appropriate German authority to retain it. Thirdly, the case states that Dr Cohn gave evidence to the following effect:

> "(a) by a decision of the Federal German Constitutional Court given in 1968, which is binding upon all Federal German courts by virtue of a subsequent decree of the Federal German Government, the decree of November 25, 1941 ..., was absolutely void ab initio; (b) the said decision had no retrospective effect; (c) the German nationality law of July 22, 1913 ..., remains in force (with certain amendments not relevant for present purposes) and was unaffected by the said decision; (d) in his opinion, under German law, if the appellant had not lost German nationality under the decree of November 25, 1941, he lost the said nationality under the German nationality law of July 22, 1913, on being naturalised a British subject in 1948."

Two points are to be particularly noted, first, that, whether or not Dr Cohn referred to it in his evidence, the case stated makes no reference to article 116 of the constitution of the Federal German Republic enacted in 1949 which, as will hereafter appear, is of vital importance in this case, and secondly, that the case stated attributes to Dr Cohn the opinion that in the 1968 decision the Federal German Constitutional Court held that the 1941 decree was void ab initio but that nevertheless the decision had no retrospective effect. It is clear from the evidence given by Dr Cohn on a later occasion that the special commissioners who signed the original case stated must have misunderstood the evidence which he was giving with regard to the 1968 decision. As a result of the absence from the case of any mention of article 116 and the presence in it of the statement that the 1968 decision had no retrospective effect the case was argued in the High Court and in the Court of Appeal and on the first occasion before this House on the footing that the only material to be considered in order to decide whether or not the appellant was a German national during the years of assessment was (a) the 1941 decree and (b) the 1913 law. The case came first before Goulding J who reversed the decision of the special commissioners. He held, first, that English law would not recognise the decree of November 25, 1941, as having any effect with regard to the appellant since it purported to alter during war time the nationality of someone who was then an enemy alien, and, secondly, that the appellant had not lost his German nationality by the law of July 22, 1913, since under German law he had already ceased to be a German national before he became a British subject – although our law regarded him as still a German national. The respondent appealed to the Court of Appeal (Lord Denning MR, Buckley and Orr LJJ) who reversed the decision of Goulding J and restored that of the commissioners. Lord Denning MR held that whatever the position might be under German law English law would not regard an enemy alien who had been naturalised as a British subject during war time as continuing thereafter to be a national of the enemy country as well as a British subject. Buckley and Orr LJJ based their judgments on a different ground – namely, that, although English law would not recognise a change in the status of an enemy alien effected by the alien's domestic law during war time, that non-recognition only lasted so long as the state of war lasted, and that consequently when the state of war between this country and Germany came to an end our law would recognise that the appellant had been deprived of his status as a German national by the decree of November 25, 1941. ...

Shortly after the collapse of the Nazi régime in May 1945, the 1941 decree was repealed by Allied military government legislation. It is, however, generally accepted by German lawyers that this repeal had no retrospective effect. When the newly established Federal Republic of Germany came to frame its constitution it had to decide what persons were to be its nationals. This was a difficult and delicate question for several different reasons. In the first place – and this, of course, is the aspect of the matter with which we are concerned in this case – it had to decide what to do about those persons who had been deprived of their German nationality by Nazi legislation. On the one hand the new Germany was anxious not to appear to treat the 1941 decree as valid in any way; but on the other hand it had to face the fact that many of those affected by it had made their homes abroad and had no intention of returning to Germany, and that such persons, many of whom had become naturalised in other countries, might well not welcome having German nationality which they thought they had lost thrust upon them without their consent. Other problems which the framers of the Basic Law had to face but which are of no relevance in this case were, of course, the status in the Federal Republic of those "Germans" who had taken refuge there in the later stages of the war and of the "Germans" in the Soviet zone of occupation.

At this point it will be convenient to refer to article 116 of the Basic Law. It runs as follows:

"(1) A German person within the meaning of this Basic Law is, subject to further legal provisions any person who possesses German nationality or has been admitted into the sphere of the German Reich according to the position on December 31, 1937, as a refugee or exile, member of the German people or as the spouse or descendant of such a person. (2) Former German citizens who were deprived of their German nationality between January 30, 1933 and May 8, 1945 for political, racial or religious reasons, and their descendants, are to be renaturalised on application. They shall be considered as not having been deprived of their nationality, provided that they have taken up their residence in Germany since May 8, 1945 and have not expressed any wish to the contrary."

It is, of course, with paragraph (2) that we are concerned. Reading the translation simply as a piece of English without the aid of a German lawyer or of a German decisions I would have interpreted it as saying that the Nazi legislation must be taken as having effectively deprived those falling within its terms of their German nationality unless they had returned to live in Germany after the war, and had not expressed a wish not to be German nationals. On the other hand, those still abroad could regain the German nationality which they had lost whenever they wished by applying for it to the appropriate authority. The appellant, though he has now made such an application, did not make it until after the years of assessment with which we are concerned.

Accordingly if the meaning of article 116(2) was what I have suggested – and it appears that for some time after 1949 it was widely thought in Germany that that was its true meaning – it would be clear that he was not a German national in the years of assessment. It would also be clear that the 1913 law could have had no application in his case since he would not have been a German national when he was naturalised here. But the 1968 decision of the Federal Constitutional Court shows that it is wrong to interpret article 116(2) as saying – even if only by implication – that the Nazi legislation had deprived anyone of his German nationality. The court in that case had to decide whether someone affected by the 1941 decree who died before the end of the war – that is, May 8, 1945 – and had not been naturalised in another country died a German national or a stateless person. It held that he died a German national because the 1941 decree was "... to so intolerable a degree irreconcilable with justice that it must be considered to have been null and void ab initio". It was common ground between Dr Cohn and Dr Jacques that this decision had retrospective effect and that in the light of it the appellant remained a German national notwithstanding the 1941 decree at least until he became a British subject in 1948.

Accordingly the questions to be decided were (1) did he lose his German nationality under the 1913 law when he became a British subject, and (2), if he did not, did he lose it in 1949 by reason of the enactment of article 116 of the Basic Law? Dr Cohn answered both these questions in the affirmative while Dr Jacques answered them in the negative. The special commissioners preferred the views of Dr Cohn on both points and since foreign law is a question of fact it might be argued that the view taken by the commissioners was binding on us even if we disagreed with it – unless indeed it was one which we thought no one could reasonably entertain. But in a case of this sort it would, I think, be unfortunate if we were obliged to give effect to a view as to the relevant foreign law which we thought to be wrong and we did in fact hear a full argument from Sir John Foster in support of the opinion of Dr Jacques. I propose therefore to proceed on the footing that it is open to us to decide the questions at issue for ourselves but for reasons which will hereafter appear I shall assume in favour of the appellant that he did not lose his German nationality on becoming naturalised here in 1948 and confine myself to the question whether he lost it by reason of the enactment of the Basic Law in 1949. The passage in the judgment of the Federal Constitutional Court in the 1968 case which deals with the position of persons affected by the 1941 decree who were alive when the Basic Law took effect ran as follows:

> "In formulating this article the constitutional legislator proceeded from the assumption that the 11th ordinance was void ab initio. This means that the persecutees have never lost their German nationality by virtue of the expatriation. They may of course have lost it for some other reason, especially through acquisition of a foreign nationality. The effect of article 116(2) of the constitution in such a case is that even these persons can regain German nationality by taking up residence in the Federal German Republic or by making an application. For persecutees who have not acquired a foreign nationality the effect of article 116(2) is that notwithstanding the fact that they did not lose their German nationality by expatriation the German state does not treat them as Germans unless they assert their German nationality by taking up residence or making an application. Thus far article 116(2) gives effect to the idea that no persecutee should have German nationality forced upon him against his will."

If one looked simply at the language of article 116(2) – in particular at the word "renaturalised" – the first sentence quoted above might be difficult to justify. But the Federal Constitutional Court supported its interpretation by reference to the views expressed during the preparation of the law by members of the committee of the parliamentary council responsible for its wording. The part of the quoted passage which is, of course, particularly relevant for present purposes is the sentence:

> "For persecutees who have not acquired a foreign nationality" – and I am assuming that the appellant's naturalisation here in 1948 can be disregarded – "the effect of article 116(2) is that notwithstanding the fact that they did not lose their German nationality by expatriation the German state does not treat them as Germans unless they assert their German nationality by taking up residence or making an application."

The effect of Dr Cohn's evidence was that no distinction could sensibly be drawn between not being treated as a German by the German state and not being a German and that accordingly the appellant, assuming that he was a German national immediately before May 23, 1949, ceased then to be a German national until he either applied to become a German national again or took up residence in Germany. The effect of Dr Jacques's evidence on the other hand was that article 116 of the

Basic Law could not be taken to have deprived anyone of his German nationality and that the appellant continued to be a German national after the enactment of the Basic Law although he would not be recognised as such by the German authorities unless he applied to be recognised or took up residence.

Applying my mind as best I can to the problem of interpreting article 116(2) of the Basic Law in the light of the 1968 decision of the Federal Constitutional Court I prefer – as did the special commissioners – the view of Dr Cohn to the view of Dr Jacques. I find the conception of a man being by German law a German national but at the same time not being by German law treated or recognised as a German national very hard to grasp and although it may look at first sight odd that a man who had not lost his German nationality by the 1941 decree should lose it in 1949 under the operation of the Basic Law this apparent oddity disappears if one bears in mind the conflicting considerations which the framers of the Basic Law had to try to reconcile. On the one hand they were unwilling to admit that the 1941 decree had ever been part of the law of Germany but at the same time they did not wish to thrust German nationality on people who did not want it. As a compromise – if one reads the Basic Law as the Federal Constitutional Court read it – they drew a line at the date of the enactment of the Basic Law. Up to that date people who fell within the scope of the 1941 decree retained their German nationality unless they had given some positive indication that they rejected it; but after the date of the coming into force of the new constitution it was up to the persons concerned to give some positive indication that they wished to be nationals of the new Germany either by living there or by applying for German nationality.

That Dr Cohn's reading of the 1968 decision is the right one is, I think, confirmed by two decisions of other German courts dealing with persons affected by the 1941 decree who died after the enactment of the Basic Law. The first (called in argument the "mental defective" case) was decided by the Berlin District Court in 1971. The question to be decided was whether a German Jew who left Germany in 1933 to settle in this country and died here in 1956 in a psychiatric institution died a German national. He had not been naturalised here and from before the date of the enactment of the Basic Law until the date of his death he had been continuously under mental disability. The court held that as he had never been able to apply his mind to the question whether or not to apply for German nationality under the provisions of article 116(2) he remained clothed with his original German nationality of which the 1941 decree had not deprived him. "Article 116(2)", to quote a passage from the judgment –

> "can be applied only to those cases in which the persons in question have or have had the possibility of making known their intention by complying with one or other of the set of requirements referred to."

It is however implicit in the decision that had the propositus not been mentally incapable on May 23, 1949, he would have lost his German nationality on that date. It might, I suppose, be argued that the conception of a "possibility of making known their intention" included not only mental capacity but also actual knowledge of the terms of article 116(2) and that no one should lose his German nationality under the article until the lapse of a reasonable time for making his application after the date when he became aware of the terms of the article; but such an interpretation might obviously give rise to disputes of fact which would be very hard to resolve and it is not surprising that, so far as the evidence before us goes, it has never been advocated by anyone.

The other decision (called in argument the "Hong Kong dentist" case) was decided by the Berlin District Court in 1968. The "propositus" in that case was a Jewish dentist who left Germany in 1937 and eventually settled in Hong Kong where he died in 1954. He never became naturalised in any other country and according to Dr Cohn's view of the meaning of the 1968 decision of the Federal Constitutional Court he died a stateless person since he had not applied for German nationality after the enactment of the Basic Law. The District Court held that he died a German national because there was no evidence that had done anything to show that he wished to renounce his German nationality. But as I read the decision this was not because the court interpreted the 1968 decision of the Federal Constitutional Court differently from Dr Cohn but because it thought that the Constitutional Court had been wrong to draw a line at the date of the enactment of the Basic Law and to say that, whereas up to that date "persecutees" were German nationals unless they had done something to show that they wished to renounce German nationality, after that date they ceased to be German nationals unless and until they took steps to acquire German nationality. The District Court may have been entitled to take a different view on this point from the Federal Constitutional Court since in the 1968 decision the point at issue was the status of persons within the scope of the 1941 decree who had died before the end of the war and what the court said about those who were alive when the Basic Law was enacted was only an obiter dictum; but I think that we should follow any views expressed by the Constitutional Court on the meaning of the Basic Law even if not part of the ratio decidendi unless they conflict with dicta of the same court in other cases. For these reasons I think that even if one assumes that the appellant did not lose his German nationality when he became naturalised in this country in 1948 he ceased to be a German national from May 23, 1949, until he applied to become a German national after the years of assessment.

Logically, of course, the question whether the appellant lost his German nationality when he became a British subject in 1948 comes before the question whether he lost it on the coming into force of the Basic Law – for it is common ground that if he ceased to be a German national on naturalisation here in 1948 he did not become one again until he applied under article 116(2) after the years of assessment. At first sight the passage from the 1968 decision quoted above would seem to point conclusively to the view that he *did* lose his German nationality in 1948 by the operation of the 1913 law. The court after saying that "the persecutees" had not lost their German citizenship by their expatriation under the 1941 decree went on to say: "They may of course have lost it for some other reason, especially through acquisition of a foreign nationality". But against this one has to set what was said by the Federal Constitutional Court itself in a decision in 1958 on which Dr Jacques strongly relied. The propositus there was a German Jew who emigrated to the USA in 1934, became naturalised as an American citizen in 1946, later returned to live in Germany and had never evinced any intention not to be a German national. In 1956 the Munich Court of Appeal issued a provisional extradition warrant against him on request of the Swiss Government in respect of criminal offences of which he was accused but the Federal Constitution Court quashed the order on the ground that he was a German national. After pointing out that he had not lost his German nationality by the Nazi legislation the court dealt with the effect of his naturalisation in the USA as follows:

> "The loss of this nationality can also not be [based on] his naturalisation in the United States of America in 1946 by virtue of section 17 no 2 and section 25(1) of the Nationality Act; those provisions presuppose that the person concerned enjoyed the effective possession of German nationality at the time when he acquired a foreign nationality. That is not the case if at the material time he was not in a position to rely on his German nationality; for, if an expatriation pronounced *before* that time is only declared invalid by a law enacted *after* that time, then the person in question had no reason at the material time to take the legal consequences of the acquisition of a foreign nationality under the German nationality law into consideration. A contrary view would also have the effect of frustrating the indemnificatory purpose of article 16(2), second sentence, of the Basic Law and would result in the person in question being treated by his home country in a manner contrary to good faith."

That case differs, of course, on its facts from this case because the appellant there had returned to live in Germany whereas the appellant here has not done so. But thought the second reason for their conclusion given in the last sentence of the quoted passage would not apply here the first reason is expressed in general terms which would appear on their face to apply to Mr Oppenheimer's naturalisation as much as to that of the appellant in that case. We did not hear a full argument from Mr Vinelott on this branch of the case and it may be that he would have convinced me that there is no inconsistency between what is said as to the effect of naturalisation in another country before the enactment of the Basic Law in the 1958 and 1968 decisions respectively. But as it is I prefer to leave open the question whether had Mr Oppenheimer died between June 4, 1948, and May 23, 1949, he would have been a German national at the date of his death and to rest my decision on the point that, having survived the enactment of the Basic Law, he ceased thereupon to be a German national until he applied to be one.

. . .

As the members of the Court of Appeal in giving their judgments proceeded – through no fault of their own – on a wholly false view of the German law applicable to this case the reasons which they gave for allowing the appeal are, strictly speaking, irrelevant. In particular, of course, the shocking character of the 1941 decree upon which so much of the argument in the courts below and in the first hearing before us centred ceased to have any bearing on the case when once one appreciates that the problem posed by that degree was tackled by the Federal Republic before the years of assessment in the Basic Law of 1949. But as the judgments below have been reported and I do not in all respects agree with them I shall state as briefly as I can what conclusion I would have reached if the relevant German law had consisted, as we thought that it did, simply and solely of the 1941 decree and the 1913 law.

There are four arguments to be considered. The first ran as follows: (A) at the outbreak of the war in 1939 Mr Oppenheimer, who was then undoubtedly a German national resident in this country, became an "enemy alien"; (B) *Rex* v *Home Secretary, ex parte L* [1945] KB 7 and *Lowenthal* v *Attorney-General* [1948] 1 All ER 295 show that the courts of this country will not recognise a change in the status of an "enemy alien" effected during the war under the law of the enemy country; and (C) this non-recognition does not end with the war. The first two steps in the argument are plainly right but the third is, I think, wrong. In reaching the conclusion that our courts should continue to refuse recognition to the change of nationality affected by the 1941 decree even after the end of the war because it was a change effected during the war Goulding J was to some extent influenced by the character of the decree (see [1972] Ch 585, 595), but the character of the decree has no relevance to this argument. The refusal of our courts to recognise a change in the status of an "enemy alien" effected during war time is not confined to changes effected by laws passed by the enemy state during the war and may operate to deny recognition to changes effected by legislation of a wholly unobjectionable character. For example, if under a law of the enemy state passed before the war a female national loses her nationality on marrying a national of another state a female national of the enemy state who was living in this country and married during the war a national of this or of some third country would be regarded by our courts as remaining an "enemy alien" even after her marriage so long as the war continued, at all events so far as regards matters connected with the conduct of the war. But there is no reason in sense or logic why our courts should continue to regard her as a national of the former enemy state for any purpose after the end of the war although by the law of that state she is no longer a national of it. I agree with Buckley and Orr LJJ that the doctrine of public policy in question merely suspends recognition during war time. I would add, however, that I incline to think that "during war time" for this purpose should be interpreted in a common sense way as "until the end of the fighting". It appears to have been assumed in the courts below that the relevant date would be not May 8, 1945, but July 9, 1951, when the government of this country declared that the state of war had ended. The man in the street would have been very surprised to be told in 1950 that we were still at war with Germany; and as at present advised I can see no reason why the suspension of recognition of changes of nationality should be artificially extended in this way. It is not clear from the report of *Lowenthal* v *Attorney-General* whether the relevant date was April 28, 1944, when the summons under s18 of the Patents and Designs Acts 1907-1946 was issued or some date after May 8, 1945. If the latter was the case I doubt whether the decision was right.

The second ground upon which it was argued that English law should deem Mr Oppenheimer to have remained a German national notwithstanding the 1941 decree was that the decree was "confiscatory". "Confiscatory legislation" is a somewhat vague phrase which is sometimes used to cover not only expropriation with no or only inadequate compensation but also compulsory acquisition for full compensation. But it is clear that if foreign legislation on its true construction purports to divest the owner of particular property here of his title to it our courts will not give effect to the transfer even if the foreign legislation provides for full compensation. I cannot see, however, how this rule could have assisted Mr Oppenheimer here. Even if one regards his status as a German national as being a bundle of rights and duties those rights and duties were not themselves locally situate here. The right to claim exemption from United Kingdom tax given to him by the Convention if he was a German national at the relevant time was no doubt situate here. In the same way if a testator who died in 1953 had left him a legacy if he was *not* a German national at the date of his death the right to claim the legacy if he could fulfil the condition would have been a right situate here. If the 1941 decree deprived him of his German nationality in the eyes of English law that no doubt would entail the consequences that his position with regard to rights then existing or subsequently arising in this country which were dependent on his being or not being a German national would have been changed by the decree; but I do not think that the fact that the legislation by which a foreign state deprives a man of his status as one of its nationals can be described as "confiscatory" necessarily entails the consequence that our law should deem him to remain a citizen of that state for the purpose of deciding whether or not he is entitled to property rights in this country. Suppose, for example, that it was the law of Ruritania that any Ruritanian citizen who was convicted of treason by a Ruritanian court should forfeit all his property wherever situate to the Ruritanian state and should also cease to be a citizen of Ruritania. Our courts would certainly refuse to entertain an action by the Ruritanian state to obtain possession of the traitor's property here; but I can see no sufficient reason why we should continue to regard him as a Ruritanian citizen for the purpose of deciding whether or not he was entitled to property here, his right to which depended on his being or not being a Ruritanian citizen at some point of time.

The third ground on which it was argued that English law should pay no regard to the 1941 decree was that it was contrary to international law.

In his judgment Buckley LJ says [1973] Ch 264 273:

> "... the answer to the question whether or not the person is a national or citizen of the country must be answered in the light of the law of that country however inequitable, oppressive or objectionable it may be."

With all respect I cannot agree that that is the law. If a foreign country purported to confer the benefit of its protection on and to exact a duty of allegiance for persons who had no connection or only a very slender connection with it our courts would be entitled to pay no regard to such legislation on the ground that the country in question was acting beyond the bounds of any jurisdiction in matters of nationality which international law would recognise. In this respect I think that our law is the same as that of the United States as stated by the Court of Appeals (Second Circuit), in *United States; ex rel Schwarzkopf v Uhl* (1943), 137 Fed Rep 2d 898. Schwarzkopf who was then an Austrian national came to the United States in 1936 with the intention of living there permanently. By a decree of July 3, 1938, the German state – which had annexed Austria on May 13, 1938 – purported to make him a German citizen and on December 9, 1941 he was arrested by the American authorities as a German citizen under a presidential decree made in view of the imminence of war between the United States and Germany. The court held in reliance on a number of authorities referred to in the judgment that the German decree of July 3, 1938, so far as it purported to impose German nationality on persons who at that time had no connection with Germany, must be disregarded by the American courts. It may be said, perhaps, that though international law sets limits to the jurisdiction of sovereign states so far as concerns the granting of nationality it sets no limits whatever to their power to withdraw it. I am not prepared to accept that this is so. I think, for example, that Martin Wolff, *Private International Law*, 2nd ed, p129, may well be right in saying that, if a state withdraws its citizenship from some class of its citizens living within its borders to which it has taken a dislike and of whom it would be glad to be rid, other states are not obliged to regard such people as "stateless". Mr Vinelott was prepared to concede that this might be so; but he pointed out that the 1941 decree was only aimed at persons who had already left Germany for good and that emigration was a common and well-recognised ground for the withdrawal of nationality. This is, of course, true, and if the decree had simply provided that all Germans who had left Germany since Hitler's advent to power with the intention of making their homes elsewhere should cease to be German nationals it may be that our courts would have had to recognise it even though many of those concerned were not in truth voluntary emigrants but had been driven from their native land. But the 1941 decree did not deprive *all* "emigrés" of their status as German nationals. It only deprived *Jewish* emigrés of their citizenship. Further, as the later paragraphs of the decree show, this discriminatory withdrawal of their rights of citizenship was used as a peg upon which to hang a discriminatory confiscation of their property. A judge should, of course, be very slow to refuse to give effect to the legislation of a foreign state in any sphere in which, according to accepted principles of international law, the foreign state had jurisdiction. He may well have an inadequate understanding of the circumstances in which the legislation was passed and his refusal to recognise it may be embarrassing to the branch of the executive which is concerned to maintain friendly relations between this country and the foreign country in question. But I think – as Upjohn J thought (see *In re Claim by Helbert Wagg & Co Ltd* [1956] Ch 323, 334) – that it is part of the public policy of this country that our courts should give effect to clearly establish rules of international law. Of course on some points it may be by no means clear what the rule of international law is. Whether, for example, legislation of a particular type is contrary to international law because it is "confiscatory" is a question upon which there may well be wide differences of opinion between communist and capitalist countries. But what we are concerned with here is legislation which takes away without compensation from a section of the citizen body singled out on racial grounds all their property on which the state passing the legislation can lay its hands and, in addition, deprives them of their citizenship. To my mind a law of this sort constitutes so grave an infringement of human rights that the courts of this country ought to refuse to recognise it as a law at all. There are, no doubt, practical objections to adopting that course with this law, for in many, if not most, cases the persons affected by the 1941 decree would not have wished to remain German nationals. Dr Mann in his article ("The Present Validity of Nazi Nationality Laws", 89 LQR 194) quotes several cases in which courts in different countries, while characterising the 1941 decree as "atrocious" or "barbarous", have yet given effect to it for this reason. But it surely cannot be right for the question whether the decree should be recognised or not to depend on the circumstances of the particular case. Moreover, in some cases – as for instance where the propositus is dead and what is in issue is the law to be applied to the devolution of his estate – it might be impossible to say which law he would have wished to govern the matter. If one held – as I would have held – that Mr Oppenheimer remained a German national in the eyes of our law notwithstanding the 1941 decree the further question would have arisen whether in the eyes of our law he lost his German nationality in 1948 under the law of 1913, although by German law as it then was he was not a German national when he was naturalised here. It would not, however, have been necessary for me to form a view of my own on this point since Mr Vinelott was prepared to accept as correct the view expressed by Goulding J in the following words [1972] Ch 585, 596:

> "... I cannot see that the non-recognition of one foreign law on grounds of public policy either demands or justifies imputing to a later foreign law an operation which, on its true construction in its own system, it evidently could not have."

Finally, it is necessary to consider the reason given by Lord Denning MR for allowing the appeal from Goulding J. It was, as I understand it, that even if Mr Oppenheimer was a German national by German law in the years of assessment, English law, which is the law to be applied in construing the convention, would not regard him as a German national as well as a British subject in view of the circumstances in which he became a British subject. Our law is, of course, familiar with the concept of dual nationality – indeed the relevant part of the tax convention proceeds on the footing that a man may be at one and the same time a British subject and a German national – and the English law which is to be applied in deciding whether or not Mr Oppenheimer was a German national at the relevant time is not simply our municipal law but includes the rule which refers the question whether a man is a German national to the municipal law of Germany. Of course, the fact that our law recognises that a man as well as being a British subject is also a German national does not in the least affect either his rights or his duties as a British subject. Consequently, in time of war between the countries concerned a man with dual nationality may find himself in a very unenviable position. As Viscount Cave LC pointed out in *Kramer* v *Attorney-General* [1923] AC 528, 532 he may be forced to fight in the British army and yet have his property confiscated under the peace treaty as the property of a German national.

Lord Denning MR was not, I am sure, intending to deny any of this; but he thought that the particular circumstances in which Mr Oppenheimer became a British subject made it impossible for him thereafter to be considered by our law as having German nationality whatever German law might say on the point. His judgment, as I read it, contains two different reasons for this conclusion – though they are not, if I may say so, very clearly distinguished. The first depended on the character of the 1941 decree. By it – the argument runs – Germany repudiated its obligations to Mr Oppenheimer and he accepted the repudiation by applying for British citizenship, so that even if the 1941 decree were to be declared 'void ab initio' by German law he would be in the eyes of English law precluded from asserting that he had remained a German national. For my part I cannot accept that concepts drawn from the law of contract can be imported in this way into the law of nationality. The second reason was a more general one – namely, that if the Secretary of State grants a certificate in naturalisation to a national of a country with whom this country is then at war English law will deem him to have thereupon lost his previous nationality for good whatever the law of the foreign country may say. If a certificate of naturalisation is granted in peace time Lord Denning MR would, I think, accept that the man in question would in the eyes of English law retain his other nationality if he did so by the law of the other country. But he considered that the conception of an enemy alien being granted a certificate of naturalisation in war time and still remaining thereafter in the eyes of our law under a duty of allegiance to the enemy sovereign as well as to the Queen of England was an impossible one and that accordingly after the grant our law would regard him as having only a single nationality – namely, British nationality – even after the end of the war. I do not myself see any need to draw a distinction between naturalisation in time of peace and naturalisation in time of war. In either case the man in question comes under a duty of allegiance to the Queen which is not affected in any way by the fact – if it be a fact – that by the law of the foreign country in question he remains a national of it.

In the result, therefore, if the relevant German law had been what we assumed it to be when the appeal was first argued I would have been in favour of allowing it; but in the light of the German law as we now know it I would, as I have said, dismiss it.

I turn now to consider the appeal *Nothman* v *Cooper*. Miss Nothman was born in 1915 in Frankfurt. She went to a grammar school and obtained distinction in mathematics. As she was a Jewess she could not go to Frankfurt University but she took a teacher's training course at a Jewish teachers' training college where she passed an examination in March 1936. During the next three years she held various teaching posts in the dwindling and persecuted Jewish community in Germany and eventually – in April 1939 – came to this country. The respondent accepts for the purposes of this appeal that she has become a British subject. Under a law enacted in 1951 by the Federal Government of Germany former public servants who had suffered injury in their careers through the "Nazi" persecution became entitled to apply for compensation (Wiedergutmachung). Article 31(d)(1) of the law provided that former employees of Jewish communities or public organisations who had or but for the persecutions would have attained a right to retirement benefits against their employers should be entitled from October 1, 1952, onwards to pension payments on the basis of their former salary payments. In 1956 Miss Nothman was awarded as from 1952 a basic monthly compensation under this article. She was assessed to United Kingdom income tax in respect of the payments which she received in the tax year 1953/54 to 1964/65 inclusive on the footing that they were income arising from possessions out of the United Kingdom. She appealed to the special commissioners against the assessments arguing (1) that she was a German national in the years in question and therefore exempt from United Kingdom income tax under the tax convention previously mentioned and (2) that for various reasons the payments which she received were not subject to United Kingdom tax. The special commissioners held that she was liable to United Kingdom tax and this decision was upheld both by Goulding J and the Court of Appeal. On her appeal to this House Miss Nothman, who presented her case with ability and courtesy, was prepared on the first point to adopt the arguments which had been submitted by Sir John Foster on behalf of Mr Oppenheimer; but on the second point she addressed to us – as she had to the court below – several arguments with which it is necessary to deal. In the first place she pointed out that the payments in question were not really pension payments at all but were in truth compensation for having been deprived of the opportunity of following her chosen career. They were therefore in the nature of damages and should not be treated as income payments. But the payments, even if not properly described as "pension" payments, are not instalments of any ascertained capital sum, and I cannot see any more than could the commissioners or the courts below why they are not received by Miss Nothman as income. Her second contention was that the payments were not assessable to tax because they were "voluntary payments". It is, of course, true that she received them because the Federal Republic decided of its own volition to do something towards making good to persons in the position of Miss Nothman the wrong done to them by the Nazi government, and no doubt what the Federal Republic has given it could if it wished take away. But the payments which Miss Nothman receives under the law while it is in force cannot be regarded as a series of voluntary gifts. Then she argued that the payments were not income from a "foreign possession",[7] but those words mean simply income derived from a source outside the United Kingdom and I think that Miss Nothman's rights under the German law in question constitute such a source. Finally Miss Nothman referred us to section 22(1) of the Finance Act 1961, which says:

> "Annuities payable under the law of the Federal German Republic relating to the compensation of victims of National-Socialist persecution, being annuities which under any such law relating to the taxation of such compensation are specifically exempted from tax of a character similar to that of income tax, shall not be regarded as income for any income tax purposes."

Unfortunately, however, as Miss Nothman admits, the German authorities have not granted to the payments being made to her any 'specific exemption' from tax – although according to her they ought, consistently with their approach in other cases, to have exempted them.

In the result, therefore, I think as the courts below thought that the decision of the special commissioners in Miss Nothman's case was correct and that her appeal must also be dismissed.'

LORD SALMON: 'My Lords, I am in entire agreement with all the views expressed in the speech of my noble and learned friend, Lord Cross of Chelsea. I wish to add only a few observations of my own.

The original case stated made no mention of article 116(2) of the Basic Law enacted by the Federal German Republic in 1949. Neither your Lordships at the first hearing of this appeal, nor the Court of Appeal, nor Goulding J had any opportunity of considering this vitally important enactment. Accordingly, in the courts below and at the first hearing before your Lordships, the appeal was necessarily conducted on the basis that the principal point for decision was whether or not our courts were bound to recognise the Nazi decree of November 1941 as effective in English law to deprive Mr Oppenheimer of his German nationality. On that basis, I was unhesitatingly in favour of allowing the appeal. The relevant parts of the Nazi decree read as follows:

> "2. A Jew loses German citizenship (a) if at the date of entry into force of this regulation he has his usual place of abode abroad, with effect from the entry into force of this decree; (b) if at some future date his usual place of abode is abroad, from the date of transfer of his usual place of abode abroad. 3(a) Property of Jews deprived of German nationality by this decree to fall to the state. (b) Such confiscated property to be used to further aims connected with the solution of the Jewish problem."

The expense of transporting large numbers of men, women and children, in all about 6,000,000, even without heat, food or sanitary arrangements must have been considerable. So no doubt was the expense of erecting, equipping and staffing concentration camps and gas chambers for their extermination. Evidently, the Nazis

---

[7] Reporter's note. See Income Tax Act 1952, s123(1), Case V.

considered it only natural that the confiscated assets of those who had been lucky enough to escape the holocaust should be used to finance it.

The Crown did not question the shocking nature of the 1941 decree, but argued quite rightly that there was no direct authority compelling our courts to refuse to recognise it. It was further argued that the authorities relating to penal or confiscatory legislation, although not directly in point, supported the view that our courts are bound by established legal principles to recognise the 1941 decree in spite of its nature. The lack of direct authority is hardly surprising. Whilst there are many examples in the books of penal or confiscatory legislation which according to our views is unjust, the barbarity of much of the Nazi legislation, of which this decree is but an example, is happily unique. I do not consider that any of the principles laid down in any of the existing authorities require our courts to recognise such a decree and I have no doubt that on the grounds of public policy they should refuse to do so.

I recognise that it is particularly within the province of any state to decide who are and who are not its nationals. If a foreign state deprives one of its nationals of his nationality, *as a rule* our courts will follow the foreign law and hold that the man in question shall be treated as not being a national of that foreign state. That principle was re-stated by Russell J in *Stoeck* v *Public Trustee* [1921] 2 Ch 67, 82. Russell J recognised, however, that circumstances could arise in which a man might be treated as a national of a foreign state for the purpose of English law although he was not a national of that state according to its own municipal law. I do not suppose that in 1921 it would have been possible for anyone to have been sufficiently imaginative or pessimistic to foresee anything like the decree of 1941. But, had Russell J been able to do so, he might well have concluded that there could be nothing which could afford a stronger justification for English law treating a man as a German national in spite of the fact that by German law he had lost his German nationality.

The principle normally applied by our courts in relation to foreign penal or confiscatory legislation was correctly stated by Goulding J: see [1972] Ch 585, 592. The comity of nations normally requires our courts to recognise the jurisdiction of a foreign state over all its own nationals and all assets situated within its own territories. Ordinarily, if our courts were to refuse to recognise legislation by a sovereign state relating to assets situated within its own territories or to the status of its own nationals on the ground that the legislation was utterly immoral and unjust, this could obviously embarrass the Crown in its relations with a sovereign state whose independence it recognised and with whom it had and hoped to maintain normal friendly relations. In *Aksionairnoye Obschestvo A M Luther* v *James Sagor & Co* [1921] 3 KB 532, the Soviet Republic by a decree passed in June 1918 declared all mechanical sawmills of a certain capital value and all woodworking establishments belonging to private or limited companies to be the property of the Soviet Republic. In 1919 agents of the Soviet Republic seized the plaintiff's mill in Russia and the stock of wood it contained. In 1920 the Soviet Republic sold a quantity of this stock to the defendants who imported it into England. The plaintiffs claimed a declaration that they were entitled to this stock on the ground that the 1918 decree of confiscation was so immoral and contrary to the principles of justice as recognised by this country that our courts ought not to pay any attention to it. It was held however that, as the government of this country had recognised the Soviet government as the de facto government of Russia prior to the 1918 decree, neither the decree nor the sale of the wood to the defendants in Russia could be impugned in our courts. The reasons for this decision are illuminating, since they illustrate one of the important differences between the present case and the host of other cases (of which *Aksionairnoye Obschestvo A M Luther* v *James Sagor & Co* [1921] 3 KB 532 is an example) in which foreign penal or confiscatory legislation has been considered in our courts. Scrutton LJ said, at pp 558-559:

> "But it appears a serious breach of international comity, if a state is recognised as a sovereign independent state, to postulate that its legislation is 'contrary to essential principles of justice and morality'. Such an allegation might well with a susceptible foreign government become a casus belli; and should in my view be the action of the Sovereign through his ministers, and not of the judges in reference to a state which their Sovereign has recognised. ... Individuals must contribute to the welfare of the state, and at present British citizens who may contribute to the state more than half their income in income tax and super tax, and a large proportion of their capital in death duties, can hardly declare a foreign state immoral which considers (though we may think wrongly) that to vest individual property in the state as representing all the citizens is the best form of proprietary right. I do not feel able to come to the conclusion that the legislation of a state recognised by my Sovereign as an independent sovereign state is so contrary to moral principle that the judges ought not to recognise it."

The alleged immorality of the Soviet Republic's 1918 decree was different in kind from the Nazi decree of 1941. The latter was without parallel. But, even more importantly, England and Russia were not at war in 1918 whilst England was at war with Germany in 1941 – a war which, as Goulding J points out [1972] Ch 585, 595, was presented in its later stages as a crusade against the barbarities of the Nazi régime of which the 1941 decree is a typical example. I do not understand how, in these circumstances, it could be regarded as embarrassing to our government in its relationship with any other sovereign state or contrary to international comity or to any legal principles hitherto enunciated for our courts to decide that the 1941 decree was so great an offence against human rights that they would have nothing to do with it.

It is for those reasons that I respectfully disagree with the finding of Buckley LJ in which Orr LJ concurred, that our courts would have been obliged to recognise the decree of 1941 as effective to deprive Mr Oppenheimer of his German nationality. It has been said that this decree conferred a positive benefit upon many of those whom it deprived of their German nationality. This may be so but there is no such finding in the case stated and it is not permissible to travel outside the case to explore these possibilities. In any event, I doubt whether the question as to whether an enactment is so great an offence against human rights that it ought not to be recognised by any civilised system of law can depend upon its impact upon the facts of any particular case.

62 *The Nature of Morality*

Mr Oppenheimer was exempt from English income tax in respect of his German pension if, but only if, he had a German as well as an English nationality during the tax years in question. He undoubtedly had no German nationality at the relevant period because of the decree of 1941 – if that decree was effective to prevent him from being treated in English law as a German national. As I have, however, already indicated, the decree, in my judgment, should not be recognised by our courts as having any effect in English law for any purpose. Although this view would have entitled Mr Oppenheimer to succeed on the case as originally stated, it is of no avail to him on the case as now re-stated.

The findings in the case, as re-stated, relating to German law, and in particular to article 116(2) of the Basic Law of 1949, throw an entirely new light upon this appeal. It is now clear that, during the tax years in question, Mr Oppenheimer's nationality under German municipal law did not in any way depend upon the decree of 1941. Indeed, by enacting the Basic Law of 1949 the German Federal Republic cleansed German municipal law of its contamination by the Nazis and did everything possible to rectify the injustice which the Nazi decrees had perpetrated. The German Federal Government were careful, however, not to thrust German nationality upon anyone against their will if the decree of 1941 had purported to deprive him of it. The Basic Law accordingly enabled anyone affected by the decree who wished to be a German national to be "re-nationalised" and treated for all purposes as a German national by German municipal law. Such a person had only to apply, at any time, for German nationality and his application would automatically be granted. Alternatively if he returned to and resided in Germany without declaring a wish not to be a German national he would be regarded, in German law, as a German national. If he did neither of these things, it would be assumed that he did not wish to be a German national and his wish would be respected. In such circumstances, German law would treat him as not being a German national – which as the commissioners have found in the re-stated case would mean that, in German law, he was not a German national. Mr Oppenheimer did not return to Germany, nor did he make any application under article 116(2) until after the tax years in question. Had he made any such application at any time between those years and 1949, he would immediately from the date of his application have been regarded by German municipal law as a German national and therefore also treated in English law as a German national. It was not the odious Nazi decree of 1941 but his own failure to apply in time under the benevolent article 116(2) of the Basic Law enacted in 1949 which deprived him of exemption from United Kingdom income tax for the tax years in question.

My Lords, I would accordingly dismiss Mr Oppenheimer's appeal. I would also, for the reasons given by my noble and learned friend Lord Cross of Chelsea, dismiss Miss Nothman's appeal.'

5. THE OBLIGATION
TO OBEY THE LAW

STEPHEN
A History of the Criminal Law of England [1]
(1883)

'The infliction of punishment bylaw gives definite expression and a solemn ratification and justification to the hatred which is excited by the commission of the offence, and which constitutes the moral or popular as distinguished from the conscientious sanction of that part of morality which is also sanctioned by the criminal law. The criminal law thus proceeds upon the principle that it is morally right to hate criminals, and it confirms and justifies the sentiment by inflicting upon criminals, punishments which express it ... I am also of the opinion that this close alliance between criminal law and moral sentiment is in all ways healthy and advantageous to the community. I think it highly desirable that criminals should be hated, that the punishment inflicted upon them should be so contrived as to give expression to that hatred, and to justify it so far as the public provision of means for expressing and gratifying a healthy natural sentiment can justify and encourage it.'

M COHEN
Moral Aspects of the Criminal Law [2]
(1940)

'The most popular theory today is that the proper aim of criminal procedure is to reform the criminal so that he may become adjusted to the social order. A mixture of sentimental and utilarian motives gives this view its great vogue. With the spread of humane feeling and the waning of faith in the old conception of the necessity of inflicting pain in the treatment of children and those suffering from mental disease, there has come a revulsion at the hardheartedness of the old retributive theory. The growing belief in education and in the healing powers of medicine encourages people to suppose that the delinquent may be re-educated to become a useful member of

[1] Stephen (1883) *A History of the Criminal Law of England.* Stevens, London, pp81–82.
[2] Cohen, M 'Moral Aspects of the Criminal Law' (1940) *Yale Law Journal* pp1012–1014.

society. Even from the strictest economic point of view, individual men and women are the most valuable assets of any society. It is not better to save them for a life of usefulness rather than punish them by imprisonment which generally makes them worse after they leave than before they entered?'

GERALD GARDINER
The Purposes of Criminal Punishment [3]
(1958)

'The belief in the value of deterrence rests on the assumption that we are rational beings who always think before we act, and then base our actions on a careful calculation of the gains and losses involved. These assumptions, dear to many lawyers, have long since been abandoned in the social sciences.

Amongst criminals, foresight and prudent calculation is even more conspicuous by its absence ... Even though there is no consensus amongst doctors about the exact description of the so-called "psycopaths", experienced Prison Medical Officers, and for that matter, Prison Governors, are agreed that there is a type of prisoner who is quite incapable of foresight, who cannot learn even from the experience of punishment, much less from the threat of it. Yet other offenders, notably some sex-offenders (but also others subject to compulsive behaviour) are sometimes at the mercy of their impulses, and unable, without proper help and treatment, to control themselves adequately. Such persons are frequently in conflict, not only with society, but also with themselves.

Another factor on which the effectiveness of deterrence depends is the certainty of conviction. But according to the latest official Criminal Statistics, only 48 per cent of the offences known to the police are "cleared up". Offences cleared up include those for which a person is arrested or summoned, or for which he is cautioned, those taken into consideration by a court when the offender is found guilty on another charge, and even some which are strongly suspected but which cannot be definitely cleared up; for instance, where the suspect dies or commits suicide before the case has been tried. Even so, this still leaves an unknown quantity of offences which remain undetected altogether, so the chances of your not being caught are distinctly better than those of your being apprehended and brought to trial. Add to this the fact that by no means all those who come before the courts are found guilty, and it is clear that the threat of punishment loses something of its persuasive force.'

---

[3] Gardiner, G 'The Purposes of Criminal Punishment' (1958) *21 Modern Law Review*, pp122–125.

LORD DEVLIN
The Enforcement of Morals [4]
(1965)

The Report of the Committee on Homosexual Offences and Prostitution, generally known as the Wolfenden Report, is recognized to be an excellent study of two very difficult legal and social problems. But it has also a particular claim to the respect of those interested in jurisprudence; it does what law reformers so rarely do; it sets out clearly and carefully what in relation to its subjects it considers the function of the law to be.[5] ... The greater part of the law relating to sexual relationship between it and the moral ideas which most of us uphold. Adultery, fornication, and prostitution are not, as the Report[6] points out, criminal offences: homosexuality between males is a criminal offence, but between females it is not. Incest was not an offence until it was declared so by statute only fifty years ago. Does the legislature select these offences haphazardly or are there some principles which can be used to determine what part of the moral law should be embodied in the criminal? ...

What is the connection between crime and sin and to what extent, if at all, should the criminal law of England concern itself with the enforcement of morals and punish sin or immorality as such? ...

Early in the Report[7] the Committee put forward:

Our own formulation of the function of the criminal law so far as it concerns the subjects of this enquiry. In this field, its function, as we see it, is to preserve public order and decency, to protect the citizen from what is offensive or injurious, and to provide sufficient safeguards against exploitation and corruption of others, particularly those who are specially vulnerable because they are young, weak in body or mind, inexperienced, or in a state of special physical, official or economic dependence.

It is not, in our view, the function of the law to intervene in the private lives of citizens, or to seek to enforce any particular pattern of behaviour, further than is necessary to carry out the purposes we have outlined. ...

Unless a deliberate attempt is to be made by society, acting through the agency of the law, to equate the sphere of crime with that of sin, there must remain a realm of private morality and immorality which is, in brief and crude terms, not the law' business. To say this is not to condone or encourage private immorality.

---

[4] From *The Enforcement of Morals* by Patrick Devlin, published by Oxford University Press. © Oxford University Press 1965, reprinted by permission of the author and publisher.

[5] The Committee's 'statement of juristic philosophy' (to quote Lord Pakenham) was considered by him in a debate in the House of Lords on 4 December 1957, reported in *Hansard Lords Debates*, vol. ccvi at 738; and also in the same debate by the Archbishop of Canterbury at 753 and Lord Denning at 806.

[6] Para. 14.

[7] Para. 13.

'We are agreed that private immorality should not be the concern of the criminal law except in the special circumstances therein mentioned.' They quote[8] with approval the report of the Street Offences Committee,[9] which says: 'As a general proposition it will be universally accepted that the law is not concerned with private morals or with ethical sanctions ... It is not the duty of the law to concern itself with immorality as such ... it should confine itself to those activities which offend against public order and decency or expose the ordinary citizen to what is offensive or injurious.[10]

These statements of principle are naturally restricted to the subject-matter of the Report. But they are made in general terms and there seems to be no reason why, if they are valid, they should not be applied to the criminal law in general. They separate very decisively crime from sin, the divine law from the secular, and the moral from the criminal. They do not signify any lack of support for the law, moral or criminal, and they do not represent schools of thought among those who may think that morals are not the law's business. There is first of all the agnostic or free-thinker ... Then there is the deeply religious person who feels that the criminal law is sometimes more of a hindrance than a help in the sphere of morality, and that the reform of the sinner – at any rate when he injures only himself – should be a spiritual rather than a temporal work. Then there is the man who without any strong feeling cannot see why, where there is freedom in religious belief, there should not logically be freedom in morality as well. All these are powerfully allied against the equating of crime with sin. ...

I must admit that I begin with a feeling that a complete separation of crime from sin (I use the term throughout this lecture in the wider meaning) would note good for the moral law and might be disastrous for the criminal. But can this sort of feeling be justified as a matter of jurisprudence? And if it be a right feeling, how should the relationship between the criminal and the moral law be stated? Is there a good theoretical basis for it, or is it just a practical working alliance, or is it a bit of both? That is the problem which I want to examine, and I shall begin by considering the standpoint of the strict logician. It can be supported by cogent arguments, some of which I believe to be unanswerable and which I put as follows.

Morals and religion are inextricably joined – the moral standards generally accepted in Western civilization being those belonging to Christianity. Outside Christendom other standards derive from other religions. None of these moral codes can claim any validity except by virtue of the religion on which it is based. Old Testament morals differ in some respects from New Testament morals. Even within Christianity there are differences. Some hold that contraception is an immoral practice and that a man who has carnal knowledge of another woman while his wife is alive is in all circumstances a fornicator; others, including most of the English-

---

[8] Para. 227.
[9] Cmd. 3231 (1928).
[10] Para. 257.

speaking world, deny both these propositions. Between the great religions of the world, of which Christianity is only one, there are much wider differences. It may or may not be right for the State to adopt one of these religions as the truth, to found itself upon its doctrines, and to deny to any of its citizens the liberty to practise any other. If it does, it is logical that it should use the secular law wherever it thinks it necessary to enforce the divine. If it does not, it is illogical that it should concern itself with morals as such. But if it leaves matters of religion to private judgment, it should logically leave matters of morals also. A State which refuses to enforce Christian beliefs has lost the right to enforce Christian morals.

If this view is sound, it means that the criminal law cannot justify any of its provisions by reference to the moral law. It cannot say, for example, that murder and theft are prohibited because they are immoral or sinful. The State must justify in some other way the punishments which it imposes on wrongdoers and a function for the criminal law independent of morals must be found. This is not difficult to do. The smooth functioning of society and the preservation of order require that a number of activities should be regulated. The rules that are made for that purpose and are enforced by the criminal law are often designed simply to achieve uniformity and convenience and rarely involve any choice between good and evil. Rules that impose a speed limit or prevent obstruction on the highway have nothing to do with morals. Since so much of the criminal law is composed of rules of this sort, why bring morals into it all? Why not define the function of the criminal law in simple terms as the preservation of order and decency and the protection of the lives and property of citizens, and elaborate those terms in relation to any particular subject in the way in which it is done in the Wolfenden Report? The criminal law in carrying out these objects will undoubtedly overlap the moral law. Crimes of violence are morally wrong and they are also offences against good order; therefore they offend against both laws. But this is simply because the two laws in pursuit of different objectives happen to cover the same area. Such is the argument.

Is the argument consistent or inconsistent with the fundamental principles of English criminal law as it exists today? ...

It is true that for many centuries the criminal law was much concerned with keeping the peace and little, if at all, with sexual morals. But it would be wrong to infer from that that it had no moral content or that it would ever have tolerated the idea of a man being left to judge for himself in matters of morals. The criminal law of England has from the very first concerned itself with moral principles. A simple way of testing this point is to consider the attitude which the criminal law adopts towards consent.

Subject to certain exceptions inherent in the nature of particular crimes, the criminal law has never permitted consent of the victim to be used as a defence. In rape, for example, consent negatives an essential element. But consent of the victim is no defence to a charge of murder. It is not a defence to any form of assault that the victim thought his punishment well deserved and submitted to it; to make a good defence the accused must prove that the law gave him the right to chastise and that he exercised it reasonably. Likewise, the victim may not forgive the aggressor and require the prosecution to desist; the right to enter a *nolle prosequi* belongs to the Attorney-General alone.

Now, if the law existed for the protection of the individual, there would be no reason why he should avail himself of it if he did not want it. The reason why a man may not consent to the commission of an offence against himself beforehand or forgive it afterwards is because it is an offence against society. It is not that society is physically injured; that would be impossible. Nor need any individual be shocked, corrupted, or exploited; everything may be done in private. Nor can it be explained on the practical ground that a violent man is a potential danger to others in the community who have therefore a direct interest in his apprehension and punishment as being necessary to their own protection. That would be true of a man whom the victim is prepared to forgive but not of one who gets his consent first; a murderer who acts only upon the consent, and maybe the request, of his victim is no menace to others, but he does threaten one of the great moral principles upon which society is based, that is, the sanctity of human life. There is only one explanation of what has hitherto been accepted as the basis of the criminal law and that is that there are certain standards of behaviour or moral principles which society requires to be observed; and the breach of them is an offence not merely against the person who is injured but against society as a whole.

Thus, if the criminal law were to be reformed so as to eliminate from it everything that was not designed to preserve order and decency or to protect citizens (including the protection of youth from corruption), it would overturn a fundamental principle. It would also end a number of specific crimes. Euthanasia or the killing of another at his own request, suicide, attempted suicide, and suicide pacts, duelling, abortion, incest between brother and sister, are all acts which can be done in private and without offence to others and need not involve the corruption or exploitation of others. Many people think that the law on some of these subjects is in need of reform, but no one hitherto has gone so far as to suggest that they should all be left outside the criminal law as matters of private morality. They can be brought within it only as a matter of moral principle. It must be remembered also that although there is much immorality that is not punished by the law, there is none that is condoned by the law. The law will not allow its processes to be used by those engaged in immorality of any sort. For example, a house may not be let for immoral purposes; the lease is invalid and would not be enforced. But if what goes on inside there is a matter of private morality and not the law's business, why does the law inquire into it all?

I think it is clear that the criminal law as we know it is based upon moral principle. In a number of crimes its function is simply to enforce a moral principle and nothing else. The law, both criminal and civil, claims to be able to speak about morality and immorality generally. Where does it get its authority to do this and how does it settle the moral principles which it enforces? Undoubtedly, as a matter

of history, it derived both from Christian teaching. But I think that the strict logician is right when he says that the law can no longer rely on doctrines in which citizens are entitled to disbelieve. It is necessary therefore to look for some other source
... I have framed three interrogatories addressed to myself to answer:

1. Has society the right to pass judgment at all on matters of morals? Ought there, in other words, to be a public morality, or are morals always a matter for private judgment?
2. If society has the right to pass judgment, has it also the right to use the weapon of the law to enforce it?
3. If so, ought it to use that weapon in all cases or only in some; and if only in some, on what principles should it distinguish?

I shall begin with the first interrogatory and consider what is meant by the right of society to pass a moral judgment, that is a judgment about what is good and what is evil. The fact that a majority of people may disapprove of a practice does not of itself make it a matter for society as a whole. Nine men out of ten may disapprove of what the tenth man is doing and still say that it is not their business. There is a case for a collective judgment (as distinct from a large number of individual opinions which sensible people may even refrain from pronouncing at all if it is upon somebody else's private affairs) only if society is affected. Without a collective judgment there can be no case at all for intervention ...

This view – that there is such a thing as public morality – can also be justified by *a priori* argument. What makes a society of any sort is community of ideas, not only political ideas but also ideas about the way its members should behave and govern their lives; these latter ideas are its morals. Every society has a moral structure as well as a political one: or rather, since that might suggest two independent systems, I should say that the structure of every society is made up both of politics and morals. Take, for example, the institution of marriage. Whether a man should be allowed to take more than one wife is something about which every society has to make up its mind one way or the other. In England we believe in the Christian idea of marriage and therefore adopt monogamy as a moral principle. Consequently the Christian institution of marriage has become the basis of family life and so part of the structure of our society. It is there not because it is Christian. It has got there because it is Christian, but it remains there because it is built into the house in which we live and could not be removed without bringing it down. The great majority of those who live in this country accept it because it is the Christian idea of marriage and for them the only true one. But a non-Christian is bound by it, not because it is part of Christianity but because, rightly or wrongly, it has been adopted by the society in which he lives. It would be useless for him to stage a debate designed to prove that polygamy was theologically more correct and socially preferable; if he wants to live in the house, he must accept it as built in the way in which it is. ...

I return to the statement that I have already made, that society means a community of ideas; without shared ideas on politics, morals, and ethics no society can exist. Each one of us has ideas about what is good and what is evil; they cannot be kept private from the society in which we live. If men and women try to create a society in which there is no fundamental agreement about good and evil they will fail; if, having based it on common agreement, the agreement does, the society will disintegrate. For society is not something that is kept together physically; it is held by the invisible bonds of common thought. If the bonds were too far relaxed the members would drift apart. A common morality is part of the bondage. The bondage is part of the price of society; and mankind, which needs society, must pay its price. ...

You may think that I have taken far too long in contending that there is such a thing as public morality, a proposition which most people would readily accept, and may have left myself too little time to discuss the next question which to many minds may cause greater difficulty; to what extent should society use the law to enforce its moral judgments? ...

But if society has the right to make a judgment and has it on the basis that a recognized morality is as necessary to society as, say, a recognized government, then society may use the law to preserve morality in the same way as it uses it to safeguard anything else that is essential to its existence. If therefore the first proposition is securely established with all its implications, society has a prima facie right to legislate against immorality as such. ...

I think, therefore, that it is not possible to set theoretical limits to the power of the State to legislate against immorality. It is not possible to settle in advance exceptions to the general rule or to define inflexibly areas of morality into which the law is in no circumstances to be allowed to enter. Society is entitled by means of its laws to protect itself from dangers, whether from within or without. Here again I think that the political parallel is legitimate. The law of treason is directed against aiding the king's enemies and against sedition from within. The justification for this is that established government is necessary for the existence of society and therefore its safety against violent overthrow must be secured. But an established morality is as necessary as good government to the welfare of society. Societies disintegrate from within more frequently than they are broken up by external pressures. There is disintegration when no common morality is observed and history shows that the loosening of moral bonds is often the first stage of disintegration, so that society is justified in taking the same steps to preserve its moral code as it does to preserve its government and other essential institutions. The suppression of vice is as much the law's business as the suppression of subversive activities; it is no more possible to define a sphere of private morality than it is to define one of private subversive activity. It is wrong to talk of private morality or of the law not being concerned with immorality as such or to try to set rigid bounds to the part which the law may play in the suppression of vice. There are no theoretical limits to the power of the State to legislate against treason and sedition, and likewise I think there can be no theoretical limits to legislation against immorality. You may argue that if a man's sins affect only himself it cannot be the concern of society. If he chooses to get drunk every night in the privacy of his own home, is anyone except himself the worse for it? But suppose a quarter or a half of the population got drunk every night, what sort of society would it be? You cannot set a theoretical limit to the number of people who can get drunk before society is entitled to legislate against drunkenness. The same may be said of gambling. The Royal Commission on Betting, Lotteries, and Gaming took as their test the character of the citizen as a member of society. They said: 'Our concern with the ethical significance of gambling is confined to the effect which it may have on the character of the gambler as a member of society. If we were convinced that whatever the degree of gambling this effect must be harmful we should be inclined to think that it was the duty of the State to restrict gambling to the greatest extent practicable.[11]

In what circumstances the State should exercise its power is the third of the interrogatories I have framed. But before I get to it I must raise a point which might have been brought up in any one of the three. How are the moral judgments of society to be ascertained? By leaving it until now, I can ask it in the more limited form that is now sufficient for my purpose. How is the law-maker to ascertain the moral judgments of society? It is surely not enough that they should be reached by the opinion of the majority; it would be too much to require the individual assent of every citizen. English law has evolved and regularly uses a standard which does not depend on the counting of heads. It is that of the reasonable man. He is not to be confused with the rational man. He is not expected to reason about anything and his judgment may be largely a matter of feeling. It is the viewpoint of the man in the street – or to use an archaism familiar to all lawyers – the man in the Clapham omnibus. He might also be called the right-minded man. For my purpose I should like to call him the man in the jury box, for the moral judgment of society must be something about which any twelve men or women drawn at random might after discussion be expected to be unanimous. This was the standard the judges applied in the days before Parliament was as active as it is now and when they laid down rules of public policy. They did not think of themselves as making law but simply as stating principles which every right-minded person would accept as valid. It is what Pollock called 'practical morality', which is based not on theological or philosophical foundations but 'in the mass of continuous experience half-consciously or unconsciously accumulated and embodies in the morality of common sense'. He called it also 'a certain way of thinking on questions of morality which we expect to find in a reasonable civilized man or a reasonable Englishman, taken at random'.[12]

Immorality then, for the purpose of the law, is what every right-minded person is presumed to consider to be immoral. Any immorality is capable of affecting society injuriously and in effect to a greater or lesser extent it usually does; this is what gives the law its *locus standi*. It cannot be shut out. But – and this brings me to the third question – the individual has a *locus standi* too; he cannot be expected to

[11] (1951) Cmd. 8190, para. 159.
[12] *Essays in Jurisprudence and Ethics* (1882), Macmillan, pp278 and 353.

surrender to the judgment of society the whole conduct of his life. It is the old and familiar question of striking a balance between the rights and interests of society and those of the individual ...

I do not think that one can talk sensibly of a public and private morality any more than one can of a public or private highway. Morality is a sphere in which there is a public interest and a private interest, often in conflict, and the problem is to reconcile the two. This does not mean that it is impossible to put forward any general statements about how in our society the balance ought to be struck. Such statements cannot of their nature be rigid or precise; they would not be designed to circumscribe the operation of the law-making power but to guide those who have to apply it. While every decision which a court of law makes when it balances the public against the private interest is an *ad hoc* decision, the cases contain statements of principle to which the court should have regard when it reaches its decision. In the same way it is possible to make general statements of principle which it may be thought the legislature should bear in mind when it is considering the enactment of laws enforcing morals.

I believe that most people would agree upon the chief of these elastic principles. There must be toleration of the maximum individual freedom that is consistent with the integrity of society. It cannot be said that this is a principle that runs all through the criminal law. Much of the criminal law that is regulatory in character – the part of it that deals with *malum prohibitum* rather than *malum in se* – is based upon the opposite principle, that is, that the choice of the individual must give way to the convenience of the many. But in all matters of conscience the principle I have stated is generally held to prevail. It is not confined to thought and speech; it extends to action, as is shown by the recognition of the right to conscientious objection in wartime; this example shows also that conscience will be respected even in times of national danger. The principle appears to me to be peculiarly appropriate to all questions or morals. Nothing should be punished by the law that does not lie beyond the limits of tolerance. It is not nearly enough to say that a majority dislike a practice; there must be a real feeling of reprobation. ... But matters of this sort are not determined by rational argument. Every moral judgment, unless it claims a divine source, is simply a feeling that no right-minded man could behave in any other way without admitting that he was doing wrong. It is the power of a common sense and not the power of reason that is behind the judgments of society. But before a society can put a practice beyond the limits of tolerance there must be a deliberate judgment that the practice is injurous to society. There is, for example, a general abhorrence of homosexuality. We should ask ourselves in the first instance whether, looking at it calmly and dispassionately, we regard it as a vice so abominable that its mere presence is an offence. If that is the genuine feeling of the society in which we live, I do not see how society can be denied the right to eradicate it. Our feeling may not be so intense as that. We may feel about it that, if confined, it is tolerable, but that if it spread it might be gravely injurious; it is in this way that most societies look upon fornication, seeing it as a natural weakness which must be kept within bounds but which cannot be rooted out. It becomes then a question of balance, the danger to society in one scale and the extent of the restriction in the other. On this sort of point the value of an investigation by such a body as the Wolfenden Committee and of its conclusions is manifest.

The limits of tolerance shift. This is supplementary to what I have been saying but of sufficient importance in itself to deserve statement as a separate principle which law-makers have to bear in mind. I suppose that moral standards do not shift; so far as they come from divine revelation they do not, and I am willing to assume that the moral judgments made by a society always remain good for that society. But the extent to which society will tolerate – I mean tolerate, not approve – departures from moral standards varies from generation to generation ... Laws, especially those which are based on morals, are less easily moved. It follows as another good working principle that in any new matter of morals the law should be slow to act. By the next generation the swell of indignation may have abated and the law be left without the strong backing which it needs. But it is then difficult to alter the law without giving the impression that moral judgment is being weakened. This is now one of the factors that is strongly militating against any alteration to the law on homosexuality.

A third elastic principle must be advanced more tentatively. It is that as far as possible privacy should be respected. This is not an idea that has ever been made explicit in the criminal law. Acts or words done or said in public or in private are all brought within its scope without distinction in principle. But there goes with this a strong reluctance on the part of judges and legislators to sanction invasions of privacy in the detection of crime. This indicates a general sentiment that the right to privacy is something to be put in the balance against the enforcement of the law. Ought the same sort of consideration to play any part in the formation of the law? Clearly only in a very limited number of cases. When the help of the law is invoked by an injured citizen, privacy must be irrelevant; the individual cannot ask that his right to privacy should be measured against injury criminally done to another. But when all who are involved in the deed are consenting parties and the injury is done to morals, the public interest in the moral order can be balanced against the claims of privacy. The restriction on police powers of investigation goes further than the affording of a parallel; it means that the detection of crime committed in private and when there is no complaint is bound to be rather haphazard and this is an additional reason for moderation. These considerations do not justify the exclusion of all private immorality from the scope of the law. I think that, as I have already suggested, the test of 'private behaviour' should be substituted for 'private morality' and the influence of the factor should be reduced from that of a definite limitation to that of a matter to be taken into account ...

Invoked by an injured citizen, privacy must be irrelevant; the individual cannot ask that his right to privacy should be measured against injury criminally done to another. But when all who are involved in the deed are consenting parties and the injury is done to morals, the public interest in the moral order can be balanced against the claims of privacy. The restriction on police powers of investigation goes further than the affording of a parallel; it means that the detection of crime committed in private and when there is no complaint is bound to be rather haphazard and this is an additional reason for moderation. These considerations do not justify the exclusion of all private immorality from the scope of the law. I think that, as I have already suggested, the test of 'private behaviour' should be substituted for 'private morality' and the influence of the factor should be reduced from that of a definite limitation to that of a matter to be taken into account ...

The last and the biggest thing to be remembered is that the law is concerned with the minimum and not with the maximum; there is much in the Sermon on the Mount that would be out of place in the Ten Commandments. We all recognize the gap between the moral law and the law of the land. No man is worth much who regulates his conduct with the sole object of escaping punishment, and every worthy society sets for its members standards which are above those of the law. We recognize the existence of such higher standards when we use expressions such as 'moral obligation' and 'morally bound'. The distinction was well put in the judgment of African elders in a family dispute: 'We have power to make you divide the crops, for this is our law, and we will see this is done. But we have not power to make you behave like an upright man.'[13]

Shaw v Director of Public Prosecutions [1961] 2 WLR 897[14]

There is such an offence known to our law as a conspiracy to corrupt public morals.

Shaw and others produced the *Ladies' Directory* in which prostitutes advertised their services. Shaw was charged with and convicted of, inter alia, a conspiracy to corrupt public morals. He unsuccessfully appealed to the Court of Criminal Appeal and thence to the House of Lords.

VISCOUNT SIMONDS: '... Need I say, my Lords, that I am no advocate of the right of the judges to create new criminal offences? ... But I am at a loss to understand how it can be said either that the law does not recognise a conspiracy to corrupt public morals or that, though there may not be an exact precedent for such a conspiracy as this case reveals, it does not fall fairly within the general words by which it is described ...

In the sphere of criminal law, I entertain no doubt that there remains in the courts of law a residual power to enforce the supreme and fundamental purpose of the law, to conserve not only the safety and order but also the moral welfare of the state, and that it is their duty to guard it against attacks which may be the more insidious because they are novel and unprepared for ... I will say a final word on an

13 A case in the Saa-Katengo at Lialiu, August 1942, quoted in *The Judicial Process among the Barotse of Northern Rhodesia* by Max Gluckna (Manchester University Press, 1955), p172
14 *Shaw v Director of Public Prosecutions* [1961] 2 WLR 897; [1962] AC 220.

aspect of the case which was urged by counsel. No one doubts – and I have put it in the forefront of this opinion – that certainty is a most desirable attribute of the criminal and civil law alike. Nevertheless, there are matters which must ultimately depend on the opinion of a jury. In the civil law I will take an example which comes, perhaps, nearest to the criminal law – the tort of negligence. It is for a jury to decide not only whether the defendant has committed the act complained of but whether, in doing it, he has fallen short of the standard of care which the circumstances require. Till their verdict is given, it is uncertain what the law requires ... There are still, as has recently been said, "unravished remnants of the common law". So, in the case of a charge of conspiracy to corrupt public morals, the uncertainty that necessarily arises from the vagueness of general words can only be resolved by the opinion of twelve chosen men and women. I am content to leave it to them.

The appeal ... should, in my opinion, be dismissed.'

Knuller (Publishing, Printing and Promotions) Ltd v Director of Public Prosecutions [1972] 3 WLR 143

The accused were concerned in the publication of a magazine which contained advertisements designed to attract readers who were prepared to indulge in homosexual practices with the advertisers. They were charged on an indictment containing two counts; one for a conspiracy to corrupt public morals, and the other for a conspiracy to outrage public decency. The accused were convicted on both counts. They appealed unsuccessfully to the Court of Appeal. On their appeal to the House of Lords a majority of four to one upheld the conviction on the first count, but, though for differing reasons, a majority of three to two was for quashing the conviction based on the second count.

LORD REID: '... It was decided by this House in *Shaw* v *Director of Public Prosecutions* that conspiracy to corrupt public morals is a crime known to the law of England. So if the appellants are to succeed on this count, either this House must reverse that decision or there must be sufficient grounds for distinguishing this case. The appellants' main argument is that we should reconsider that decision; alternatively they submit that it can and should be distinguished ...

I can turn now to the appellants' second argument.

They say that homosexual acts between adult males in private are now lawful so it is unreasonable and cannot be the law that other persons are guilty of an offence if they are merely put in touch with one another two males who wish to indulge in such acts. There is a material difference between merely exempting certain conduct from criminal penalties and making it lawful in the full sense. Prostitution and gaming afford examples of this difference ...

I find nothing in the Act to indicate that Parliament thought or intended to lay down that indulgence in these practices is not corrupting. I read the Act as saying that even though it may be corrupting, if people choose to corrupt themselves in this way that is their affair and the law will not interfere. But no licence is given to others to encourage the practice. So if one accepts *Shaw's* case as rightly decided it must be left to each jury to decide in the circumstances of each case whether people were likely to be corrupted ...

To my mind questions of public policy of the utmost importance are at stake here.

I think that the objections to the creation of this generalised offence are similar in character to but even greater than the objections to the generalised offence of conspiracy to corrupt public morals. In upholding the decision in *Shaw's* case we are, in my view, in no way affirming or lending any support to the doctrine that the courts still have some general or residual power either to create new offences or so to widen existing offences as to make punishable conduct of a type hitherto not subject to punishment.'

6. UTILITARIANISM

J BENTHAM
Of Laws in General [1]
(1783)

I

A LAW DEFINED AND DISTINGUISHED

A law may be defined as an assemblage of signs declarative of a volition conceived or adopted by the *sovereign* in a state, concerning the conduct to be observed in a certain *case* by a certain person or class of persons, who in the case in question are or are supposed to be subject to this power: such volition trusting for its accomplishments to the expectation of certain events which it is intended such declaration should upon occasion be a means of bringing to pass, and the prospect of which it is intended should act as a motive upon those whose conduct is in question.

According to this definition, a law may be considered in eight different respects.

(1) In respect of its *source*: that is in respect to the person or persons of whose will it is the expression.

(2) In respect to the quality of its *subjects*: by which I mean the persons and things to which it may apply.

(3) In respect of its *objects*: by which I mean the *acts*, as characterized by the *circumstances*, to which it may apply.

(4) In respect to its *extent*, the generality or the amplitude of its application: that is in respect to the determinateness of the persons whose conduct it may seek to regulate.

(5) In respect to its *aspects*: that is in respect to the various manners in which the will whereof it is the expression may apply itself to the acts and circumstances which are its objects.

(6) In respect of its *force*: that is, in respect to the *motives* it relies on for enabling it to produce the effect it aims at, and the laws or other means which it relies on for bringing those motives into play: such laws may be styled its *corroborative appendage*s.

(7) In respect of its *expression*: that it is in respect to the nature of the *signs* by which the will whereof it is the expression may be made known.

[1] Bentham, J (1783) 'Of Laws in General'. Republished (1945) in *The Limits of Jurisprudence Defined*, ed C W Everett. Columbia University Press, Chapter 2.

(8) In respect to its *remedial appendages*, where it has any: by which I mean certain other laws which may occasionally come to be subjoined to the principal law in question; and of which the design is to obviate the mischief that stands connected with any individual act of the number of those which are made offences by it, in a more perfect manner than can be done by the sole efficacy of the subsidiary appendages to which it stands indebted for its force.

The latitude here given to the import of the word *law* is it must be confessed rather greater than what seems to be given to it in common: the definition being such as is applicable to various objects which are not commonly characterized by that name. Taking this definition for the standard it matters not whether the expression of will in question, so as it have but the authority of the sovereign to back it, were his by immediate conception or only by adoption: whether it be of the most public or of the most private or even domestic nature: whether the sovereign from whom it derives its force be an individual or a body: whether it be a command or a countermand: whether it be expressed in the way of statute, or of customary law. Under the term 'law' then if this definition be admitted of, we must include a judicial order, a military or any other kind of executive order, or even the most trivial and momentary order of the domestic kind, so it be not illegal: that is, so as the issuing of it be not forbidden by some other law.

Judging however from analogy, it would naturally be expected that the signification given to the word *law* should be correspondent to that of its conjugates legislation and *legislative power*: for what, it will be said, is legislation but the act of making laws? or legislative power but the power of making them? that consequently the term *law* should be applied to every expression of will, the uttering of which was an act of legislation, an exertion of legislative power; and that on the other hand it should not be applied to any expression of will of which those two propositions could not be predicted. Accordingly in the former of these points it does indeed quadrate with these two expressions: but it can not be said to do so in the latter. It has all the amplitude which they have, but the import of it is not every where confined within the bounds which limit theirs. This will be seen in a variety of examples.

(1) In the first place, according to the definition, the word *law* should be applicable to any of the most trivial order supposing it to be not illegal, which a man may have occasion to give for any of the most inconsiderable purposes of life: to any order which a master may have occasion to give to his servant, a parent to his child, or (where the request of a husband assumes the harsh form of a command) of a husband to his wife. Yet it would seem a strange catachresis to speak of the isssuing of any such order as an act of legislation, or as an exercise of legislative power. Not but that in cases like these the word *law* is frequently enough employed: but then it is in the way of figure. Even where there is no such legal superiority, a man may say to another out of compliment, 'your commands are laws to me': but on occasions like these the impropriety of the expression is the very reason of its being chosen.

(2) With equal propriety (according to the definition) would the word *law* be applicable to a temporary order issued by any magistrate who is spoken of as exercising thereby a branch of *executive* power, or as exercising the functions belonging to any department of *administration*. But the executive power is continually mentioned as distinct from the legislative: and the business of administration is as constantly opposed to that of legislation. Let the Board of Treasury order a sum of money to be paid or issued to such or such a person, let the Commander in chief order such or such a body of troops to march to such a place, let the Navy Board order such or such a ship to be fitted out, let the Board of Ordnance order such or such a train of artillery to be dispatched to such a destination – Who would ever speak of any of these orders as acts of legislative power, as acts of legislation?

(3) With equal propriety again would the word law according to the definition be applicable to any *judicial* order, to any order which in the course of a cause of any kind a man might have occasion to issue in the capacity of a judge. Yet the business of judicature is constantly looked upon as essentially distinct from the business of legislation and as constantly opposed to it: and the case is the same between the judicial and the legislative power. Even suppose the order to have been ever so general, suppose the persons to whom it is addressed to be ever so numerous and indeterminate, and the duration of it ever so indefinite, still if issued in the course of a forensic contestation, the act of issuing it would not be looked upon in general as coming under the notion of an act of legislation, or as an exercise of legislative power. The fate of a province may be determined by a judicial decree: but the pronouncing of the decree will not on that account be looked upon as being capable with any sort of propriety of being termed an act of legislation ...

Such then are the various sorts of expressions of will to which men would be apt for one reason or other to deny the appellation of *a* law: such therefore are the points in which the definition here given of that important word outstretches the idea which common usage has annexed to it. And these excluded objects have in every point except that of the manner of their appertaining to the sovereign, in every point in short except their immediate *source*, the same nature with those whose title to the appellation stands clearest of dispute. They are all referrable *ultimately* to one common source: they have all of them alike their subjects and their objects, their local extent and their duration: in point of logical extent as it may be called they must all of them be either general or particular, and they may in most instances be indifferently either the one or the other: they are all of them susceptible of the same diversities with respect to the *parties* whom they may affect, and the *aspects* which they have present to the acts which are their objects: they require all of them the same *force* to give them effect, and the same *signs* to give them utterance.

SOURCE OF A LAW

First then with respect to its *source*. Considered in this point of view, the will of which it is the expression must, as the definition intimates, be the will of the sovereign in *a* state.

H L A HART
Positivism and the Separation of Law and Morals [2]
(1958)

I

Undoubtedly, when Bentham and Austin insisted on the distinction between law as it is and as it ought to be, they had in mind *particular* laws the meanings of which were clear and so not in dispute, and they were concerned to argue that such laws, even if morally outrageous, were still laws. It is, however, necessary, in considering the criticisms which later developed, to consider more than those criticisms which were directed to this particular point if we are to get at the root of the dissatisfaction felt; we must also take account of the objection that, even if what the Utilitarians said on this particular point were true, their insistence on it, in a terminology suggesting a general cleavage between what is and ought to be law, obscured the fact that at other points there is an essential point of contract between the two. So in what follows I shall consider not only criticisms of the particular point which the Utilitarians had in mind, but also the claim that an essential connection between law and morals emerges if we examine how laws, the meanings of which are in dispute, are interpreted and applied in concrete cases; and that this connection emerges again if we widen our point of view and ask, not whether every particular rule of law must satisfy a moral minimum in order to be a law, but whether a system of rules which altogether failed to do this could be a legal system.

There is, however, one major initial complexity by which criticism has been much confused. We must remember that the Utilitarians combined with their insistence on the separation of law and morals two other equally famous but distinct doctrines. One was the important truth that a purely analytical study of legal concepts, a study of the meaning of the distinctive vocabulary of the law, was as vital to our understanding of the nature of law as historical or sociological studies, though of course it could not supplant them. The other doctrine was the famous imperative theory of law – that law is essentially a command.

[2] From 71 *Harvard Law Review* 593 (1958). © 1958 The Harvard Law Review Association. Professor Lon L Fuller replied to this essay in 'Positivism and Fidelity to Law – A Reply to Professor Hart' (1958) 71 *Harvard Law Review* 630.

These three doctrines constitute the utilitarian tradition in jurisprudence; yet they are distinct doctrines. It is possible to endorse the separation between law and morals and to value analytical inquiries into the meaning of legal concepts and yet think it wrong to conceive of law as essentially a command. One source of great confusion in the criticism of the separation of law and morals was the belief that the falsity of any one of these three doctrines in the utilitarian tradition showed the other two to be false; what was worse was the failure to see that there were three quite separate doctrines in this tradition. The indiscriminate use of the label 'positivism' to designate ambiguously each one of these three separate doctrines (together with some others which the Utilitarians never professed) has perhaps confused the issue more than any other single factor.[3] Some of the early American critics of the Austinian doctrine were, however, admirably clear on just this matter. Gray, for example, added at the end of the tribute to Austin, which I have already quoted, the words, 'He may have been wrong in treating the Law of the State as being the command of the sovereign'[4] and he touched shrewdly on many points where the command theory is defective. But other critics have been less clearheaded and have thought that the inadequacies of the command theory which gradually came to light were sufficient to demonstrate the falsity of the separation of law and morals.

This was a mistake, but a natural one. To see how natural it was we must look a little more closely at the command idea. The famous theory that law is a command was a part of a wider and more ambitious claim. Austin said that the notion of a command was 'the *key* to the sciences of jurisprudence and morals',[5] and contemporary attempts to elucidate moral judgments in terms of 'imperative' or 'prescriptive' utterances echo this ambitious claim. But the command theory, viewed as an effort to identify even the quintessence of law, let alone the quintessence of morals, seems breathtaking in its simplicity and quite inadequate. There is much, even in the simplest legal system, that is distorted if presented as a command. Yet the Utilitarians thought that the essence of a legal system could be conveyed if the notion of a command were supplemented by that of a habit of obedience. The simple scheme was this: What is a command? It is simply an expression by one

[3] It may help to identify five (there may be more) meanings of 'positivism' bandied about in contemporary jurisprudence:

(1) the contention that laws are commands of human beings.

(2) the contention that there is no necessary connection between law and morals, or law as it is and ought to be.

(3) the contention that the analysis (or study of the meaning) of legal concepts is (a) worth pursuing and (b) to be distinguished from historical inquiries into the causes or origins of laws, from sociological inquiries into the relation of law and other social phenomena, and from the criticism or appraisal of law whether in terms of morals, social aims, 'functions', or otherwise.

(4) the contention that a legal system is a 'closed logical system' in which correct legal decisions can be deduced by logical means from predetermined legal rules without reference to social aims, policies, moral standards, and

(5) the contention that moral judgments cannot be established or defended, as statements of facts can, by rational argument, evidence, or proof ('noncognitivism' in ethics).

Bentham and Austin held the views described in (1), (2), and (3) but not those in (4) and (5). Opinion (4) is often ascribed to analytical jurists, but I know of no 'analyst' who held this view.

[4] Gray (1921) *The Nature and Source of the Law*, 2nd edn, pp94–5.

[5] Austin (1954) *The Province of Jurisprudence Determined*. Library of Ideas edn, p13.

person of the desire that another person should do or abstain from some action, accompanied by a threat of punishment which is likely to follow disobedience. Commands are laws if two conditions are satisfied: first, they must be general; second, they must be commanded by what (as both Bentham and Austin claimed) exists in every political society whatever its constitutional form, namely, a person or a group of persons who are in receipt of habitual obedience from most of the society but pay no such obedience to others. These persons are its sovereign. Thus law is the command of the uncommanded commanders of society – the creation of the legally untrammelled will of the sovereign who is by definition outside the law.

It is easy to see that this account of a legal system is threadbare. One can also see why it might seem that its inadequacy is due to the omission of some essential connection with morality. The situation which the simple trilogy of command, sanction, and sovereign avails to describe, if you take these notions at all precisely, is like that of a gunman saying to his victim, 'Give me your money or your life'. The only difference is that in the case of a legal system the gunman says it to a large number of people who are accustomed to the racket and habitually surrender to it. Law surely is not the gunman situation writ large, and legal order is surely not to be thus simply identified with compulsion.

This scheme, despite the points of obvious analogy between a statute and a command, omits some of the most characteristic elements of law. Let me cite a few. It is wrong to think of a legislature (and *a fortiori* an electorate) with a changing membership, as a group of persons habitually obeyed: this simple idea is suited only to a monarch sufficiently long-lived for a 'habit' to grow up. Even if we waive this point, nothing which legislators do makes law unless they comply with fundamental accepted rules specifying the essential lawmaking procedures. This is true even if a system having a simple unitary constitution like the British. These fundamental accepted rules specifying what the legislature must do to legislate are not commands habitually obeyed, nor can they be expressed as habits of obedience to persons. They lie at the root of a legal system, and what is most missing in the utilitarian scheme is an analysis of what it is for a social group and its officials to accept such rules. This notion, not that of a command as Austin claimed, is the 'key to the science of jurisprudence', or at least one of the keys.

Again, Austin, in the case of a democracy, looked past the legislators to the electorate as 'the sovereign' (or in England as part of it). He thought that in the United States the mass of the electors to the state and federal legislatures were the sovereign whose commands, given by their 'agents' in the legislatures, were law. But on this footing the whole notion of the sovereign outside the law being 'habitually obeyed' by the 'bulk' of the population must go: for in this case the 'bulk' obeys the bulk, that is, it obeys itself. Plainly the general acceptance of the authority of a lawmaking procedure, irrespective of the changing individuals who operate it from time to time, can be only distorted by an analysis in terms of mass habitual obedience to certain persons who are by definition outside the law, just as the cognate but much simpler phenomenon of the general social acceptance of a rule, say of taking off the hat when entering a church, would be distorted if represented as habitual obedience by the mass to specific persons.

Other critics dimly sense a further and more important defect in the command theory, yet blurred the edge of an important criticism by assuming that the defect was due to the failure to insist upon some important connection between law and morals. This more radical defect is as follows. The picture that the command theory draws of life under law is essentially a simple relationship of the commander to the commanded, of superior to inferior, of top to bottom; the relationship is vertical between the commanders or authors of the law conceived of as essentially outside the law and those who are commanded and subject to the law. In this picture no place, or only an accidental or subordinate place is afforded for a distinction between types of legal rules which are in fact radically different. Some laws require men to act in certain ways or to abstain from acting whether they wish to or not. The criminal law consists largely of rules of this sort: like commands they are simply 'obeyed' or 'disobeyed'. But other legal rules are presented to society in quite different ways and have quite different functions. They provide facilities more or less elaborate for individuals to create structures of rights and duties for the conduct of life within the coercive framework of the law. Such are the rules enabling individuals to make contracts, wills and trusts, and generally to mould their legal relations with others. Such rules, unlike the criminal law, are not factors designed to obstruct wishes and choices of an antisocial sort. On the contrary, these rules provide facilities for the realization of wishes and choices. They do not say (like commands) 'do this whether you wish it or not', but rather 'if you wish to do this, here is the way to do it'. Under these rules we exercise powers, make claims, and assert rights. These phrases mark off characteristic features of laws that confer rights and powers; they are laws which are, so to speak, put at the disposition of individuals in a way in which the criminal law is not. Much ingenuity has gone into the task of 'reducing' laws of this second sort to some complex variant of laws of the first sort. The effort to show that laws conferring rights are 'really' only conditional stipulations of sanctions to be exacted from the person ultimately under a legal duty characterizes much of Kelsen's work.[6] Yet to urge this is really just to exhibit dogmatic determination to suppress one aspect of the legal system in order to maintain the theory that the stipulation of a sanction, like Austin's command, represents the quintessence of law. One might as well urge that the rules of baseball were 'really' only complex conditional directions to the scorer and that this showed their real or 'essential' nature.

One of the first jurists in England to break with the Austinian tradition, Salmond, complained that the analysis in terms of commands left the notion of a right unprovided with a place.[7] But he confused the point. He argued first, and correctly,

[6] See eg Kelsen (1945) *General Theory of Law and State*, pp58-61, 143-4. According to Kelsen, all laws, not only those conferring rights and powers, are reducible to such 'primary norms' conditionally stipulating sanctions.

[7] Salmond (1893) *The First Principles of Jurisprudence*, pp97-8. He protested against 'the creed of what is termed the English school of jurisprudence', because it 'attempted to deprive the idea of law of that ethical significance which is one of its most essential elements'. Id at 9, 10.

that if laws are merely commands it is inexplicable that we should have come to speak of legal rights and powers as conferred or arising under them, but then wrongly concluded that the rules of a legal system must necessarily be connected with moral rules or principles of justice and that only on this footing could the phenomenon of legal rights be explained. Otherwise, Salmond thought, we would have to say that a mere 'verbal coincidence' connects the concepts of legal and moral right. Similarly, continental critics of the Utilitarians, always alive to the complexity of the notion of a subjective right, insisted that the command theory gave it no place. Hägerström insisted that if laws were merely commands the notion of an individual's right was really inexplicable, for commands are, as he said, something which we either obey or we do not obey; they do not confer rights.[8] But he, too, concluded that moral, or, as he put it, commonsense, notions of justice must therefore be necessarily involved in the analysis of any legal structure elaborate enough to confer rights.[9]

Yet, surely these arguments are confused. Rules that confer rights, though distinct from commands, need not be moral rules or coincide with them. Rights, after all, exist under the rules of ceremonies, games, and in many other spheres regulated by rules which are irrelevant to the question of justice or what the law ought to be. Nor need rules which confer rights be just or morally good rules. The rights of a master over his slaves show us that. 'Their merit or demerit', as Austin termed it, depends on how rights are distributed in society and over whom or what they are exercised. These critics indeed revealed the inadequacy of the simple notions of command and habit for the analysis of law; at many points it is apparent that the social acceptance of a rule or standard of authority (even if it is motivated only by fear or superstition or rests on inertia) must be brought into the analysis and cannot itself be reduced to the two simple terms. Yet nothing in this showed the utilitarian insistence on the distinction between the existence of law and its 'merits' to be wrong.

II

I now turn to a distinctively American criticism of the separation of the law that is from the law that ought to be. It emerged from the critical study of the judicial process with which American jurisprudence has been on the whole so beneficially occupied. The most sceptical of these critics – the loosely named 'Realists' of the 1930s – perhaps too naïvely accepted the conceptual framework of the natural sciences as adequate for the characterization of law and for the analysis of rule-guided action of which a living system of law at least partly consists. But they opened men's eyes to what actually goes on when courts decide cases, and the contrast they drew between the actual facts of judicial decision and the traditional

---

[8] Hägerström (1953) *Inquiries Into the Nature of Law and Morals*, Olivecrona edn p217: '[T]he whole theory of the subjective rights of private individuals ... is incompatible with the imperative theory'. See also id at 221: 'The description of them [claims to legal protection] as rights is wholly derived from the idea that the law which is concerned with them is a true expression of rights and duties in the sense in which the popular notion of justice understands these terms.'

[9] Id at 218.

terminology for describing it as if it were a wholly logical operation was usually illuminating; for in spite of some exaggeration the 'Realists' made us acutely conscious of one cardinal feature of human language and human thought, emphasis on which is vital not only for the understanding of law but in areas of philosophy far beyond the confines of jurisprudence. The insight of this school may be presented in the following example. A legal rule forbids you to take a vehicle into the public park. Plainly this forbids an automobile, but what about bicycles, roller skates, toy automobiles? What about aeroplanes? Are these, as we say, to be called 'vehicles' for the purpose of the rule or not? If we are to communicate with each other at all, and if, as in the most elementary form of law, we are to express our intentions that a certain type of behaviour be regulated by rules, then the general words we use – like 'vehicle' in the case I consider – must have some standard instance in which no doubts are felt about its application. There must be a core of settled meaning, but there will be, as well, a penumbra of debatable cases in which words are neither obviously applicable nor obviously ruled out. These cases will each have some features in common with the standard case; they will lack others or be accompanied by features not present in the standard case.

. . .

We may call the problems which arise out of the hard core of standard instances or settled meaning 'problems of the penumbra'; they are always with us whether in relation to such trivial things as the regulation of the use of the public park or in relation to the multidimensional generalities of a constitution. If a penumbra of uncertainty must surround all legal rules, then their application to specific cases in the penumbral area cannot be a matter of logical deduction, and so deductive reasoning, which for generations has been cherished as the very perfection of human reasoning, cannot serve as a model for what judges, or indeed anyone, should do in bringing particular cases under general rules. In this area men cannot live by deduction alone. And it follows that if legal arguments and legal decisions of penumbral questions are to be rational, their rationality must lie in something other than a logical relation to premises. So if it is rational or 'sound' to argue and to decide that for the purposes of this rule an aeroplane is not a vehicle, this argument must be sound or rational without being logically conclusive. What is it then that makes such decisions correct or at least better than alternative decisions? Again, it seems true to say that the criterion which makes a decision sound in such cases is some concept of what the law ought to be; it is easy to slide from that into saying that it must be a moral judgment about what law ought to be. So here we touch upon a point of necessary 'intersection between law and morals' which demonstrates the falsity or, at any rate, the misleading character of the Utilitarians' emphatic insistence on the separation of law as it is and ought to be. Surely, Bentham and Austin could only have written as they did because they misunderstood or neglected this aspect of the judicial process, because they ignored the problems of the penumbra.

The misconception of the judicial process which ignores the problems of the penumbra and which views the process as consisting pre-eminently in deductive reasoning is often stigmatized as the error of 'formalism' or 'literalism'.

. . .

The villains of this piece, responsible for the conception of the judge as an automaton, are not the Utilitarian thinkers. The responsibility, if it is to be laid at the door of any theorist, is with thinkers like Blackstone and, at an earlier stage, Montesquieu. The root of this evil is preoccupation with the separation of powers and Blackstone's 'childish fiction' (as Austin termed it) that judges only 'find', never 'make', law.

But we are concerned with 'formalism' as a vice not of jurists but of judges. What precisely is it for a judge to commit this error, to be a 'formalist', 'automatic', a 'slot machine'? ... It is clear that the essence of his error is to give some general term an interpretation which is blind to social values and consequences (or which is in some other way stupid or perhaps merely disliked by critics). ... A judge has to apply a rule to a concrete case – perhaps the rule that one may not take a stolen 'vehicle' across state lines, and in this case an aeroplane had been taken. He either does not see or pretends not to see that the general terms of this rule are susceptible of different interpretations and that he has a choice left open uncontrolled by linguistic conventions. He ignores, or is blind to, the fact that he is in the area of the penumbra and is not dealing with a standard case. Instead of choosing in the light of social aims, the judge fixes the meaning in a different way. He either takes the meaning that the word most obviously suggests in its ordinary nonlegal context to ordinary men, or one which the word has been given in some other legal context, or, still worse, he thinks of a standard case and then arbitrarily identifies certain features in it – for example, in the case of a vehicle, (1) normally used on land, (2) capable of carrying a human person, (3) capable of being self-propelled – and treats these three as always necessary and always sufficient conditions for the use in all contexts of the word 'vehicle', irrespective of the social consequences of giving it this interpretation. This choice, not 'logic', would force the judge to include a toy motor car (if electrically propelled) and to exclude bicycles and the aeroplane. In all this there is possibly great stupidity but no more 'logic', and no less, than in cases in which the interpretation given to a general term and the consequent application of some general rule to a particular case is consciously controlled by some identified social aim.

Decisions made in a fashion as blind as this would scarcely deserve the name of decisions; we might as well toss a penny in applying a rule of law. But it is at least doubtful whether any judicial decisions (even in England) have been quite as automatic as this. Rather, either the interpretations stigmatized as automatic have resulted from the conviction that it is fairer in a criminal statute to take a meaning which would jump to the mind of the ordinary man at the cost even of defeating other values, and this itself is a social policy (though possibly a bad one); or much more frequently, what is stigmatized as 'mechanical' and 'automatic' is a determined choice made indeed in the light of a social aim but of a conservative social aim. Certainly any of the Supreme Court decisions at the turn of the century which have been so stigmatized[10] represent clear choices in the penumbral area to give effect to a policy of a conservative type. This is peculiarly true of Mr Justice Peckham's opinions defining the spheres of police power and due process.[11]

. . .

Clearly, if the demonstration of the errors of formalism is to show the utilitarian distinction to be wrong, the point must be drastically restated. The point must be not merely that a judicial decision to be rational must be made in the light of some conception of what ought to be, but that the aims, the social policies and purposes to which judges should appeal if their decisions are to be rational, are themselves to be considered as part of the law in some suitably wide sense of 'law' which is held to be more illuminating than that used by the Utilitarians. This restatement of the point would have the following consequence: instead of saying that the recurrence of penumbral questions shows us that legal rules are essentially incomplete, and that, when they fail to determine decisions, judges must legislate and so exercise a creative choice between alternatives, we shall say that the social policies which guide the judges' choice are in a sense there for them to discover; the judges are only 'drawing out' of the rule what, if it is properly understood, is 'latent' within it. To call this judicial legislation is to obscure some essential continuity between the clear cases of the rule's application and the penumbral decisions. I shall question later whether this way of talking is salutary, but I wish at this time to point out something obvious, but likely, if not stated to tangle the issues. It does not follow that, because the opposite of a decision reached blindly in the formalist or literalist manner is a decision intelligently reached by reference to some conception of what ought to be, we have a junction of law and morals. We must, I think, beware of thinking in a too simple-minded fashion about the word 'ought'. This is not because there is no distinction to be made between law as it is and ought to be. Far from it. It is because the distinction should be between what is and what from many different points of view ought to be. The word 'ought' merely reflects the presence of some standard of criticism; one of these standards is a moral standard but not all standards are moral.

. . .

So here intelligent and rational decision is guided however uncertainly by moral aims. But we have only to vary the example to see that this need not necessarily be so and surely, if it need not necessarily be so, the Utilitarian point remains

---

[10] See, eg Pound 'Mechanical Jurisprudence' (1908) 8 *Columbia Law Review* 605, 615-16.

[11] See, eg *Lochner v New York*, 198 US 45 (1905). Justice Peckham's opinion that there were no reasonable grounds for interfering with the right of free contact by determining the hours of labour in the occupation of a baker may indeed be a wrongheaded piece of conservation but there is nothing automatic or mechanical about it.

unshaken. Under the Nazi regime men were sentenced by courts for criticism of the regime. Here the choice of sentence might be guided exclusively by consideration of what was needed to maintain the state's tyranny effectively. What sentence would both terrorize the public at large and keep the friends and family of the prisoner in suspense so that both hope and fear would co-operate as factors making for subservience? The prisoner of such a system would be regarded simply as an object to be used in pursuit of these aims. Yet, in contrast with a mechanical decision on these grounds would be intelligent and purposive, and from one point of view the decision would be as it ought to be. Of course, I am not unaware that a whole philosophical tradition has sought to demonstrate the fact that we cannot correctly call decisions or behaviour truly rational unless they are in confirmity with moral aims and principles. But the example I have used seems to me to serve at least as a warning that we cannot use the errors of formalism as something which per se demonstrates the falsity of the utilitarian insistence on the distinction between law as it is and law as *morally* it ought to be.

We can now return to the main point. If it is true that the intelligent decision of penumbral questions is one made not mechanically but in the light of aims, purposes and policies, though not necessarily in the light of anything we would call moral principles, is it wise to express this important fact by saying that the firm utilitarian distinction between what the law is and what it ought to be should be dropped? Perhaps the claim that it is wise cannot be theoretically refuted for it is, in effect, an *invitation* to revise our conception of what a legal rule is. We have invited to include in the 'rule' the various aims and policies in the light of which its penumbral cases are decided on the ground that these aims have, because of their importance, as much right to be called law as the core of legal rules whose meaning is settled. But though an invitation cannot be refuted, it may be refused and I would proffer two reasons for refusing this invitation. First, everything we have learned about the judicial process can be expressed in other less mysterious ways. We can say laws are incurably incomplete and we must decide the penumbral cases rationally by reference to social aims. I think Holmes, who had such a vivid appreciation of the fact that 'general propositions do not decide concrete cases', would have put it that way. Second to insist on the utilitarian distinction is to emphasise that the hard core of settled meaning is law in some centrally important sense and that even if there are border-lines, there must first be lines. If this were not so the notion of rules controlling courts' decisions would be senseless as some of the 'Realists' – in their most extreme moods, and, I think, on bad grounds – claimed.[12]

[12] One recantation of this extreme position is worth mention in the present context. In the first edition of *The Bramble Bush*, Professor Llewellyn committed himself wholeheartedly to the view that 'what these officials do about disputes is, to my mind, the law itself' and that '*rules* ... are important so far as they help you ... predict what judges will do ... That is all their importance, except as pretty playthings'. Llewellyn (1930) *The Bramble Bush*, 1st edn pp3, 5. In the second edition he said that these were 'unhappy words when not more fully developed, and they are plainly at best a very partial statement of the whole truth. ... [O]ne office of law is to control officials in some part, and to guide them even ... where no thoroughgoing control is possible, or is desired ... [T]he words fail to take proper account ... of the office of the institution of law as an instrument of conscious shaping ...' Llewellyn (1951) *The Bramble Bush*, 2nd edn, p9.

By contrast, to soften the distinction, to assert mysteriously that there is some fused identity between law as it is and as it ought to be, is to suggest that all legal questions are fundamentally like those of the penumbra. It is to assert that there is no central element of actual law to be seen in the core of central meaning which rules have, that there is nothing in the nature of a legal rule inconsistent with *all* questions being open to reconsideration in the light of social policy. Of course, it is good to be occupied with the penumbra. Its problems are rightly the daily diet of the law schools. But to be occupied with the penumbra is one thing, to be preoccupied with it another. And preoccupation with the penumbra is, if I may say so, as rich a source of confusion in the American legal tradition as formalism in the English. Of course we might abandon the notion that rules have authority; we might cease to attach force or even meaning to an argument that a case falls clearly within a rule and the scope of a precedent. We might call all such reasoning 'automatic' or 'mechanical', which is already the routine invective of the courts. But until we decide that this *is* what we want, we should not encourage it by obliterating the Utilitarian distinction.

7. POSITIVISM:
THE COMMAND THEORY

J AUSTIN
The Province of Jurisprudence Determined [1]
(1839)

Every *law* or *rule* (taken with the largest signification which can be given to the term *properly*) is a *command*. Or, rather, laws or rules, properly so called, are a species of commands.

Now, since the term command comprises the term law, the first is the simpler as well as the larger of the two. But, simple as it is, it admits of explanation. And, since it is the key to the sciences of jurisprudence and morals, its meaning should be analysed with precision.

Accordingly, I shall endeavour, in the first instance, to analyse the meaning of 'command':

. . .

If you express or intimate a wish that I shall do or forbear from some act, and if you will visit me with an evil in case I comply not with your wish, the expression or intimation of your wish is a command. A command is distinguished from other significations of desire, not by the style in which the desire is signified, but by the the power and the purpose of the party commanding to inflict an evil or pain in case the desire be disregarded. If you cannot or will not harm me in case I comply not with your wish, the expression of your wish is not a command, although you utter your wish in imperative phrase. If you are able and willing to harm me in case I comply not with your wish, the expression of your wish amounts to a command, although you are prompted by a spirit of courtesy to utter it in the shape of a request. 'Preces erant, sed quibus contradicti non posset.' Such is the language of Tacitus, when speaking of a petition by the soldiery to a son and lieutenant of Vespasian.

A command, then, is a signification of desire. But a command is distinguished from other significations of desire by this peculiarity: that the party to whom it is directed is liable to evil from the other, in case he comply not with the desire.

Being liable to evil from you if I comply not with a wish which you signify, I am

[1] Austin, J (1839) 'The Province of Jurisprudence Determined'. Republished (1954) in *The Uses of the Study of Jurisprudence*, ed H L A Hart. Weidenfeld and Nicholson, London, pp296–299.

bound or *obliged* by your command, or I lie under a *duty* to obey it. If, in spite of that evil in prospect, I comply not with the wish which you signify, I am said to disobey your command, or to violate the duty which it imposes.

Command and duty are, therefore, correlative terms: the meaning denoted by each being implied or supposed by the other. Or (changing the expression) wherever a duty lies, a command has been signified; and whenever a command is signified, a duty is imposed.

The evil which will probably be incurred in case a command be disobeyed or (to use an equivalent expression) in case a duty be broken, is frequently called a sanction, or an *enforcement of obedience*. Or (varying the phrase) the command or the duty is said to be *sanctioned* or *enforced* by the chance of incurring the evil. ...

Accordingly, I distribute laws proper, with such improper laws as are closely analogous to the proper, under three capital classes.

The first comprises the laws (properly so called) which are set by God to his human creatures.

The second comprises the laws (properly so called) which are set by men as political superiors, or by men, as private persons, in pursuance of legal rights.

The third comprises laws of the two following species: 1. The laws (properly so called) which are set by men to men but not by men as political superiors, nor by men, as private persons, in pursuance of legal rights: 2. The laws, which are closely analogous to laws proper, but are merely opinions or sentiments held or felt by men in regard to human conduct. – I put laws of these species into a common class, and I mark them with the common name of positive morality or positive moral rules.

POSITIVE LAW AND MORALITY

My reasons for using the two expressions '*positive* law' and '*positive* morality', are the following:

There are two capital classes of human laws. The first comprises the laws (properly so called) which are set by men as political superiors, or by men, as private persons, in pursuance of legal rights. The second comprises the laws (proper and improper) which belong to the two species above mentioned.

As merely distinguished from the second, the first of those capital classes might be named simply *law*. As merely distinguished from the first, the second of those capital classes might be named simply *morality*. But both must be distinguished from the law of God: and, for the purpose of distinguishing both from the law of God, we must qualify the names *law* and *morality*. Accordingly, I style the first of those capital classes 'positive law': and I style the second of those capital classes 'positive morality'. By the common epithet *positive*, I denote that both classes flow from human sources. By the distinctive names *law* and *morality*, I denote the difference between the human sources from which the two classes respectively emanate.

Strictly speaking, every law properly so called is a positive law. For it is put or set by individual or collective author, or it exists by the position or institution of its individual or collective author.

But, as opposed to the law of nature (meaning the law of God), human law of the first of those capital classes is styled by writers on jurisprudence 'positive law'. This application of the expression 'positive law' was manifestly made for the purpose of obviating confusion; confusion of human law of the first of those capital classes with that Divine law which is the measure or test of human.

And, in order to obviate similar confusion, I apply the expression 'positive morality' to human law of the second capital class. For the name *morality*, when standing unqualified or alone, may signify the law set by God, or human law of that second capital class. If you say that an act or omission violates morality, you speak ambiguously. You may mean that it violates the law which I style 'positive morality', or that it violates the Divine law which is the measure or test of the former. ...

From the expression *positive law* and the expression *positive morality*, I pass to certain expressions with which they are closely connected.

The *science of jurisprudence* (or, simply and briefly, *jurisprudence*) is concerned with positive laws, or with laws strictly so called, as considered without regard to their goodness or badness.

Positive morality, as considered without regard to its goodness or badness, *might* be the subject of a science closely analogous to jurisprudence. I say '*might* be'; since it is only in one of its branches (namely, the law of nations or international law) that positive morality, as considered without regard to its goodness or badness, has been treated by writers in a scientific or systematic manner. – For the science of positive morality, as considered without regard to its goodness or badness, current or established language will hardly afford us a name. The name *morals*, or *science of morals*, would denote it ambiguously: the name *morals*, or *science of morals*, being commonly applied (as I shall show immediately) to a department of ethics or deontology. But, since the science of jurisprudence is not unfrequently styled 'the science of positive law', the science in question might be styled analogically 'the science of positive morality'. ...

The *science of ethics* (or, in the language of Mr Bentham, *the science of deontology*) may be defined in the following manner. – It affects to determine the test of positive law and morality. In other words, it affects to expound them as they should be: as they would be if they were good or worthy of praise; or as they would be if they conformed to an assumed measure.

The science of ethics (or, simply and briefly, ethics) consists of two departments: one relating specially to positive law, the other relating specially to positive morality.

R COTTERRELL
The Politics of Jurisprudence [2]
(1989)

John Austin's wife wrote that he lived 'a life of unbroken disappointment and failure'.[3] Yet Austin, more than any other writer, provided the compact and systematic formulation of a conception of law which allowed an escape from the tradition-bound theory implicit in classical common law thought. Equally, Austin provided what historical jurisprudence could not: a clear designation of the scope of legal knowledge, an orderly theory of law which allowed the legal to be distinguished from the non-legal and the logical connections between legal ideas to be made explicit. Finally, he offered a way of looking at law which made legislation central rather than peripheral. Thus, his legal theory recognised the reality of the modern state as a massive organisation of power. It tried to show law's relationship with this centralised and extensive power structure. It seemed in tune with modern times in which government, not community, was the apparent source of law. Thus, noting Sarah Austin's comment quoted above, one of Austin's most important successors goes on to remark that 'within a few years of his death it was clear that his work had established the study of jurisprudence in England' (Hart 1955: xvi). Austin died in 1859, believing that his neglected writings and unsuccessful lectures had made no mark whatsoever. Four years later all of his most important work had been republished, largely through the efforts of his widow. For reasons to be considered in this chapter, it caught the legal mood of the times. It established or clarified ideas about the nature of law which still provide basic elements in the vocabulary of concepts which lawyers in the Anglo-American world use (cf Dworkin 1977: 16).

Austin's legal theory is contained primarily in the lectures he prepared as the first professor of jurisprudence in what was to become the University of London. Much of his legal philosophy is heavily indebted to earlier writers. It represents the packaging of a set of ideas distilled from a long tradition of political theory concerned with the concept of sovereignty, together with a selective plundering of the legal theory of Austin's original mentor, the English philosopher and law reformer, Jeremy Bentham. Today, the received wisdom is that Austin's work is much less important than Bentham's and, indeed, there is no doubt that its intellectual range is far more limited. But, partly because of the accidents of publication, Austin exerted an influence on the development of legal theory and on wider concerns in legal scholarship far beyond that of Bentham.

The fact that all of Austin's major work in legal theory was in print from the 1860s, whereas the major writings of Bentham which cover similar ground were not,

---

[2] Cotterrell, R (1989) *The Politics of Jurisprudence*. Butterworths, London, pp52–57.
[3] In a letter quoted in Rumble 1985, 56.

is, however, only part of the explanation. The form of Austin's legal theory and the ordering of its concerns enables it to offer a normative legal theory which was particularly appropriate to the political and legal professional concerns of its time. Further, it exemplifies a certain general conception of law in an extremely concise and straightforward manner. In fact, Austin's 'failure' in so many worldly things may have been the condition of his success in this. He pursued with apparently total singlemindedness a distinct image of how a 'science' of law might be possible. Lacking Bentham's restless intellectual curiosity – which diverted the greater writer into an immense diversity of projects – Austin meticulously worked on the theory of law which had been merely a part of Bentham's concerns. Where his ideas differ from Bentham's it is often because he prefers a stubborn logic (for example, on the nature of sovereignty) or a hard-headed realism (for example, in discussing judicial law-making), where Bentham equivocates or tries to develop more radical analyses in the cause of legal or political reform.

For the moment it will be necessary to keep an open mind about the relative merits of Bentham and Austin in their development of normative legal theory – the theory which is the exclusive concern of this book. But it will be argued in the following pages that a strong defence can be made on Austin's behalf against many of the most serious criticisms which are routinely made of his legal theory. In this chapter he occupies centre stage simply because it is he rather than Bentham who has exerted by far the greater influence on later jurists and on legal scholarship generally, and he who offers a version of normative legal theory which in its clear (even dogmatic) pronouncement provides an effective contrast to the vague theory underpinning the common law tradition. In considering Austin's ideas and their political and professional consequences, however, comparisons with Bentham's theories will be made. And it will be necessary to trace the roots of Austin's thinking beyond Bentham to make the point that the evolution of common law thought, considered in Chapter 2, is paralleled by a long tradition of quite different thinking about the nature of law.

THE EMPIRE OF DARKNESS AND THE REGION OF LIGHT

A key to understanding the motivation behind and orientation of the legal theories of Austin and Bentham is to recognise the profound hostility of both writers to the methods and outlook of English common law, and the profound difference between their reactions to it. Towards the end of his life Austin may well have modified his views but his London University lectures on jurisprudence, originally written for presentation at the end of the 1820s and the basis of his reputation in legal philosophy, are full of vitriolic comments on the absurdities of common law thought and the irrationality of a legal system – if system it could be called – developed primarily by piecemeal judicial interventions. Bentham viewed judge-made law as like waiting for one's dog to do something wrong and then beating it (cf Stein 1980: 70). Austin, however, was not opposed to judicial law-making. What offended him was the total lack of systematic organisation or of a structure of clearly definable rational principles in common law. In his lectures he was determined to map out a rational, scientific approach to legal understanding – a modern view of law which would replace archaic, confused, tradition-bound common law thought but would be able to encompass both legislation and judge-made law.

This aim immediately distinguishes Austin from Bentham. Always the more radical thinker, Bentham has no patience in his writings with the idea that judicial decisions are an appropriate source of law. He pins his faith on the kind of codification Savigny despised. All law should be purposively, deliberately, rationally created by legislative means. As far as possible, law should be expressed in rational, systematically organised codes. Austin also favoured codification and writes extensively in his lectures of its merits and of the absurdity of most of Savigny's objections to it. But he also shows a cool realism about the possibilities. Austin's views on judge-made law, or 'judicary law' as he prefers to call it, will be discussed later. For the moment it is enough to say that he recognises that judge-made law is an inevitable component of a modern legal system, and that – despite many disadvantages – it has some virtues and is often the only practical means of legal development at certain times and in certain fields. Codification is admirable in theory but, in practice, requires immense legislative skill, juristic knowledge and political vision. What is needed, therefore, is a view of law which can accommodate realistically all these aspects but present them within the framework of the rational, centralised governmental structure of the modern state.

Although a matter is often ignored or under-emphasised in commentaries on Austin, it is important to note that he found models of legal scholarship, to help in this task, quite outside Benthamite influences. Austin saw in Roman law – especially as interpreted and developed by continental civil law jurists – the epitome of a rational legal order vastly superior to English common law in its logical organisation. 'Turning from the study of the English to the study of the Roman law, you escape from the empire of chaos and darkness, to a world which seems, by comparison, the region of order and light' (Austin 1885: 58). The 'extraordinary merit' of Roman law scholarship was in the way scholars had 'seized its general principles with great clearness and penetration, ... applied these principles with admirable logic to the explanation of details and ... thus reduced this positive system of law to a compact and coherent whole' (Austin 1832: 188). By contrast, English law was full of 'useless and misleading jargon' often employed inconsistently (Austin 1885: 686). While distancing himself in his writings from the legal philosophies informing Roman law and, indeed, from that law's actual content, Austin rarely fails to sing the praises of Romanist legal scholarship. He spent several months in Germany, studying the writings of the German scholars of Roman law and German legal philosophy, in preparation for his own lectures.

How important is this in understanding the orientation of Austin's legal philosophy? It suggests that, although he 'was accepted as the heir apparent of Bentham in the special department of jurisprudence' (Stephen 1900: 317) and undoubtedly saw himself, at the time he wrote his lectures, as a disciple (though a critical one) of Bentham, his model of a science of law was not wholly Benthamite. He quoted with approval other writers' praise of the 'scientific method' of the Romanists which had made them 'models to all succeeding ages' (1832: 377). As already indicated, for Austin this method – which could allow the rationalisation of law from many sources, including judicial decisions and custom, as well as legislation – involved identifying general principles, applying them logically to explain detail, and so demonstrating order and coherence in law.

Certainly, Bentham had already supplied many other elements needed. He had recognised the need for a coherent doctrine to guide the rational reform of law and to dispose of common law archaism and had found this in the principle of utility. Utility required that law-making and legal institutions be designed to promote the greatest happiness of the greatest number of people. Utility would replace traditional, self-serving or subjectively moral evaluations with a rational evaluation of the worth of particular practices, institutions and policies in terms of how far they served the common good, measured in terms of maximisation of satisfaction of the actual desires of the greatest possible number of the population. Austin's lectures presuppose the doctrine of utility as elaborated by Bentham and warmly – even fanatically – defend it. But Austin's course was devoted to the theory of law *as it is* (which he called the science of law), not the theory of law as it should or might be (which he termed the science of legislation). Consequently, although several of Austin's lectures directly discuss the principle of utility, it does not occupy the central place in the body of his writings which it does in Bentham's. Bentham's 'expository jurisprudence' (his term for the science of law), upon which Austin drew extensively, was an offshoot of his concern with the working out of the principle of utility in its application to law reform. Thus, the science of legislation (he calls it censorial jurisprudence) is central to Bentham and expository jurisprudence is a necessary basis of knowledge upon which censorial jurisprudence can be pursued. By contrast, Austin is known through a set of lectures devoted to elaborating a theory of existing law. In them he apologetically justifies bringing in the principle of utility as necessary to help to explain why law has taken particular forms (Austin 1832: 59; 1863: 373). In the particular context of Austin's lectures, therefore, the science of legislation is *subordinate* to the science of law.

. . .

POSITIVE LAW AND POSITIVE MORALITY

From one viewpoint, the most valuable contribution of Austin's legal theory is its attempt to distinguish clearly *law* from other phenomena (for example, moral rules, social customs) with which it could be confused. ... Classical common law thought did not do this. For Austin, clear thinking about law necessitates such a demarcation of the subject-matter of legal science. Bentham had poured scorn on the way moral notions and legal principles were mixed up in Blackstone's *Commentaries*, the famous eighteenth century treatise on English law (Bentham 1977: 3–33). To Bentham the result seemed thoroughly unscientific, allowing Blackstone to preach moral sermons or indulge his prejudices under cover of stating the law. Thus, when Austin – strongly influenced by Bentham's critique of Blackstone – came to write his lectures it seemed obvious to him that the starting point for the science of law must be a clear analytical separation of law and morality.

Madzimbamuto v Lardner-Burke [1968] 3 WLR 1229[4]

PRIVY COUNCIL

Southern Rhodesia was annexed to the Crown in 1923, being given the status of a colony. In 1948 the British Nationality Act, 1948, created Southern Rhodesian citizenship. In 1961 the colony was granted a Constitution whereunder, inter alia, its legislature had power to make laws for the peace, order and good government of Southern Rhodesia and 'the executive authority ... is vested in Her Majesty and may be exercised on Her Majesty's behalf by the Governor.' The Constitution provided that the law to be administered was the law in force in the Cape of Good Hope in June 1891 (that being Roman-Dutch law), and it contained a 'Declaration of Rights' designed to secure 'the fundamental rights and freedoms of the individual'.

On 5 November, 1965, a state of emergency in Southern Rhodesia was validly proclaimed by the Governor, and emergency regulations were made under which, on the following day, the first respondent, as Minister of Justice, made an order for the detention of the appellant's husband, M, on the ground that he was 'likely to commit acts in Rhodesia ... likely to endanger the public safety, disturb or interfere with public order or interfere with the maintenance of any essential service.' Since 1959, M had from time to time been detained or placed in a restriction area under earlier emergency powers. On 11 November, 1965, the Prime Minister of Southern Rhodesia and his colleagues issued a 'Declaration of Independence' purporting to declare that Southern Rhodesia was no longer a Crown colony but was an independent sovereign state. On the same day, in a message to the people of Rhodesia, the Governor informed them that the Declaration of Independence was unconstitutional, and that the Prime Minister and his colleagues had ceased to hold office. His message called upon the people to refrain from illegal acts furthering the objects of the illegal régime, and stated as follows:

> 'It is the duty of all citizens to maintain law and order in the country and to carry on with their normal tasks. This applies equally to the judiciary, the armed services, the police and the public service.'

On 16 November, 1965, the United Kingdom Parliament passed the Southern Rhodesia Act 1965, which reasserted that Southern Rhodesia continued to be part of

[4] *Madzimbamuto* v *Lardner-Burke* [1969] 1 AC 845; [1968] 3 WLR 1229.

Her Majesty's dominions. On 18 November, 1965, the Southern Rhodesia (Constitution) Order 1965, was made, s2(1) of which provided that:

> '... any instrument made or other act done in purported promulgation of any constitution for Southern Rhodesia except as authorised by Act of Parliament is void and of no effect.'

By s3(1) the powers of the legislature to make laws, of the Legislative Assembly to transact business, and of any person or authority to take steps for the reconstitution of the Legislative Assembly or the election of members thereof, were suspended, and by s6 any law made, business transacted or step taken in contravention of the order was declared void and of no effect. The Prime Minister and his colleagues disregarded their dismissal from office, and the members of the Legislative Assembly disregarded its suspension and purported to adopt the new Constitution of 1965, established by the illegal régime, s3 of which provided that 'there shall be an officer administering the Government in and over Rhodesia'. The lawful state of emergency under which M was detained expired on 4 February 1966, but his detention was continued under fresh emergency regulations invalidly made. In proceedings for a declaration that M's detention was unlawful Lewis and Goldin JJ in the General Division held that the 1965 Constitution and the Government of the Prime Minister and his colleagues were unlawful but that, it being the only effective government, necessity required that effect be given to the fresh emergency regulations and therefore the detention was lawful. On appeal, the Appellate Division affirmed that decision in the main but held that the particular regulation under which M had been detained since 4 February 1966, was ultra vires and invalid, and therefore allowed the appeal. A fresh detention order was immediately made under a regulation which the Appellate Division had by implication held to be valid.

On appeal to the Privy Council.

LORD REID: 'The appellant's husband is detained in prison at Gwelo. The appellant contends that that determination is wrong in law and that he is unlawfully detained. For reasons which will appear later their Lordships decided that the appellant has a right to appeal ...

On 11 November 1965 Mr Smith, the Prime Minister, and his ministerial colleagues, including the first respondent, issued a declaration of independence to the effect that Southern Rhodesia was no longer a Crown colony but was an independent sovereign State. They also issued a new Constitution. On the same day the Governor issued this statement:

> "The government have made an unconstitutional declaration of independence.
>
> I have received the following message from Her Majesty's Secretary of State for Commonwealth Relations: 'I have it in command from Her Majesty to inform you that it is Her Majesty's pleasure that, in the event of an unconstitutional declaration of independence, Mr Ian Smith and the other persons holding office as Ministers of the government of Southern Rhodesia or as deputy Ministers cease to hold office. I am commanded by Her Majesty to instruct you in the event to convey Her Majesty's pleasure in this matter to Mr Smith and otherwise to publish it in such manner as you may deem fit.'

In accordance with these instructions I have informed Mr Smith and his colleagues that they no longer hold office. I call on the citizens of Rhodesia to refrain from all acts which further objectives of the illegal authorities. Subject to that, it is the duty of all citizens to maintain law and order in the country and to carry on with their normal tasks. This applies equally to the judiciary, the armed services, the police, and the public service."

On 16 November 1965, the Parliament of the United Kingdom passed the Southern Rhodesia Act 1965 the leading provisions of which were:

"1. It is hereby declared that Southern Rhodesia continues to be part of Her Majesty's dominions, and that the Government and Parliament of the United Kingdom have the responsibility and jurisdiction as heretofore for and in respect of it.
2. Her Majesty may by Order in Council make such provision in relation to Southern Rhodesia, or persons or things in any way belonging to or connected with Southern Rhodesia, as appears to Her to be necessary or expedient in consequence of any unconstitutional action taken therein" ...

Their Lordships can now turn to the three main questions in this case:

1. What was the legal effect in Southern Rhodesia of the Southern Rhodesia Act 1965 and the Order in Council which accompanied it?
2. Can the usurping government now in control in Southern Rhodesia be regarded for any purpose as a lawful government?
3. If not, to what extent, if at all, are the courts of Southern Rhodesia entitled to recognise or give effect to its legislative or administrative acts?

If the Queen in the Parliament of the United Kingdom was Sovereign in Southern Rhodesia in 1965 there can be no doubt that the Southern Rhodesia Act 1965 and the Order in Council made under it were of full legal effect there. Several of the learned judges have held that sovereignty was divided between the United Kingdom and Southern Rhodesia. Their Lordships cannot agree. So far as they are aware it has never been doubted that, when a colony is acquired or annexed following on conquest or settlement, the sovereignty of the United Kingdom Parliament extends to that colony, and its powers over the colony are the same as its powers in the United Kingdom. So in 1923 full sovereignty over the annexed territory of Southern Rhodesia was acquired. That sovereignty was not dismissed by the limited grant of self government which was then made. It was necessary to pass the Statute of Westminster 1931, in order to confer independence and sovereignty on the six Dominions therein mentioned, but Southern Rhodesia was not included. Section 4 of that Act provides:

"No Act of Parliament of the United Kingdom passed after the commencement of this Act shall extend, or be deemed to extend, to a Dominion as part of the law of that dominion unless it is expressly declared in that Act that the Dominion has requested, and consented to, the enactment thereof."

No similar provision has been enacted with regard to Southern Rhodesia ...

Subsection (3) mentions eight countries to which full independence had already been granted and also Southern Rhodesia ...

The learned judges refer to the statement of the United Kingdom government in 1961, already quoted, setting out the convention that the Parliament of the United Kingdom does not legislate without the consent of the government of Southern Rhodesia on matters within the competence of the legislative assembly. That was a very important convention but it had no legal effect in limiting the legal power of Parliament.

It is often said that it would be unconstitutional for the United Kingdom Parliament to do certain things, meaning that the moral, political and other reasons against doing them are so strong that most people would regard it as highly improper if Parliament did these things. But that does not mean that it is beyond the power of Parliament to do such things. If Parliament chose to do any of them the courts could not hold the Act of Parliament invalid. It may be that it would have been thought before 1965 that it would be unconstitutional to disregard this convention. But it may also be that the unilateral declaration of independence released the United Kingdom from any obligation to observe the convention. Their Lordships in declaring the law are not concerned with these matters. They are only concerned with the legal powers of Parliament.

Finally, on this first question their Lordships can find nothing in the 1961 Constitution which could be interpreted as a grant of limited sovereignty. Even assuming that it is possible under the British system, they did not find an indication of an intention to transfer sovereignty or any such clear cut division between what is granted by way of sovereignty and what is reserved as would be necessary if there were to be a transfer of some part of the sovereignty of the Queen in the Parliament of the United Kingdom. But they are therefore of opinion that the Act and Order in Council of 1965 had full legal effect in Southern Rhodesia ...

The provisions of the Order in Council are drastic and unqualified. With regard to the making of laws for Southern Rhodesia s3(1)(a) provides that no laws may be made by the legislature of Southern Rhodesia and no business may be transacted by the legislative assembly; then s3(1)(a) authorises Her Majesty in Council to make laws for the peace, order and good government of Southern Rhodesia: and s6 declares that any law made in contravention of any prohibition imposed by the Order is void and of no effect. This can only mean that the power to make laws is transferred to Her Majesty in Council with the result that no purported law made by any person or body in Southern Rhodesia can have any legal effect, no matter how necessary that purported law may be for the purpose of preserving law and order or for any other purpose. It is for Her Majesty in Council to judge whether any new law is required and to enact such new laws as may be thought necessary or desirable.

It was argued that the Order in Council only refers to and only makes illegal future Acts of the previously lawful legislature and has no relation to those of the unlawful regime which are thereto left to the appreciation of the courts. This would indeed be paradoxical. But in their Lordships' opinion the Act of 1965 and the Order in Council have made it clear beyond doubt that the United Kingdom

Parliament has resumed full power to legislate for Rhodesia and has removed from Rhodesia the power to legislate for itself ...

Her Majesty's judges have been put in an extremely difficult position. But the fact that the judges among others have been put in a very difficult position cannot justify disregard of legislation passed or authorised by the United Kingdom Parliament, by the introduction of a doctrine of necessity which in their Lordships' judgment cannot be reconciled with the terms of the Order in Council. It is for Parliament and Parliament alone to determine whether the maintenance of law and order would justify giving effect to laws made by the usurping government, to such extent as may be necessary for that purpose.

The issue in this case is whether emergency powers regulations made under the 1965 Constitution can be regarded as having any legal validity, force or effect. Section 2(1) of the Order in Council of 1965 provides:

> "It is hereby declared for the avoidance of doubt that any instrument made or other act done in purported promulgation of any Constitution for Southern Rhodesia except as authorised by Act of Parliament is void and of no effect."

The 1965 Constitution, made void by that provision, provides by s3 that "There shall be an Officer Administering the Government in and over Rhodesia" – an office hitherto unknown to the law. The emergency powers regulations which were determined by the High Court to be valid were made by the Officer Administering the Government. For the reasons already given their Lordships are of opinion that that determination was erroneous. And it must follow that any order for detention made under such regulations is legally invalid.

Their Lordships will therefore humbly advise Her Majesty that it should be declared that the determination of the High Court of Southern Rhodesia with regard to the validity of emergency powers regulations made in Southern Rhodesia since 11 November 1965, is erroneous, and that such regulations have no legal validity, force or effect.'

H L A HART
The Concept of Law [5]
(1961)

There are therefore two minimum conditions necessary and sufficient for the existence of a legal system. On the one hand those rules of behaviour which are valid according to the system's ultimate criteria of validity must be generally obeyed, and, on the other hand, its rules of recognition specifying the criteria of legal validity and its rules of change and adjudication must be effectively accepted as common public standards of official behaviour by its officials. The first condition is

[5] Hart, H L A (1961) *The Concept of Law.* Oxford University Press, Oxford, pp113–115.

the only one which private citizens *need* satisfy: they must obey each 'for his part only' and from any motive whatever; thought in a healthy society they will in fact often accept these rules as common standards of behaviour and acknowledge an obligation to obey them, or even trace this obligation to a more general obligation to respect the constitution. The second condition must also be satisfied by the officials of the system. They must regard these as common standards of official behaviour and appraise critically their own and each other's deviations as lapses. Of course it is also true that besides these there will be many primary rules which apply to officials in their merely personal capacity which they need only obey.

The assertion that a legal system exists is therefore a Janus-faced statement looking both towards obedience by ordinary citizens and to the acceptance by officials of secondary rules as critical common standards of official behaviour. We need not be surprised at this duality. It is merely the reflection of the composite character of a legal system as compared with a simpler decentralized pre-legal form of social structure which consists only of primary rules. In the simpler structure, since there are no officials, the rules must be widely accepted as setting critical standards for the behaviour of the group. If, there, the internal point of view is not widely disseminated there could not logically be any rules. But where there is a union of primary and secondary rules, which is, as we have argued, the most fruitful way of regarding a legal system, the acceptance of the rules as common standards for the group may be split off from the relatively passive matter of the ordinary individual acquiescing in the rules by obeying them for his part alone. In an extreme case the internal point of view with its characteristic normative use of legal language ('This is a valid rule') might be confined to the official world. In this more complex system, only officials might accept and use the system's criteria of legal validity. The society in which this was so might be deplorably sheeplike; the sheep might end in the slaughter-house. But there is little reason for thinking that it could not exist or for denying it the title of a legal system.

THE PATHOLOGY OF A LEGAL SYSTEM

Evidence for the existence of a legal system must therefore be drawn from two different sectors of social life. The normal, unproblematic case where we can say confidently that a legal system exists, is just one where it is clear that the two sectors are congruent in their respective typical concerns with the law. Crudely put, the facts are that the rules recognized as valid at the official level are generally obeyed. Sometimes, however, the official sector may be detached from the private sector, in the sense that there is no longer general obedience to the rules which are valid according to the criteria of validity in use in the courts. The variety of ways in which this may happen belongs to the pathology of legal systems; for they represent a breakdown in the complex congruent practice which is referred to when we make the external statement of fact that a legal system exists. There is here a partial failure of what is presupposed whenever, from within the particular system, we make internal statements of law. Such a breakdown may be the product of different disturbing factors. 'Revolution', where rival claims to govern are made from within the group, is only one case, and though this will always involve the breach of some of the laws of the existing system, it may entail only the legally unauthorized substitution of a new set of individuals as officials, and not a new constitution or legal system. Enemy occupation, where a rival claim to govern without authority under the existing system comes from without, is another case; and the simple breakdown of ordered legal control in the fact of anarchy or banditry without political pretensions to govern is yet another.

In each of these cases there may be half-way stages during which the courts function, either on the territory or in exile, and still use the criteria of legal validity of the old once firmly established system; but these orders are ineffective in the territory. The state at which it is right to say in such cases that the legal system has finally ceased to exist is a thing not susceptible of any exact determination. Plainly, if there is some considerable chance of a restoration or if the disturbance of the established system is an incident in a general war of which the issue is still uncertain, no unqualified assertion that it has ceased to exist would be warranted. This is so just because the statement that a legal system exists is of a sufficiently broad and general type to allow for interruptions; it is not verified or falsified by what happens in short spaces of time.

8. CONTINENTAL LEGAL POSITIVISM: KELSEN'S THEORY

HANS KELSEN
The Pure Theory of Law [1]
(1934)

I

1)   The Pure Theory of Law is a theory of the positive law. As a theory it is exclusively concerned with the accurate definition of its subject-matter. It endeavours to answer the question, What is the law? but not the question, What ought it to be? It is a science and not a politics of law.

That all this is described as a 'pure' theory of law means that it is concerned solely with that part of knowledge which deals with law, excluding from such knowledge everything which does not strictly belong to the subject-matter law. That is, it endeavours to free the science of law from all foreign elements. This is its fundamental methodological principle. It would seem a self-evident one. Yet a glance at the traditional science of law in its nineteenth and twentieth century developments shows plainly how far removed from the requirement of purity that science was. Jurisprudence, in a wholly uncritical fashion, was mixed up with psychology and biology, with ethics and theology. There is today hardly a single social science into whose province jurisprudence feels itself unfitted to enter, even thinking, indeed, to enhance its scientific status by such conjunction with other disciplines. The real science of law, of course, is lost in such a process.

2)   The Pure Theory of Law seeks to define clearly its objects of knowledge in these two directions in which its autonomy has been most endangered by the prevailing syncretism of methods. Law is a social phenomenon. Society, however, is something wholly different from nature, since an entirely different association of elements. If legal science is not to disappear into natural science, then law must be distinguished in the plainest possible manner from nature. The difficulty about such a distinction is that law, or what is generally called law, belongs with at least a part of its being to nature and seems to have a thoroughly natural existence. If, for instance, we analyse any condition of things

[1] Kelsen, H 'The Pure Theory of Law' (translated by C H Wilson) (1934) 50 *Law Quarterly Review* 474; (1935) 50 *Law Quarterly Review* 517.

such as is called law – a parliamentary ruling, a judicial sentence, a legal process, a delict – we can distinguish two elements. The one is a sensible act in time and place, an external process, generally a human behaviour; the other is a significance attached to or immanent in this act or process, a specific meaning. People meet together in a hall, make speeches, some rise from their seats, others remain seated; that is the external process. Its meaning: that a law has been passed. A man, clothed in a gown, speaks certain words from an elevated position to a person standing in front of him. This external process means a judicial sentence. One merchant writes to another a letter with a certain content; the other sends a return letter. This means they have concluded a contract. Someone, by some action or other, brings about the death of another. This means, legally, murder.

3) We cannot immediately perceive this 'significance' in the act, as an external condition, in the same way in which we perceive in an object its natural characteristics and functions, its colour, hardness and weight. The act may, indeed, in so far as it is expressed in written or in spoken words, itself indicate something of its significance, may declare its own meaning. This is a special characteristic of the material dealt with in social and in particular in juristic knowledge. A plant can convey nothing about itself to the research worker who is trying to define it. It makes no attempt to explain itself scientifically. But a social act can very well carry with it an indication of its own meaning. The person instituting the act himself attaches to it a definite meaning which he expresses in some fashion or other and which is understood by those towards whom the act is directed. The persons assembled in parliament can give explicit directions as to the law which they are passing. Two private persons can declare their intention of instituting a legal relationship. Legal science generally finds some self-explanation of its material which precedes that meaning with which it, as a science, has to endow it.

4) In all this there emerges the necessity of distinguishing between the subjective and the objective meaning of an act. The subjective may but need not coincide with the objective meaning, which adheres to the act by virtue of its place among all legal acts, that is, in the legal system. The act of the celebrated Commander of Kopenick was in its intention, and in its subjective meaning, an administrative order. Objectively, however, it was not this at all but a delict. When a secret society, with the intention of freeing the motherland of subversive characters, condemns to death some person whom it holds to be a traitor, and entrusts to one of its members the execution of what it holds, subjectively, to be a death sentence (and it calls it such), objectively, that is, in the system of the objective law, this is not a death sentence at all but a vehmic murder, although the external circumstances of the act differ in no way from the execution of a death sentence.

5)   These external circumstances, since they are sensible, temporospatial events, are in every case a piece of nature and as such causally determined. But as elements of the system nature, they are not objects of specifically juristic knowledge, are, indeed not legal matter at all. That which makes the process into a legal (or illegal) act is not its factuality, not its natural, causal existence, but the objective significance which is bound up with it, its meaning. Its characteristically legal meaning it receives from a norm whose content refers to it. The norm functions as a schema of meaning. It itself is born of a legal act which in its turn receives its meaning from another norm. That a certain condition of fact is the execution of a death sentence and not a murder, this quality, which is not perceptible to the senses, is arrived at only by a mental process: by confronting the act with the penal statute book and penal administration. That the above-mentioned correspondence meant the conclusion of a contract resulted solely from the fact that this circumstance fell under certain rulings in the civil statute book. That an assembly of persons is a parliament and that the result of their activities is a law is only to say that the whole condition of fact corresponds to definite prescriptions in the constitution. That is to say, the content of some factual occurrence coincides with the content of some norm which is presupposed as valid.

6)   Towards these norms, then, which confer on certain circumstances their character of legal (or illegal) acts, and which are themselves born of such legal acts, is legal knowledge directed. At the same time, it must be observed, the norm, as a specific content, is something other than the physical act in which it is willed or imagined. We must clearly distinguish between the willing or the thinking of the norm and the norm itself which is willed or thought. When we speak of 'making' (setting up) a norm we mean thereby a factual process which carries the norm as content. The Pure Theory Of Law is not concerned with any such mental processes or physical movements when it seeks to review norms or to comprehend something legally. To comprehend something legally can mean only to comprehend something as law. To say that only legal norms can make up the subject-matter of legal knowledge is a tautological statement. For law, the sole object of legal knowledge, is Norm. The norm, however, is a category which has no application in the sphere of nature. When natural acts are characterized as legal processes, this means only that certain norms are asserted as valid whose content stands in a definite correspondence to that of the factual circumstance. When the judge determines that some concrete condition of fact, say a delict, is present, his examination is directed in the first place to some natural, existent reality. But his knowledge only becomes juristic when he brings this condition of fact into relation with the statute which he has to apply, when he designates it as 'theft' or 'fraud.' And he can only so designate it when the content of the actual circumstance is recognized in a quite definite fashion as the content of a norm. (At the same time, it must be remembered, the activity of the judge is in no way exhausted by the act of recognition: this is only the

forerunner of an act of will by which is to be set up the individual norm of the judicial sentence.)

7) In defining the law as norm, and in restricting legal science (whose function is different from that of the legislative and executive organs) to knowledge of norms, we at the same time delimit law from nature and the science of law, as a normative science, from all other sciences which aim at explaining causal, natural processes. In particular, we delimit it from one science which sets itself the task of examining the causes and effects of these natural processes which, receiving their designation from legal norms, appear as legal acts. If such a study be called sociology, or sociology of law, we shall make no objection. Neither shall we say anything here of its value or its prospects. This only is certain, that such legal-sociological knowledge has nothing to do with the norms of the law as specific contents. It deals only with certain processes without reference to their relation to any valid or assumed norms. It relates the circumstances to be examined not to valid norms but to other circumstances, as causes to effects. It inquires by what causes a legislator is determined in constituting these and not other norms, and what effects his ordinances have had. It inquires in what way economic facts and religious views actually influence the activities of the Courts, and for what motives men make their behaviour conform to the law or not. For such an inquiry law is only a natural reality, a fact in the consciousness of those who make, or of those subject to, the norms. The law itself, therefore, is not properly the subject of this study, but certain parallel processes in nature. In the same way the physiologist, examining the physical or chemical processes which condition or which accompany certain emotions, does not comprehend the emotions themselves. The emotions are not comprehensible in chemical or physiological terms. The Pure Theory of Law, as a specific science of law, considers legal norms not as natural realities, not as facts in consciousness, but as meaning-contents. And it considers facts only as the content of legal norms, that is, only as determined by the norms. Its problem is to discover the specific principles of a sphere of meaning.

8) In delimiting law from nature, the Pure Theory of Law at the same time draws the line of demarcation between Nature and Idea. The science of law is a mental and not a natural science. It can be debated whether the opposition of nature and idea coincides with that of reality and value, of the Is and the Ought, of causal law and normative law; or whether the sphere of essence is broader than that of value, or than that of the norm. But it cannot be denied that the law, as norm, is an ideal and not a natural reality. And so emerges the necessity of distinguishing law, not only from nature, but also from other spiritual phenomena, particularly from other types of norms. What is here chiefly important is to liberate law from that association which has traditionally been made for it – its association with morals. This is not of course to question the requirement that law ought to be moral, that is, good. That requirement is

self-evident. What is questioned is simply the view that law, as such, is a part of morals and that therefore every law, as law, is in some sense and in some measure moral. In looking on the law as a part-province of morals, while leaving obscure the issue as to whether this means that law ought to be constructed morally, or that it is a matter of fact moral, the attempt is made to confer on law that absolute value which morals claims. As a moral category law meant the same as justice. This is the expression from the absolutely right social order. The word, however, is often used in the sense of positive accordance with the law, particularly accordance with statute law. In this sense, if a general norm is applied in one case and not in another identical case, the procedure is termed 'unjust' and this without reference to the value of the general norm itself. In this usage the just sentence expressed only the relative value of conformity to the norm. 'Just' is only another word for 'legal' or 'legitimate.' In its proper meaning, as distinct from that which it has in law, 'justice' connotes an absolute value. Its content cannot be ascertained by the Pure Theory of Law. Indeed it is not ascertainable by rational knowledge at all. The history of human speculation for centuries has been the history of a vain striving after a solution of the problem. That striving has hitherto led only to the emptiest of tautologies, such as the formula *suum cuique* or the categoric imperative. From the standpoint of rational knowledge there are only interests and conflicts of interests, the solution of which is arrived at by an arrangement which may either satisfy the one interest at the expense of the other, or institute an equivalence or compromise between them. To determine, however, whether this or that order has an absolute value, that is, is 'just,' is not possible by the methods of rational knowledge. Justice is an irrational ideal. However indispensable it may be for the willing and acting of human beings it is not viable by reason. Only positive law is known, or more correctly is revealed, to reason. If we refrain from distinguishing these two meanings of the term justice, if we do not repudiate the claim (of the legislating authority) that the law is just law, we are lending our support to that ideological tendency which was the specific characteristic of the classical, conservative theory of natural law. This latter was concerned not so much with the knowledge of the valid law but rather with its justification. It sought to demonstrate that the positive law was simply an emanation of a natural, divine or reasonable, absolutely just order. The revolutionary natural law school, on the other hand, which in the history of legal science plays a relatively minor role, was of the opposite opinion, questioning the validity of the positive law and maintaining that it contradicted a presupposed, absolute order. Thereby they brought the actual law for a time into a more unfavourable light than it truly deserved.

9)   Even after the apparent defeat of the theory of natural law, these ideological tendencies, whose political intentions and effects are obvious, still hold sway over contemporary legal science. The Pure Theory of Law is directed against

them. This theory is concerned to show the law as it is, without legitimising it as just, or disqualifying it as unjust; it seeks the real, the positive law, not the right law. In this sense it is a radically realistic theory of law. It refuses to evaluate the positive law. As a science it considers itself bound only to comprehend the positive law according to its nature and to understand it by analysis of its structure. In particular it declines to serve any political interests by providing them with ideologies whereby to justify or disqualify the existing social order. In this point it finds itself in direct opposition to traditional legal science which, consciously or unconsciously, has always in some measure an ideological colouring. Precisely in this anti-ideological tendency the Pure Theory of Law reveals itself as a true science. For science, as a part of knowledge, is compelled, by an internal necessity, to lay bare its subject-matter. Ideology on the other hand covers up reality, by explaining it away if it wishes to defend it, by distorting it if it wishes to destroy it or replace it with a substitute. All ideology has its roots in willing and not in knowing; it springs from certain interests, or more correctly, from interests other than that of truth. In saying this, of course, nothing is implied as to the value or worth of these other interests. Knowledge must continue to tear down the veils which the will has laid about things. The authority which creates the law and is, therefore, anxious for its maintenance may well ask itself if such an unvarnished knowledge of its product is a useful thing. And the powers which desire to overthrow the existing order and replace it with one which they hold to be better may well not want to know much of such a science of law. But neither the one nor the other consideration can be allowed to prevent the emergence of a science of law such as the Pure Theory of Law desires to be.

II

10) The ideological character of traditional legal theory is clearly revealed in the customary formulation of the concept of law. It stands still today under the influence of the conservative natural law school, which operates, as I have already shown, with a transcendental concept of law. This is in complete accordance with the basic metaphysical character of philosophy during the reign of natural right theories; a period which, politically, coincides with the development of the police state of absolute monarchy. With the victory of bourgeois liberalism in the nineteenth century an outspoken reaction against meta-physic and natural law theory set in. The changeover of bourgeois legal science from natural law to positivism went hand in hand with the progress of the empirical natural sciences and with a critical analysis of religious ideology. Yet this changeover, however radical, was never a complete one. Law is indeed, no longer presumed to be an eternal and absolute category; it is recognized that its content is subject to historical change and that as positive law it is a temporally and spatially conditioned phenomenon. The idea of an absolute legal value, however, is not quite lost but lives on in the ethical notion of justice to

which positivist jurisprudence continues to cling. Even although the distinction between justice and law is firmly emphasized, the two are still bound together by more or less visible ties. If we are really to have 'law', we are told, then the positive political order must participate in some measure in the idea of justice, must realize an ethical minimum and approximate to right 'law,' that is, to justice. Since, however, the legal character of the prevailing political order is presumed to be self-evident, its legitimisation at the hands of this theory of the moral minimum (which is only a minimized theory of natural law) is an easy matter. And this minimum guarantee suffices alike for the comparatively peaceful periods of middle-class domination and for the periods of relative equilibrium of the social forces. The final consequences of the officially recognized positivist principle have not been clearly displayed. The science of law is not yet wholly positivistic, though predominantly so.

11) a) The position is clearly revealed in the concept under which positive law is subsumed – the concept of the norm, or of the Ought. The non-identity of legal and moral norms, it is true, continues to be asserted; but from the juristic side no attack is made on an absolute moral value. And even if it seems intended thereby to allow the merely relative character of law to emerge more clearly, yet the mere fact that jurisprudence does not feel itself sufficiently independent to deny the existence of an absolute value cannot be without its effects on the jurist's concept of law. And indeed when law and morals are both seen to be normative, and the meaning of both the legal and the moral norm is expressed in an 'Ought,' there remains attached to the legal norm and to the legal Ought something of the absolute value which is peculiar to morals. The judgment that some thing is according to the legal norms, that some content or other legally ought to be, is never quite free from the impression that it is therefore good, right and just. And in this sense the positivist jurisprudence of the nineteenth century, though it conceives of law as normative, is not quite free of a certain ideological element.

b) To free the theory of law from this element is the endeavour of the Pure Theory of Law. The Pure Theory of Law separates the concept of the legal completely from that of the moral norm and establishes the law as a specific system independent even of the moral law. It does this not, as is generally the case with the traditional theory, by defining the legal norm, like the moral norm, as an imperative, but as an hypothetical judgment expressing a specific relationship between a conditioning circumstance and a conditioned consequence. The legal norm becomes the legal maxim – the fundamental form of the statute law. Just as natural law links a certain circumstance to another as cause to effect, so the legal rule links the legal condition to the legal consequence. In the one case the connecting principle is causality: in the other it is imputation. The Pure Theory of Law regards this principle as the special and nature runs: If A is, then B must be. The legal rule says: If A is, then B ought to be. And thereby it says nothing as to the value, the moral or political value of the relationship. The Ought remains a pure *a priori* category for the comprehension of the empirical legal material. In this respect it is indispensable if we are to grasp at all the specific fashion in which positive law connects circumstances with one another. For it is evident that this connexion is not that of cause and effect. Punishment does not follow upon a delict as effect upon a cause. The legislator relates the two circumstances in a fashion wholly different from causality. Wholly different, yet a connexion as unshakeable as causality. For in the legal system the punishment follows always and invariably on the delict even when in fact, for some reason or other, it fails of execution. Even though it does not so fail, it still does not stand to the delict in the relation of effect to cause. When we say: If there is tort, then the consequence of tort (punishment) shall (ie ought to) follow, this Ought, the category of law, indicates only the specific sense in which the legal condition and the legal consequence are held together in the legal rule. The category has a purely formal character. Thereby it distinguishes itself in principle from any transcendental notion of law. It is applicable no matter what the content of the circumstances which it links together, no matter what the character of the acts to which it gives the name of law. No social reality can be refused incorporation in this legal category on account of its contentual structure. It is an epistemological-transcendental category in the sense of Kantian philosophy, not metaphysical-transcendental. In this it preserves its radically anti-ideological tendency, thereby incurring the most violent resistance on the part of the traditional theory of law, which finds it hard to bear that the law of the Soviet Republic should be considered every bit as much as legal order as that of Fascist Italy or that of democratic, capitalist France.

c) Since the inception of the widespread social changes caused by the World War the traditional theory of law has been preparing for a wholesale return to natural law theory, just as philosophy is in full reaction to the pre-Kantian metaphysic. The middle classes, in the same political situation now in the middle of the twentieth century as the feudal nobility at the beginning of the nineteenth, are harking back to the identical political ideologies which the feudal nobility defended against these very middle classes. The Pure Theory of Law finds itself, therefore, in the strongest opposition to the Epigones who repudiate Kantian transcendental philosophy and legal positivism, precisely because it draws the final conclusions from the original, positive, anti-ideological philosophy and theory of law of the nineteenth century.

12) In the formal category of the Ought or the norm, however, we have discovered only the chief concept, not the specific difference, of law. The legal theory of the nineteenth century was in the main united in defining the legal norm as a norm of compulsion, that is, as a norm instituting compulsion, and in holding that in this very point it distinguished itself from other norms. In this respect

the Pure Theory of Law continues the tradition. It makes the consequence, which is linked in the legal rule to a definite condition, a state act of compulsion, that is, punishment and its civil or administrative execution. Solely by this means is the conditioning circumstance qualified as delict and the conditioned as the consequence of delict. It is the result of no inherent quality, of no relation to some extra-legal norm or moral value transcending positive law, that a definite behaviour is designated illegal, a delict in the widest sense of the term. This result follows solely from the fact that the positive legal order reacts to the behaviour with an act of compulsion.

13) Seen from the immanental standpoint which the Pure Theory of Law adopts, the concept of delict undergoes a radical change in meaning. It is not the motive of the legislator, nor that some circumstance is held by the authority constituting the norms to be undesirable or, to use an obscure expression, socially harmful, which determines the concept of delict. That which alone is regulative is the position of the circumstance in question within the legal rule; whether or not it is the condition for the specific reaction of law, the act of compulsion. Delict is a particular behaviour – appearing in the legal rule as condition – of a person, against whom is directed the act of compulsion – appearing in the legal rule as consequence. If, as in the case of primitive legal systems, or as in the case of a delict attributed to a juristic person, the consequence falls on some person other than the one responsible for the condition, there is always the presupposition that there exists between the two some connexion, real or fictitious, which is accepted by the lawgiver. We are speaking here of responsibility for another's crime. Thus the family of the murderer is held responsible in the place of the later, the prince answers for the delict committed by his subjects, the people for breaches of the law made by other state organs (collective responsibility). Between the real subject of the delict and the object of the consequence there exists always physical or juristic identity.

Here, again, the Pure Theory of Law finds itself in opposition to the contemporary legal theory, which, consonant with its reversal to natural law doctrine, would like to renounce compulsion as the empirical criterion of law, since it holds that law can be recognized by its inherent significance, by its coincidence with an idea of law. Only in so far as the obligatory nature of law is held to proceed from direct insight into its value, when the positive law is simply the demonstrant of an absolute, that is, divine or natural order, can the element of compulsion appear as unessential; the validity of the law rests, then, exactly as in absolutist morals, on the internal compulsion which accompanies the evidence of its authority. This is an unambiguous natural law conception.

14) If law, however, considered purely positively, is nothing else than an external, compulsive order, then it is clearly only a specific social technique. The desired social condition is brought about by attaching to its contradictory, the human behaviour, an act of compulsion, that is, the compulsory removal of a good: life,

freedom or economic utility. In this fashion we may pursue any social end whatsoever. Law is characterized not as an end but as a specific means, as an apparatus of compulsion, to which, as such, there adheres no political or ethical value, an apparatus whose value derives rather from some end which transcends the law. This too, is an interpretation of the material of the law wholly free from ideology.

15) It is often denied that the law is such an entity at all. The law is looked upon, that is, legal ordinances are looked upon, as means to evoke a specific behaviour on the part of the persons with whom it is concerned. It is thought that the legal order can thus be understood as the uniformity of a certain series of human behaviours. The normative meaning with which the ordinances appear is thus consciously ignored since it is deemed unnecessary to accept an Ought which is wholly different from the Is. The assertion of the legislator or of the legal theorist, that 'he who steals shall be (ie ought to be) punished,' is looked on simply as an attempt to bring men to forsake theft and to punish thieves, as an attempt to arouse in men certain ideals (*Vorstellungen*) which will motivate them to an adequate behaviour. The juristic position, that one ought not to steal, that thieves should be punished, is dissolved into the statement of fact, that some men are engaged in persuading others not to steal, to punish thiefs, or that men do as a general rule forsake theft and punish thieves. The law – as a relation between those making and those carrying out the ordinances – is looked on as an enterprise of the same type as that of the hunter who sets a lure to entice his quarry into a trap. The comparison is just, not only because in the two cases the motivation relation is the same, but also because this view of law, in so far as it continues to declare the law as norm, practises a deception. From such a standpoint there are no 'norms' at all; the phrase, this or that 'shall' or 'ought' to be, has no specific, positive, legal meaning such as the Pure Theory of Law accepts. From such a standpoint only the natural, pure and simple, can be considered, only the nexus of causal occurrence, the factuality of the laws not their specific meaning. This meaning – the norm or the Ought – in which the law consists, appears to this view as pure 'ideology,' even in the purified meaning of law – as free from all moral or absolute value – which the Pure Theory of Law professes. The sole 'reality' is nature, causally regulated occurrence, both physical and mental.

16) It is a question whether, from such a standpoint, social phenomena can be understood at all, whether, indeed, society as a definite subject does not entirely disappear. For there is much that leads us to think that the social is essentially ideological in character and that society is distinguished only from nature as ideology from a reality. We need not here go into this whole question. It is sufficient to say, that in such a process the specific meaning of the law vanishes completely. If the 'norm,' the 'Ought,' is rendered devoid of meaning then there is no sense in saying: this shall be legal, that illegal; this belong to me, that to

you; X shall have the right, Y shall be obliged, etc. In short, the thousand and one expressions of our daily legal life lose their meaning. For I am saying two different things when I say: A is legally bound (Ought) to do such and such for B, and when I say: There is a certain chance that A will do such and such for B. And again when I say: This behaviour is according to law a delict, and should be punished, and when I say: He who has done this will in all probability be punished. It is impossible to convey the meaning involved in the relation between the legislator and the legal administrator, between the administrator and the subject, between one subject and another, by an expression denoting the probable course of a future behaviour. Such an expression proceeds from a transcendental viewpoint. It gives no answer to the specifically juristic question: What is the law? It answers rather the 'metalegal' question: What happens, and what probably will happen? If the normative sense of law is only 'ideology,' then a theory of law which wants to grasp its inner meaning must be directed towards elucidating the principles of an ideology. The Pure Theory of Law is fully aware of this. Indeed, by depriving law of its metaphysical, absolute value it has made way for a clearer insight into the ideological character of law. But it does not therefore feel bound to renounce a normative theory of law, renounce the task of systematizing and elucidating the mental contents which, borne by natural acts, first give to those their character of law.

III

17) The general theory of law, as developed by the positivistic jurisprudence of the nineteenth century, is characterized by a dualism which cuts across all its problems and dominates the entire system. This dualism is a legacy from the theory of natural law, whose place has been taken by the general theory of law. The natural law dualism was derived from the acceptance of a divine or natural order of law, above and superior to the political order of the positive law, and essentially possessed, at least in the opinion of the classical representatives of natural law theory in the seventeenth and eighteenth centuries, of a conservative, legitimising function. It is true that the positivism of the nineteenth century does not indeed wholly renounce, as already said, a justification of the law by a supra-positive value; but it does this only indirectly, under the cover of its concepts. The justification of the positive law no longer proceeds from a higher and different law, but rather from the concept of law itself. We are to speak now not of the former immament, not manifest dualism, but of an explicit, trans-systematic dualism, appearing in the distinction between objective and subjective, public and private law and in innumerable other distinctions, not least among which is the distinction between law and the state. And the function of this manifold dualism is by no means simply to legitimise the positive legal order, but also to set certain limits to its contentual structure. The former function applies particularly to the distinction between law and the state, the latter quite unmistakably, to that between objective and subjective law.

The distinction between public and private law is inordinately ambiguous and its ideological function, too, ill-defined.

18) If the general theory of law maintains its subject, the law, to be given not only in an objective but also in a subjective sense, it introduces a contradiction of principle into the basis of the system. For thereby it asserts the law to be an objective norm or complex of norms and at the same time to be something subjective, that is, something wholly different, incapable of being subsumed under a common concept – namely, interest or will. This contradiction is not removed by asserting a relation between the objective and the subjective law, namely, that the latter is the interest protected by the former, or the will recognized or served by the former. In its original intention the dualism of objective and subjective law expressed the notion that the latter was both logically prior and prior in time to the former. First there arise subjective rights and chief among these – property, the prototype of all subjective rights, and only at a later stage does there emerge the objective law, as a political order, protecting and serving the independently arisen subjective rights. This view appears most clearly among the representatives of the historical school, who not only inaugurate the legal positivism of the nineteenth century, but also give a decisive cast to the conceptual structure of the general theory of law. Thus we read, for example, in Dernburg: 'Rights, in the subjective sense, existed historically long before any conscious political order was formed. These rights were founded on the personality of the individual and on the respect which he had been able to obtain for himself and his possessions. Only by a process of abstraction from the existing subjective rights was the notion of a legal order arrived at. It is, therefore, an incorrect and unhistorical view which refuses to see in subjective right the source of the objective law.'

19) Closely related to the notion of subjective right, indeed only another form of the same notion, is that of the legal subject or 'person' as the bearer of subjective rights. In its essentials the notion is confined in its application to the property-owner. Here again the regulative idea is that of a legal entity independent of the legal order, a legal subjectivity, which the subjective law finds, as it were, already present, whether in the individual or in certain collectivities: it has only to recognize it, and must do so if it it not to lose its character of 'law.' The contradiction between law (in the objective sense) and a subjectivity of right, which is a logical contradiction if the two be maintained conjointly existent, emerges most strikingly when we consider that the significance of the objective law, as a heteronomous norm, is its binding quality, its compulsion, while the nature of this legal personality is precisely the opposite, namely, freedom, in the sense of self-determination.

20) The fictitious character of this view of legal personality is obvious. For, in so far as we can speak at all of self-determination of the individual in the sphere of

law – namely, with regard to so-called private law and contract, autonomy exists only in a highly circumscribed and imperfect sense ...

It is not difficult to understand why the ideology of subjective right is related to the ethics values of individual freedom and autonomous personality when in this freedom property is always included. An order which did not recognize the free personality of man in this sense, that is, an order which did not serve subjective right, is in this view not fit to be a legal order at all.

21) It is perfectly consonant with such an ideology that the relation of law and society, and in particular of law and economics, should be viewed as the relation of form and content. Rights are seen as a relationship within the social material, receiving in the law only their external expression. It is a particularly sociological section of traditional jurisprudence which follows in this way what is really a natural law point of view. Again, following the dualism of subjective and objective law, legal relations between persons are distinguished from those between things, according as it is a relation between subjects, or one between subject and object (person and thing). This second relationship is demonstrated *par excellence* in property; the whole distinction is, indeed, concerned with this institution. The relationship is defined as the exclusive power of a person over a thing, a description which distinguishes it fundamentally from the obligations which are based on personal relationships. Further, this important civil law distinction has a frankly ideological character. That it continues to be maintained despite the repeated objection that the legal power of a person over a thing consists in nothing else than a specific relationship to other subjects, namely, in their duty to refrain from interferring with his right of disposal of the thing, and in his legal ability to exclude all others from the enjoyment of it, is clearly because its distinctive economic and social function is disguised by the definition of property as a relation between person and thing. Whether this definition is justly or unjustly described by socialist theory as 'exploitation' is irrelevant; it is at all events true that it consists in nothing else than a relation of the property-owner to other subjects, who are forbidden access to his property and who are compelled to respect his proprietary powers. Yet traditional jurisprudence rejects in the most decisive fashion the view that the subjective right of one is valid simply as the reflex of the legal duty of another. Again and again its representatives emphasize the primary character of the possession of a right; indeed, they go so far as to identify it with right in general.

22) The second form of subjective right, the legal duty, is handled by the general theory of law in a strikingly stepmotherly fashion. It is even from time to time maintained that duty is no legal concept at all, that there are only moral duties. Yet the essential function of a compulsive order such as the law can hardly be anything else than the exercise of normative obligation over the individuals subject to it; and such normative obligation can be designated only as duty. Moral duty is nothing else than the obligation which binds an individual by

reason of the validity of a moral order. There is, of course, little sense in extending the concept of subjective right, in the role of category of private property, to cover legal duty. Indeed, it would be to challenge all that subjective right, in the meaning of the ideological theory, stands for to confront it with duty as a concept of equal rank, let alone as the primary factor.

23) It is precisely at this point that the Pure Theory of Law begins its criticism of prevalent theory, by setting the concept of legal duty with the greatest possible emphasis in the foreground. In this, too, the Pure Theory only draws the final conclusions from certain fundamental, yet little developed ideas in the positivistic theory of the nineteenth century. It recognizes in legal duty simply the legal norm in its application to the concrete behaviour of a definite individual, that is, the individualized legal norm. Further, it emancipates the concept of legal duty completely from that of moral duty by interpreting it in the following fashion: a man is legally obliged to a certain behaviour is so far as the contradictory of that behaviour appears in the legal norm as the condition of a compulsive act, described as the penalty (consequence of tort). If the compulsive act is directed against someone other than him whose behaviour figures as the condition of the penalty (or as the content of the duty), then we can speak of responsibility, and distinguish the concepts of duty and responsibility. Responsibility appears as a special kind of duty. The legal duty emerges as the sole essential function of the objective law. Every rule of law must necessarily lay down a duty; it can also lay down a rights. Such is present when among the conditions of the penalty, and directed to these, there is included an appeal by him whose interests have been damaged by the wrong. Only in respect of this individual can the norm be said to confer a rights and to become, in a sense different from that of legal duty, subjective law, that is a subject's right, since it places itself at his disposal for the support of his interests. This subjective right, however, does not appear as something completely independent of the objective law; for there is only such a thing as subjective law at all in so far as it is included in the objective legal norm. The conferring of a right is only a possible and by no means a necessary contentual construction of the objective law, a special technique of which the law may but need not avail itself. It is the specific technique of the capitalist legal order, in so far as this is built up on the institution of private property and therefore directed specially to individual interests. Nor is this technique prevalent in every section of the capitalist legal order; it is fully developed only in so-called private law and in certain parts of administrative law. Modern penal law has dispensed with it. In the place of him whose interests have been damaged there appears as plaintiff a State organ which officially institutes proceedings. With this insight into the nature of what is called law in the subjective sense, the Pure Theory of Law disposes completely of the dualism of subjective and objective law. Subjective is not different from objective law; it is the objective

law itself in so far as the latter directs the penalty against a concrete subject (duty), or puts itself at the disposal of such (right). With this reduction of the subjective to the objective law, any ideological misuse is excluded. Above all, however, the concept of law is no longer limited to a particular technical construction. The historical restrictions of capitalist legal forms are accounted for by the concept itself.

24) We can now see our way clear to recognize in the concept of the legal subject, or person, only an auxiliary device created by the juristic mind for purposes of exposition and under the influence of an anthropomorphous, personificative, legal language. 'Person' is only the personificative expression for the unity of a bundle of legal rights and duties, that is, norm complexes. To perceive this is to avoid these misleading hypostases by which the law, as an object of knowledge, appears in a double form. Now, for the first time, the old demand of positivistic legal theory, that the physical and the juristic person should be conceived as identical in nature, can be fully realized. The 'physical person' is not, as traditional theory maintains, man. That is no juristic, but a biological and psychological concept. Physical person is the personification of the group of norms regulating the conduct of one human being. (The second meaning of the concept of the juristic person, in which it is used chiefly by the legislator – juristic person as an expression for a statutory limitation of responsibility – is not discussed here.) The assertion that the juristic person has a real existence is thus shown to be an illusion. Its duties and rights are resolved into the duties and rights of human beings, that is, into the norms regulating human behaviour and designating it as rights and duties. The freedom or autonomy of the physical person, which is the juristic parallel of the ethical dogma of freedom of the will, is rejected as an illusion from the domain of legal theory. More, the 'sovereignty' of the supreme, comprehensive, juristic person, which has been so constantly advanced by political theory as the fundamental quality of the State, appears now only as the principle of freedom of the will recurring on a higher level, and therefore as a theoretically untenable category.

25) We have now seen that the 'person' is a personification for a complex of norms and is, therefore, a more or less voluntarily individualized part of the objective legal order, which latter provides an organic, that is, a systematic unity between all the rights and duties it has set up, the rights and duties of all persons; the right of the one is always and necessarily the duty of the other.

26) Having removed from the concept of subjective right as from that of the legal subject all trace of ideological function, and thereby beaten a way through the tangle of personifications to the real legal relationships, we can more clearly see the latter as relations between human behaviours, linked by the norm in which they appear as content. This is the legal relationship: the connexion between two conditions of fact, of which the one is a human behaviour characterized as a

legal duty, the other a human behaviour characterized as a right. The Pure Theory of Law, by rejecting so-called subjective law in all its appearances – legal right, legal duty, legal subject – as an entity different in kind from the objective law, and by showing it to be only a special form of figurative exposition of the objective law, has made way for the overthrow of that subjectivistic attitude which produced the concept of subjective right, that attitude of special pleading which regards the law only from a party interest point of view, considering how it may benefit the individual and his interests. It is the specific attitude of Roman jurisprudence which, in essentials the product of the advisory practice of the jurisconsults, was received along with Roman Law. The attitude of the Pure Theory of Law is on the contrary wholly objective and universalistic. It is concerned fundamentally with the law as a whole, seeing every single phenomenon only in its systematic relation to all others, seeing in every part of the law the function of the whole. In this sense it is a truly organic view of law. But in calling law an organism the theory does not mean any supra-individual and supra-empirical, metaphysical entity of a biological nature, a conception which in general hides ethico-political postulates, but solely that the law is a system, and that all legal problems are problems of system. Legal theory thus becomes a structural analysis, as exact as possible, of the positive law, an analysis free of all ethical or political judgments of value.

A WILSON
The Imperative Fallacy in Kelsen's Theory [2]
(1981)

I

The legal norm, it was almost unanimously accepted in jurisprudence to about 1900, expressed 'the will of the state,' and what this will required was the 'law abiding conduct of the subject'; in other words, the legal norm appeared as a command 'ordering' or 'prohibiting' certain conduct to the subject. This, the Imperative Theory, had been maintained by schools of thought otherwise radically different, as by the continental advocates of Natural Law in the seventeenth century, Grotius and Puffendorf, and in nineteenth century England by Jeremy Bentham and John Austin; it was upheld in Germany in the late nineteenth century by more than one jurist, notably Binding. Kelsen, in reaction, set up in his early work a concept of his own, combining his own view of the 'will of the state' and his new, quite different view of the norm in relation to that will.

[2] Wilson, A 'The Imperative Fallacy in Kelsen's Theory' (1981) 44 *Modern Law Review* 270.

In this essay I begin by describing summarily Kelsen's treatment of the legal norm in the later stages of his career, with reference to his changing position as to the idea of command. The rest of the argument will be pursued as follows. First I elucidate the different meanings attached to the term 'ought' as it is used by Kelsen in different contexts in his work. Secondly, I shall show that Kelsen's views as to the origin and validity respectively of norms are irreconcilable. His belief in the 'ought' as ultimately traceable to the will is, to be sure, a logical consequence of his ethical subjectivism but leads him, nonetheless, into the fallacy of making an 'ought' rest ultimately on the 'is'. Commission of this fallacy, however, was never explicitly admitted by Kelsen, who remained throughout equally attached to the belief that 'an ought can only be founded on another ought.'

Though at the beginning of his career Kelsen had rejected the notion of the legal norm as conveying the 'will of the state' and had seen it, in its formal character, as a 'hypothetical judgment' not expressive of will, he came round, in the 1960 (second edition) of *The Pure Theory*, to admission of the will into his concept of the legal norm, without making the norm 'an act of will':

> 'Norm is the meaning of an act by which a certain behaviour is commanded, permitted or authorized. The norm, as the specific meaning of an act directed toward the behaviour of someone else, is to be carefully differentiated from the act of will whose meaning the norm is: the norm is an ought, but the act of will is an 'is'. Hence the situation constituted by such an act must be described by the statement: The one individual wills that the other individual ought to behave in a certain way.'[3]

The 'act' here is, typically, that of legislation, and the distinction Kelsen draws, whether or not acceptable, is clear; it does not essentially have need of what he says later about the 'existence' of the norm after the 'act of will' has taken place. He has thus drastically revised, by reformulation, the imperative or command theory of the norm. The elements which went, under that theory, to the making of a command still go to the making of the norm. But Kelsen rescues the norm from the level of command pure and simple by elevating it in itself to the realm of the 'ought' whilst leaving the act of will in the realm of 'is.'

II

In the 1960 edition of *The Pure Theory* Kelsen draws a strong and clear distinction between the 'legal norm' (Rechtsnorm) and its juristic description, ie the 'rule of law' (Rechtssatz). Whilst the legal norm is now seen as 'a qualified imperative' the rule of law retains the formal character of 'a hypothetical judgment.' This is a fact to which I recur in noting the different senses of the word 'ought' as used by Kelsen.

In his early work (1911 to 1934) Kelsen used the term 'rule of law' and the term 'legal norm' in such a way that they seemed synonymous. Yet he claims to have

---

[3] *The Pure Theory of Law* (translated by Max Knight in 1967 from the 1960 edition), p5, hereinafter referred to as *The Pure Theory*.

reached the notion of 'rule of law' from the beginning.[4] His theory indeed needs that notion, since the Kelsenian idea of legal science, as distinct from law itself, and with it the idea of the 'ought' within legal science, as correspondingly distinct from the 'ought' of the legal norm, make sense only in terms of the Rechtssatz concept. When we speak of the idea of the 'ought' within legal science making sense in such terms, we may note the way in which Kelsen draws his distinction when writing of the legal norm and the rule of law. He says that rules of law are hypothetical judgments stating that according to a national or international legal order, under the conditions determined by this order, certain consequences ought to take place; here the Rechtssatz merely reports that in a given valid legal order a particular norm prescribes a certain conduct. The norm uses 'ought' prescriptively to do so, and Kelsen explicitly acknowledges it. In the rule of law, on the contrary, the 'ought' has a special sense: it conveys, with a purely cognitive signification necessary to scientific inquiry, a principle of association between facts or events, the principle found in the legal norm but with the prescriptive element, so to speak, drained off.

Kelsen's ethical subjectivism had led him in 1923 so far as to assert: 'a moral norm is valid – ie it exists – only in so far as the individual sets it up and 'wills' its content.'[5] No further obligations, that is, exist for an individual than those he himself ultimately wills. In this formulation the will not only determines the content but provides the validity of the moral norm, and it was here that the fallacy should have been spotted.

In 1965 he continues to say 'there are no norms but those which stem from arbitrary choice,' meaning both moral and legal norms.[6] He is now only reminding us that every time a prescription is issued, there has been a choice, an arbitrary choice, since it stems directly or indirectly from the will and not from reason. Human reason, he says, does not choose. Even if thought precedes the willing and choosing of a norm this thought is not immanent in the willing and choosing when these take place.[7] But he goes on to add something quite new. He takes from the individual the possibility of validating a normative system, and lodges this with the not fully clarified moral or legal Grundnorm. Norms are now valid if they stand in

[4] It is worth noticing here that many a commentator on Kelsen has asserted that such a distinction did not exist in the earlier stages of Kelsen's career. Thus, for instance, Julius Stone argues in his *Legal System and Lawyers' Reasonings* (1964), p102, that Kelsen has 'acknowledged his previous confusion'. Kelsen himself has answered categorically to that charge, making it clear that the distinction between law, ie norms, whose essence is to stipulate that something ought to be done, and the science of law, whose object is norms, has always been present in his work. (Cf 'Reply to Professor Stone' in 17 *Stanford Law Review* pp1128 et seq.)
[5] *Hauptprobleme*, p35.
[6] 'Norms posited by human acts of will possess - in the true meaning of the word - an arbitrary character. ... The assumption that there must be norms which do not spring from "arbitrary choice" leads to the concept of norms which are not the meaning of human acts of will.' (On the Concept of Norm in *Essays in Legal and Moral Philosophy* (Ota Weinberger, ed 1973), p218.)
[7] In this, Kelsen explicitly and directly fights the Kantian notion of practical reason; for whilst Kant posited the existence of a 'practical reason' capable of willing, Kelsen adhered adamantly to a narrower definition of reason as a mere capacity for attaining knowledge. It is relevant to notice this diversion from the Kantian-cu-neo-Kantian premises upon which Kelsen avowedly worked.

proper relation to an accepted Grundnorm: thus a particular norm can be valid for me, even if I do not will it:

> 'The theory of recognition ... presupposes the ideal of individual liberty as self-determination, that is, the norm that the individual ought to do only what he wants to do. This is the basic norm of this theory. The difference between it and the theory of the basic norm of a positive legal order, as taught by the *The Pure Theory of Law*, is evident: ... the doctrine of the basic norm (in the Pure Theory) is not a doctrine of recognition as is sometimes erroneously understood. ...'[8]

In so arguing Kelsen has steered wholly clear of the 'imperative fallacy' in the crude form under which any 'thou shall' is taken to imply 'thou ought.' This is my main contention. It is in his final conception of the Basic Norm and its function as source of validity of the normative system whose foundation it is, that the imperative fallacy, in a sophisticated and disguised form, does appear in Kelsen's theory; this, however, presents matter for separate discussion elsewhere.

[8] *The Pure Theory*, p218, note 83.

9. MODERN POSITIVISM

H L A HART
The Concept of Law [1]
(1961)

A FRESH START

At various crucial points, the simple model of law as the sovereign's coercive orders failed to reproduce some of the salient features of a legal system. ...

The main ways in which the theory failed are instructive enough to merit a second summary. First, it became clear that though of all the varieties of law, a criminal statute, forbidding or enjoining certain actions under penalty, most resembles orders backed by threats given by one person to others, such as statute nonetheless differs from such orders in the important respect that it commonly applies to those who enact it and not merely to others. Secondly, there are other varieties of law, notably those conferring legal powers to adjudicate or legislate (public powers) or to create or vary legal relations (private powers) which cannot, without absurdity, be construed as orders backed by threats. Thirdly, there are legal rules which differ from orders in their mode of origin, because they are not brought into being by anything analogous to explicit prescription. Finally, the analysis of law in terms of the sovereign, habitually obeyed and necessarily exempt from all legal limitation, failed to account for the continuity of legislative authority characteristic of a modern legal system, and the sovereign person or persons could not be identified with either the electorate or the legislature of a modern state.

It will be recalled that in thus criticizing the conception of law as the sovereign's coercive orders we considered also a number of ancillary devices which were brought in at the cost of corrupting the primitive simplicity of the theory to rescue it from its difficulties. But these too failed. One device, the notion of a *tacit* order, seemed to have no application to the complex actualities of a modern legal system, but only to very much simpler situations like that of a general who deliberately refrains from interferring with orders given by his subordinates. Other devices, such as that of treating power-conferring rules as mere fragments of rules imposing duties, or treating all rules as directed only to officials, distort the ways in which these are spoken of, thought of, and actually used in social life. This had no better claim to our assent than the theory that all the rules of a game are 'really' directions to the umpire and the scorer. The device, designed to reconcile the self-binding character

[1] Hart, H L A (1961) *The Concept of Law*. Oxford University Press, Oxford, pp77-81, 102-107, 112-113.

of legislation with the theory that a statute is an order given to *others*, was to distinguish the legislators acting in their official capacity, as *one* person ordering *others* who include themselves in their private capacities. This device, impeccable in itself, involved supplementing the theory with something it does not contain: this is the notion of a rule defining what must be done to legislate; for it is only in conforming with such a rule that legislators have an official capacity and a separate personality to be contrasted with themselves as private individuals.

... The root cause of failure is that the elements out of which the theory was constructed, viz the ideas of orders, obedience, habits and threats, do not include, and cannot by their combination yield, the idea of a rule, without which we cannot hope to elucidate even the most elementary forms of law. It is true that the idea of a rule is by no means a simple one: we have already seen the need, if we are to do justice to the complexity of a legal system, to discriminate between two different though related types. Under rules of the one type, which may well be considered the basic or primary type, human beings are required to do or abstain from certain actions, whether they wish to or not. Rules of the other type are in a sense parasitic upon or secondary to the first; for they provide that human beings may by doing or saying certain things introduce new rules of the primary type, extinguish or modify old ones, or in various ways determine their incidence or control their operations. Rules of the first type impose duties; rules of the second type confer powers, public or private. Rules of the first type concern actions involving physical movement or changes; rules of the second type provide for operations which lead not merely to physical movement or change, but to the creation or variation of duties or obligations.

We have already given some preliminary analysis of what is involved in the assertion that rules of these two types exist among a given social group, and in this chapter we shall not only carry this analysis a little farther but we shall make the general claim that in the combination of these two types of rule there lies what Austin wrongly claimed to have found in the notion of coercive orders, namely, 'the key to the science of jurisprudence'. We shall not indeed claim that wherever the word 'law' is 'properly' used this combination of primary and secondary rules is to be found; for it is clear that the diverse range of cases of which the word 'law' is used are not linked by any such simple uniformity, but by less direct relations – often of analogy of either form or content – to a central case. What we shall attempt to show, in this and the succeeding chapters, is that most of the features of law which have proved most perplexing and have both provoked and eluded the search for definition can best be rendered clear, if these two types of rule and the interplay between them are understood. We accord this union of elements a central place because of their explanatory power in elucidating the concepts that constitute the framework of legal thought. The justification for the use of the word 'law' for a range of apparently heterogeneous cases is a secondary matter which can be undertaken when the central elements have been grasped.

THE IDEA OF OBLIGATION

It will be recalled that the theory of law as coercive orders, notwithstanding its errors, started from the perfectly correct appreciation of the fact that where there is law, there human conduct is made in some sense non-optional or obligatory. In choosing this starting-point the theory was well inspired, and in building up a new account of law in terms of the interplay of primary and secondary rules we too shall start from the same idea. It is, however, here, at this crucial first step, that we have perhaps most to learn from the theory's errors.

Let us recall the gunman situation. A orders B to hand over his money and threatens to shoot him if he does not comply. According to the theory of coercive orders this situation illustrates the notion of obligation or duty in general. Legal obligation is to be found in this situation writ large; A must be the sovereign habitually obeyed and the orders must be general, prescribing courses of conduct not single actions. The plausibility of the claim that the gunman situation displays the meaning of obligation lies in the fact that it is certainly one in which we would say that B, if he obeyed, was 'obliged' to hand over his money. It is, however, equally certain that we should misdescribe the situation if we said, on these facts, that B 'had an obligation' or a 'duty' to hand over the money. So from the start it is clear that we need something else from an understanding of the idea of obligation. There is a difference, yet to be explained, between the assertion that someone *was obliged* to do something and the assertion that he *had an obligation* to do it. The first is often a statement about the beliefs and motives with which an action is done; B was obliged to hand over his money may simply mean, as it does in the gunman case, that he believed that some harm or other unpleasant consequences would befall him if he did not hand it over and he handed it over to avoid those consequences. In such cases the prospects of what would happen to the agent if he disobeyed has rendered something he would otherwise have preferred to have done (keep the money) less eligible.

Two further elements slightly complicate the elucidation of the notion of being obliged to do something. It seems clear that we should not think of B as obliged to hand over the money if the threatened harm was, according to common judgments, trivial in comparison with the disadvantage or serious consequences, either for B or for others, of complying with the orders, as it would be, for example, if A merely threatened to pinch B. Nor perhaps should we say that B was obliged, if there were no reasonable grounds for thinking that A could or would probably implement his threat of relatively serious harm. Yet, though such references to common judgments of comparative harm and reasonable estimates of likelihood, are implicit in this notion, the statement that a person was obliged to obey someone is, in the main, a psychological one referring to the beliefs and motives with which an action was done. But the statements that someone *had an obligation* to do something is of a very different type and there are many signs of this difference. Thus not only is it the case that the facts about B's action and his beliefs and motives in the gunman case, though sufficient to warrant the statement that B was obliged to hand over his purse, are *not sufficient* to warrant the statement that he had an obligation to do this; it is also the case that facts of this sort, ie facts about beliefs and motives, are *not necessary* for the truth of a statement that a person had an obligation to do something. Thus the statement that a person had an obligation, eg to tell the truth or report for military service, remains true even if he believed (reasonably or unreasonably) that he would never be found out and had nothing to fear from disobedience. Moreover, whereas the statement that he had this obligation is quite independent of the question whether or not he in fact reported for service, the statement that someone was obliged to do something, normally carries the implication that he actually did it.

Some theorists, Austin among them, seeing perhaps the general irrelevance of the person's beliefs, fears, and motives to the question whether he had an obligation to do something, have defined this notion not in terms of these subjective facts, but in terms of the *chance* or *likelihood* that the person having the obligation will suffer a punishment or 'evil' at the hands of others in the event of disobedience. This, in effect, treats statements of obligation not as psychological statements but as predictions or assessments of chances of incurring punishment or 'evil'. To many later theorists this has appeared as a revelation, bring down to earth an elusive notion and restating it in the same clear, hard, empirical terms as are used in science. It has, indeed, been accepted sometimes as the only alternative to metaphysical conceptions of obligation or duty. ...

THE FOUNDATIONS OF A LEGAL SYSTEM

The rule of recognition providing the criteria by which the validity of other rules of the system is assessed is in an important sense, which we shall try to clarify, an *ultimate* rule: and where, as is usual, there are several criteria ranked in order of relative subordination and primacy one of them is *supreme*. These ideas of the ultimacy of the rule of recognition and the supremacy of one of its criteria merit some attention. It is important to disentangle them from the theory, which we have rejected, that somewhere in every legal system, even though it lurks behind legal forms, there must be a sovereign legislative power which is legally unlimited.

Of these two ideas, supreme criterion and ultimate rule, the first is the easiest to define. We may say that a criterion of legal validity or source of law is supreme if rules identified by reference to it are still recognised as rules of the system, even if they conflict with rules identified by reference to the other criteria, whereas rules identified by reference to the latter are not so recognised if they conflict with the rules identified by reference to the supreme criterion. A similar explanation in comparative terms can be given of the notions of 'superior' and 'subordinate' criteria which we have already used. It is plain that the notions of a superior and a supreme criterion merely refer to a *relative* place on a scale and do not import any notion of legally *unlimited* legislative power. Yet 'supreme' and 'unlimited' are easy to confuse – at least in legal theory. One reason for this is that in the simpler forms of legal system the ideas of ultimate rule of recognition, supreme criterion, and legally unlimited legislature seem to converge. For where there is a legislature subject to no constitutional limitations and competent by its enactment to deprive all other rules of law emanating from other sources of their status as law, it is part of the rule of recognition in such a system that enactment by that legislature is the supreme criterion of validity. This is, according to constitutional theory, the position in the United Kingdom. But even systems like that of the United States in which there is no such legally unlimited legislature may perfectly well contain an ultimate rule of recognition which provides a set of criteria of validity, one of which is supreme. This will be so, where the legislative competence of the ordinary legislature is limited by a constitution which contains no amending power, or places some clauses outside the scope of that power. Here there is no legally unlimited legislature, even in the widest interpretation of 'legislature'; but the system of course contains an ultimate rule of recognition and, in the clauses of its constitution, a supreme criterion of validity.

The sense in which the rule of recognition is the *ultimate* rule of a system is best understood if we pursue a very familiar chain of legal reasoning. If the question is raised whether some suggested rule is legally valid, we must, in order to answer the question, use a criterion of validity provided by some other rule. Is this purported by-law of the Oxfordshire County Council valid? Yes: because it was made in exercise of the powers conferred, and in accordance with the procedure specified, by a statutory order made by the Minister of Health. At this first stage the statutory order provides the criteria in terms of which the validity of the by-law is assessed. There may be no practical need to go farther; but there is a standing possibility of doing so. We may query the validity of the statutory order and assess its validity in terms of the statute empowering the minister to make such orders. Finally when the validity of the statute has been queried and assessed by reference to the rule that what the Queen in Parliament enacts is law, we are brought to a stop in inquiries concerning validity: for we have reached a rule which, like the intermediate statutory order and statute, provides criteria for the assessment of the validity of other rules; but it is also unlike them in that there is no rule providing criteria for the assessment of its own legal validity.

There are, indeed, many questions which we can raise about this ultimate rule. We can ask whether it is the practice of courts, legislatures, officials, or private citizens in England actually to use this rule as an ultimate rule of recognition. Or has our process of legal reasoning been an idle game with the criteria of validity of a system now discarded? We can ask whether it is a satisfactory form of legal system which has such a rule at its root. Does it produce more good than evil? Are there prudential reasons for supporting it? If there a moral obligation to do so? These are plainly very important questions' but, equally plainly, when we ask them about the rule of recognition, we are no longer attempting to answer the same kind of question about it as those which we answered about other rules with its aid. When we move from saying that a particular enactment is valid, because it satisfies the rule that what the Queen in Parliament enacts is law, to saying that in England this last rule is used by courts, officials and private persons as the ultimate rule of recognition, we have moved from an internal statement of law asserting the validity of a rule of the system to an external statement of fact which an observer of the system might make even if he did not accept it. So too when we move from the statement that a particular enactment is valid, to the statement that the rule of recognition of the system is an excellent one and the system based on it is one worthy of support, we have moved from a statement of legal validity to a statement of value.

Some writers, who have emphasised the legal ultimacy of the rule of recognition, have expressed this by saying that, whereas the legal validity of other rules of the system can be demonstrated by reference to it, its own validity cannot be demonstrated but is 'assumed' or 'postulated' or is a 'hypothesis'. This may, however, be seriously misleading. Statements of legal validity made about particular rules in the day-to-day life of a legal system whether by judges, lawyers, or ordinary citizens do indeed carry with them certain presuppositions. They are internal statements of law expressing the point of view of those who accept the rule of recognition of the system and, as such, leave unstated much that could be stated in external statements of fact about the system. What is thus left unstated forms the normal background or context of statements of legal validity and is thus said to be 'presupposed' by them. But it is important to see precisely what these presupposed matters are, and not to obscure their character. They consist of two things. First, a person who seriously asserts the validity of some given rule of law, say a particular statute, himself makes use of a rule of recognition which he accepts as appropriate for identifying the law. Secondly, it is the case that this rule of recognition, in terms of which he assesses the validity of a particular statute, is not only accepted by him but is the rule of recognition actually accepted and employed in the general operation of the system. If the truth of this presupposition were doubted, it could be established by reference to actual practice: to the way in which courts identify what is to count as law, and to the general acceptance of or acquiescence in these identifications.

Neither of these two presuppositions are well described as 'assumptions' of a 'validity' which cannot be demonstrated. We only need the word 'validity', and commonly only use it, to answer questions which arise *within* a system of rules where the status of a rule as a member of the system depends on its satisfying certain criteria provided by the rule of recognition. No such question can arise as to the validity of the very rule of recognition which provides the criteria; it can neither be valid nor invalid but is simply accepted as appropriate for use in this way. To express this simple fact by saying darkly that its validity is 'assumed but cannot be demonstrated', is like saying that we assume, but can never demonstrate, that the standard metre bar in Paris which is the ultimate test of the correctness of all measurement in metres, is itself correct.

A more serious objection is that talk of the 'assumption' that the ultimate rule of recognition is valid conceals the essentially factual character of the second presupposition which lies behind the lawyers' statements of validity. No doubt the practice of judges, officials and others, in which the actual existence of a rule of recognition consists, is a complex matter. As we shall see later, there are certainly situations in which questions as to the precise content and scope of this kind of rule, and even as to its existence, may not admit of a clear or determinate answer. Nonetheless it is important to distinguish 'assuming the validity' from 'presupposing the existence' of such a rule; if only because failure to do this obscures what is meant by the assertion that such a rule *exists*.

In the simple system of primary rules of obligation sketched in the last chapter, the assertion that a given rule existed could only be an external statement of fact such as an observer who did not accept the rules might make and verify by ascertaining whether or not, as a matter of fact, a given mode of behaviour was generally accepted as a standard and was accompanied by those features which, as we have seen, distinguish a social rule from mere convergent habits. It is in this way also that we should now interpret and verify the assertion that in England a rule – though not a legal one – exists that we must bare the head on entering a church. If such rules as these are found to exist in the actual practice of a social group, there is no separate question of their validity to be discussed, though of course their value or desirability is open to question. Once their existence has been established as a fact we should only confuse matters by affirming or denying that they were valid or by saying that 'we assumed' but could not show their validity. Where, on the other hand, as in a mature legal system, we have a system of rules which includes a rule of recognition so that the status of a rule as a member of the system now depends on whether it satisfies certain criteria provided by the rule of recognition, this brings with it a new application of the word 'exist'. The statement that a rule exists may now no longer be what it was in the simple case of customary rules – an external statement of the *fact* that a certain mode of behaviour was generally accepted as a standard in practice. It may now be an internal statement applying an accepted but unstated rule of recognition and meaning (roughly) no more than 'valid given the system's criteria of validity'. In this respect, however, as in others a rule of recognition is unlike other rules of the system. The assertion that it exists can only be an external statement of fact. For whereas a subordinate rule of a system may be valid and in that sense 'exist' even if it is generally disregarded, the rule of recognition exists only as a complex, but normally concordant, practice of the courts, officials, and private persons in identifying the law by reference to certain criteria. Its existence is a matter of fact.

NEW QUESTIONS

Once we abandon the view that the foundations of a legal system consist in a habit of obedience to a legally unlimited sovereign and substitute for this the conception of an ultimate rule of recognition which provides a system of rules with its criteria of validity, a range of fascinating and important questions confronts us. They are relatively new questions; for they were veiled so long as jurisprudence and political theory were committed to the older ways of thought. They are also difficult questions, requiring for a full answer, on the one hand a grasp of some fundamental issues of constitutional law and on the other an appreciation of the characteristic manner in which legal forms may silently shift and change. We shall therefore investigate these questions only so far as they bear upon the wisdom or unwisdom of insisting, as we have done, that a central place should be assigned to the union of primary and secondary rules in the elucidation of the concept of law.

. . .

What makes 'obedience' misleading as a description of what legislators do in conforming to the rules conferring their powers, and of what courts do in applying an accepted ultimate rule of recognition, is that obeying a rule (or an order) *need* involve no thought on the part of the person obeying that what he does is the right thing both for himself and for others to do: he need have no view of what he does as a fulfilment of a standard of behaviour for others of the social group. He need not think of his confirming behaviour as 'right', 'correct', or 'obligatory'. His attitude, in other words, need not have any of that critical character which is involved whenever social rules are accepted and types of conduct are treated as general standards. He need not, though he may, share the internal point of view accepting the rules as standards for all to whom they apply. Instead, he may think of the rule only as something demanding action from *him* under threat of penalty; he may obey it out of fear of the consequences, or from inertia, without thinking of himself or others as having an obligation to do so and without being disposed to criticise either himself or others for deviations. But this merely personal concern with the rules, which is all the ordinary citizen *may* have in obeying them, cannot characterise the attitude of the courts to the rules with which they operate as courts. This is most patently the case with the ultimate rule of recognition in terms of which the validity of other rules is assessed. This, if it is to exist at all, must be regarded from the internal point of view as a public, common standard of correct judicial decision, and not as something which each judge merely obeys for his part only. Individual courts of the system though they may, on occasion, deviate from these rules must, in general, be critically concerned with such deviations as lapses from standards, which are essentially common or public. This is not merely a matter of the efficiency or health of the legal system, but is logically a necessary condition of our ability to speak of the existence of a single legal system. If only some judges acted 'for their part only' on the footing that what the Queen in Parliament enacts is law, and made no criticisms of those who did not respect this rule of recognition, the characteristic unit and continuity of a legal system would have disappeared. For this depends on the acceptance, at this crucial point, of common standards of legal validity. In the interval between these vagaries of judicial behaviour and the chaos which would ultimately ensue when the ordinary man was faced with contrary judicial orders, we would be at a loss to describe the situation. We would be in the presence of a lusus naturae worth thinking about only because it sharpens our awareness of what is often too obvious to be noticed.

There are therefore two minimum conditions necessary and sufficient for the existence of a legal system. On the one hand those rules of behaviour which are valid according to the system's ultimate criteria of validity must be generally obeyed, and, on the other hand, its rules of recognition specifying the criteria of legal validity and its rules of change and adjudication must be effectively accepted as common public standards of official behaviour by its officials. The first condition is the only one which private citizens *need* satisfy: they may obey each 'for his part only' and from any motive whatever; though in a healthy society they will in fact often accept these rules as common standards of behaviour and acknowledge an obligation to obey them, or even trace this obligation to a more general obligation to respect the constitution. The second condition must also be satisfied by the officials of the system. They must regard these as common standards of official behaviour and appraise critically their own and each other's deviations as lapses. Of course it is also true that besides these there will be many primary rules which apply to officials in their merely personal capacity which they need only obey.

The assertion that a legal system exists is therefore a Janus-faced statement looking both towards obedience by ordinary citizens and to the acceptance by officials of secondary rules as critical common standards of official behaviour. We need not be surprised at this duality. It is merely the reflection of the composite character of a legal system as compared with a simpler decentralised pre-legal form of social structure.

P MILTON
Review of H L A Hart 'Essays in Jurisprudence and Philosophy' and of Neil MacCormick 'H L A Hart' [2]
(1984)

Hart's particular contribution to the history of jurisprudence was to bring together two quite different intellectual traditions which had hitherto remained apart and might have continued their separate ways but for his appointment to the Oxford chair. The first of these was the native analytical–utilitarian–positivist tradition of Bentham and Austin which, though somewhat moribund by the nineteen fifties, remained, in the absence of any real competition, the mainstream of English jurisprudence. Hart's response to this tradition can best be seen in his Holmes Lecture 'Positivism and Separation of Law and Morals', reprinted here. For Hart the central issue is the conceptual separation of law and morals – the existence of a law is one thing, its merit another – and on this the positivists were quite right. But

[2] Milton, P, Review of H L A Hart 'Essays in Jurisprudence and Philosophy', and of Neil MacCormick 'H L A Hart' (1984) 44 *Modern Law Review*, 751.

if the foundations were sound the theories erected upon them were not: in particular there was an over simple picture of law as command, a radically defective analysis of obligation, and a misplaced emphasis on sovereignty. In short, the Austinian theory was much too crude. What was needed was to dismantle it carefully noting both merits and defects, and to replace it by something much more sound. This was the programme of *The Concept of Law*.

How was this to be done? Here we have to introduce the other tradition, one that is frequently called linguistic philosophy. This influence is discussed by MacCormick in his opening chapter, and is more briefly mentioned by Hart in his introductory essay and in the essay on Jhering. Both use the term *linguistic philosophy* to denote not just the movement which flourished at Oxford in the two decades after the last war but also the conception of philosophy to be found in Wittgenstein's later writings. Here one has to be careful.

Throughout his life Wittgenstein rejected the view that philosophy was, or ought to aim to be, a science – that is, a body of doctrine supported by evidence, proofs or arguments and involving such things as theories, explanations or hypotheses. This is what lies behind the famous remark that philosophy leaves everything as it is: it is purely descriptive. There are no genuine philosophical problems, if by that one means real problems with real answers, but just an intricate mass of conceptual muddle that needs to be disentangled. As somebody else's slogan had it, philosophical problems were to be dissolved not solved. (Of course this is itself a philosophical thesis of some kind and therefore falls under its own ban. Thus the reader of the *Tractatus* who has struggled through to the end is told there that the propositions that he has read are in fact nonsensical, as one who understands them will realise. In his later writings we find Wittgenstein covertly putting forward philosophical theses: there is a deeply obscure and contentious one that all languages are intrinsically social so that a logically private language is impossible.)

Wittgenstein's conception of philosophy, which lies right at the heart of his thought and is responsible for most of its peculiarities, including the way it is written, has had no influence on Hart that I can discern. Hart believes that legal philosophy contains many genuine and important problems, and he discusses what they are in the *Encyclopaedia of Philosophy* article 'Problems of the Philosophy of Law', reprinted here. Furthermore he believes, quite reasonably, that he has himself solved, or at least contributed to the solution of, some of them.

A second and much more real influence was J L Austin. Unlike Wittgenstein, who seems to have had no influence on him, Austin was a classicist who was fascinated by the minutiae of ordinary linguistic usage, something which, despite his occasional panegyrics on ordinary language, interested Wittgenstein hardly at all. For Austin the reason why philosophers so often failed to make any real progress was not that all their problems were spurious, though some were, but that they were usually badly formulated and, above all, *complex*. The occupational disease of philosophers was giving simple answers to complicated problems on the basis of a small number of examples, all too often the same old ones. Part of the cure for this was a detailed and painstaking examination of ordinary language and the immense number of subtle distinctions it contains.

In addition Austin was deeply interested in what he called performatives – speech acts in which something is *done* rather than merely described or reported. Whether performatives are of general philosophical importance is, I think, doubtful, but there is one area of discourse where they appear with especial frequency, and that is the law. Performatives can be spotted by the express or implied use of the word *hereby*: 'I John Doe hereby revoke all wills and testamentary dispositions ...' Of course, as Austin found in his later investigations, the notion of performatives is not free from problems of its own; nevertheless there is something there which, for the lawyer at least, is important and illuminating.

. . .

What we observe, therefore, is a subtle tension between Hart the linguistic philosopher and Hart the legal positivist. Legal positivism is more than the mere application of conceptual analysis to legal problems; it is a theory, or to be more accurate a group of theories, about the nature of law and the structure of legal systems. And as there is more than one positivist theory on the market – Kelsen's is the leading competitor – we are faced with problems if we are to choose between them. Is it merely a matter of personal whim, as one might choose rival football clubs, or are there, as one would hope, more rational criteria? On questions of this kind neither Hart nor MacCormick provide much guidance.

Consider the case of someone starting from scratch to construct a general theory of law. Should he start with an empirical investigation of actual legal systems, or should he try and work out a priori the structure that any legal system must necessarily have? The latter has an obvious appeal to the philosophically trained and greatly cuts down on the footwork. The most extreme version of this approach is, of course, Kelsen's Pure Theory which indeed has no discernible empirical content. And one can find more modest versions of the same thing in England. Austin's argument that every legal system must contain an unlimited sovereign is based not primarily on experience – though it fitted the British constitution quite well – but on the a priori argument that to do otherwise would generate an infinite regress. There is a curious parallel here with the Aristotelian argument for the Unmoved Mover. Hart's method is more cautious and more empirical, but the argument that the transition from the pre-legal to the legal state must involve the creation of rules of recognition, adjudication and change is itself a priori. It is that an effective system of decision making and social control in a complex society must have these characteristics. A related argument produces what he calls the maximum content of natural law: if human society is to persist then certain rules are necessary.

It is illuminating to range legal theories along a continuum with monistic a priori theories at one end and more pluralist empirical theories at the other. Kelsen is an example of the former and the American realists the latter, with Hart somewhere in the middle. Most of the argument in *The Concept of Law* is against the monistic theories of Austin and (to a lesser extent) Kelsen, whereas most of the criticism subsequently aimed at it has come from the opposite direction. The argument is that Hart has not gone far enough, that he has remained too committed to legal positivism.

The most notable exponent of this has been Ronald Dworkin. He started in his 1967 article 'Is Law a System of Rules?' with an attack from the pluralist side: Hart had failed to distinguish rules from principles, policies and other standards. This was followed by a series of articles developing a novel and unusual theory of judicial decision according to which there is, or may be, a right answer in hard cases, even though no-one, not even the superhuman Hercules J, can demonstrate what this right answer is. *This* theory is radically monistic and is, and is intended to be, in complete contrast to Hart's theory of judicial discretion. Hart's response is scrupulously polite, even complimentary, but on the crucial points he has not budged an inch.

M ZANDER
A Matter of Justice [3]
(1989)

QUASI LAW-MAKING

Even more striking as examples of law-making by Whitehall are the techniques of governing a code of practice, guidance note, circular, approved code, outline scheme, statement of advice or departmental circular – the list is long and seems constantly to be growing. A recent valuable comment on this trend by two academic writers, Dr Robert Baldwin and Mr John Houghton, suggested that it represents 'a discernible retreat from primary legislation in favour of government by informal rules'. Each time government confronts a difficult regulatory task, 'it seems to come up with a new device'. One view of such rules was that they offered a useful structuring of discretion; another was that they were often used cynically so as to make law without resort to Parliament, to instruct judges on the meaning of statutes, and to insulate bureaucracies from review. Thus, for instance, the rules on picketing were contained in a code not an Act; the rules on police stop and search, detention and questioning were set out in lengthy codes of practice, parole policy had been drastically altered by ministerial pronouncement; and in fields such as planning, housing, matrimonial proceedings and health and safety at work there had been a distinct movement towards regulation by informal rules. In other areas such as prisons, immigration and criminal injuries compensation, the status and force of important rules was unclear. The authors argued:

[3] Zander, M (1989) *A Matter of Justice*. Oxford University Press, Oxford, pp264–266.

For bureaucrats, the attractions of informality are plain. Such rules inexpensively and swiftly routinise the exercise of discretion; they provide easy justifications for statutory powers; they 'get the job done' whilst offering something to critics (irregular police questioning leads to disciplinary action, not exclusion of evidence); they give a flexibility that primary legislation does not offer; and they are largely immune from judicial review.

Their concern was that informed rules were 'too free from control by Parliament, executive, judiciary or any other source and that this freedom is increasingly open to exploitation'. Often there was little indication from any statute as to whether the rule was authorised and, if so, what was its effect or scope. Judges therefore had considerable latitude in deciding whether to give the rules legal effect. Often they are published hapharzardly or not at all. There was little opportunity for consultation or public input in such rule-making, and lobbying might be limited to certain favoured interest groups.

It was true, of course, that informal rules had some virtues. They encouraged consistency in bureaucratic decision-making; they simplified complex issues and notified the public as to how it was being treated; they were flexible and could be issued quickly; they were less liable than formal rules to get snared in litigation; they allowed control of official action where legislation was inappropriate or politically undesirable.

The point made by the two authors, therefore, is not that informal rule-making is necessarily wrong, but that more should be done by legislators to clarify the status of rules and that the judiciary should be more prepared than it is to hold the makers of such rules to account. Thus there should be a duty normally to publish the rules so as to make them available to the persons affected. In some instances the courts might be able to construe a duty to consult with interested parties at the rule-making stages and to apply the tests of fairness and reasonableness to the rules created. The science of informal rule-making is still in its infancy. The first stage is a recognition of a problem and the mapping of its contours. The next stage, of developing a coherent approach to its solutions, is for the future. In the meanwhile, government by Whitehall continues and grows apace.

10. NATURAL LAW

PLATO
Republic [1]
(c.380BC)

A State, I said, arises, out of the needs of mankind; no one is self-sufficing, but all of us have many wants. Can any other origin of a State be imagined? There can be no other.

Then, as we have many wants, and many persons are needed to supply them, one takes a helper for one purpose and another for another; and when these partners and helpers are gathered together in one habitation the body of inhabitants is termed a State.

True, he said.

And they exchanged with one another, and one gives, and another receives, under the idea that the exchange will be for their good.

Very true.

Then, I said, let us begin and create in idea a State; and yet the true creator is necessity, which is the mother of our invention.

. . .

... our aim in founding the State was not the disproportionate happiness of any one class, but the greatest happiness of the whole; we thought that in a State which is ordered with a view to the good of the whole we should be most likely to find justice, and in the ill-ordered State injustice: and, having found them, we might then decide which of the two is the happier. At present, I take it, we are fashioning the happy State, not piecemeal, or with a view of making a few happy citizens, but as a whole; and by-and-by we will proceed to view the opposite kind of State.

. . .

How then may we devise one of those needful falsehoods of which we lately spoke — just one royal lie which may deceive the rulers, if that be possible, and at any rate the rest of the city?

What sort of lie? he asked.

Nothing new, I replied; only an old Phoenician tale of what has often occurred before now in other places, (as the poets say, and have made the world believe though not in our time, and I do not know whether such an event could ever

[1] Plato, *Republic, Book II*, ed B Jowett (1888) Oxford University Press, Oxford.

happen again, or could now even be made probable, if it did).

How your words seem to hesitate on your lips!

. . .

True, I replied, but there is more coming: I have only told you half. Citizens, we shall say to them in our tale, you are brothers, yet God has framed you differently. Some of you have the power of command, and in the composition of these he has mingled gold, wherefore also they have the greatest honour; others he has made of silver, to be auxiliaries; others again who are to be husbandmen and craftsmen.

. . .

THOMAS JEFFERSON
American Declaration of Independence
(1776)

We hold these truths to be self-evident; that all men are created equal; that they are endowed by their creator with certain inalienable rights; that among these are life, liberty, and the pursuit of happiness; that to secure these rights, governments are instituted among men, deriving their just powers from the consent of the governed; that whenever any form of government becomes destructive of these ends, it is the right of the people to alter or to abolish it, and to institute new government, laying its foundation on such principles and organizing its powers in such form, as to them shall seem most likely to effect their safety and happiness.

CONSTITUTION OF THE UNITED STATES
(1791)

AMENDMENT I (1791)
Freedom of Religion, of Speech, and the Press

Congress shall make no law respecting an establishment of religion or prohibiting the free exercise thereof; or abridging the freedom of speech, or of the press; or the right of the people peaceably to assemble, and to petition the Government for a redress of grievances.

AMENDMENT II (1791)
Right to Keep and Bear Arms

A well regulated Militia being necessary to the security of a free State, the right of the people to bear Arms shall not be infringed.

AMENDMENT III (1791)
Quartering of Soldiers

No soldier shall, in time of peace be quartered in any house, without the consent of the owner, nor in time of war, but in a manner to be prescribed by law.

AMENDMENT IV (1791)
Security from Unwarrantable Search and Seizure

The right of the people to be secure in their persons, houses, papers and effects, against unreasonable searches and seizures, shall not be violated, and no Warrants shall issue, but upon probable cause, supported by Oath or affirmation, and particularly describing the place to be searched, and the persons or things to be seized.

AMENDMENT V (1791)
Rights of Accused in Criminal Proceedings

No person shall be held to answer for a capital, or otherwise, infamous crime, unless on a presentment or indictment of a Grand Jury except in cases arising in the land or naval forces, or in the Militia when in actual service in time of War or public danger; nor shall any person be subject for the same offense to be twice put in jeopardy of life and limb; nor shall be compelled in any criminal case to be a witness against himself, nor be deprived of life, liberty, or property, without due process of law; nor shall private property be taken for public use, without just compensation.

AMENDMENT VI (1791)
Right to Speedy Trial, Witnesses, etc

In all criminal prosecutions, the accused shall enjoy the right to speedy and public trial, by an impartial jury of the State and district wherein the crime shall have been committed, which district shall have been previously ascertained by law, and to be informed of the nature and cause of the accusation; to be confronted with the witnesses against him; to have compulsory process for obtaining witnesses in his favour, and to have the Assistance of Counsel for his defence.

AMENDMENT VII (1791)
Trial by Jury in Civil Cases

In Suits at common law, where the value in controversy shall exceed twenty dollars, the right of trial by jury shall be preserved, and no one tried by a jury, shall be otherwise re-examined in any Court of the United States, than according to the rules of the common law.

AMENDMENT VIII (1791)
Bails, Fines, Punishments

Excessive bail shall not be required, nor excessive fines imposed, nor cruel and unusual punishments inflicted.

AMENDMENT IX (1791)
Reservation of Rights of the People

The enumeration in the Constitution, of certain rights, shall not be construed to deny or disparage others retained by the people.

AMENDMENT X (1791)
Powers Reserved to States or People

The powers not delegated to the United States by the Constitution, nor prohibited by it to the States, are reserved to the States respectively, or to the people.

NEW TESTAMENT
GOSPEL ACCORDING TO ST LUKE CH 10

And behold, a man versed in the law stood up, making trial of him and saying: Master, what shall I do to inherit everlasting life? He said to him: What is written in the law? How do you read it? The man answered and said: You shall love the Lord your God from all your heart and in all your spirit and in all your strength and in all your mind; and you shall love your neighbour as yourself. He said to him: You have answered right. Do this and you will live. But the man, wishing to justify himself, said to Jesus: And who is my neighbour?

Donoghue (or McAlister) v Stevenson [1932] AC 562, 580

LORD ATKIN: 'The rule that you are to love your neighbour becomes in law: You must not injure your neighbour, and the lawyer's question: Who is my neighbour? receives a restricted reply. You must take reasonable care to avoid acts or omissions which you can reasonably foresee would be likely to injure your neighbour. Who then, in law, is my neighbour? The answer seems to be persons who are so closely and directly affected by my act that I ought reasonably to have them in contemplation as being so affected when I am directing my mind to the acts or omissions which are called in question.'

J M FINNIS
Natural Law and Natural Rights [2]
(1980)

What, then, are the basic forms of good for us?

A LIFE

A first basic value, corresponding to the drive for self-preservation, is the value of life. The term 'life' here signifies every aspect of the vitality (*vita*, life) which puts a human being in good shape for self-determination. Hence, life here includes bodily (including cerebral) health, and freedom from the pain that betokens organic malfunctioning or injury. And the recognition, pursuit, and realisation of this basic human purpose (or internally related group of purposes) are as various as the crafty struggle and prayer of a man overboard seeking to stay afloat until his ship turns back for him; the teamwork of surgeons and the whole network of supporting staff, ancillary services, medical schools, etc.; road safety laws and programmes; famine relief expeditions; farming and rearing and fishing; food marketing; the resuscitation of suicides; watching out as one steps off the kerb ...

Perhaps we should include in this category the transmission of life by procreation of children.

B KNOWLEDGE

The second basic value I have already discussed: it is knowledge, considered as desirable for its own sake, not merely instrumentally.

C PLAY

The third basic aspect of human well-being is play. A certain sort of moralist analysing human goods may overlook this basic value, but an anthropologist will not fail to observe this large and irreducible element in human culture. More importantly, each one of us can see the point of engaging in performances which have no point beyond the performance itself, enjoyed for its own sake. The performance may be solitary or social, intellectual or physical, strenuous or relaxed, highly structured or relatively informal, conventional or ad hoc in its pattern ... An element of play can enter into any human activity, even the drafting of enactments, but is always analytically distinguishable from its 'serious' context; and some activities, enterprises, and institutions are entirely or primarily pure play. Play, then, has and is its own value.

[2] Finnis, J M (1980) *Natural Law and Natural Rights*. Oxford University Press, Oxford, pp206–211.

D AESTHETIC EXPERIENCE

The fourth basic component in our flourishing is aesthetic experience. Many forms of play, such as dance or song or football, are the matrix or occasion of aesthetic experience. But beauty is not an indispensable element of play. Moreover, beautiful form can be found and enjoyed in nature. Aesthetic experience, unlike play, need not involve an action of one's own; what is sought after and valued for its own sake may simply be the beautiful form 'outside' one, and the 'inner' experience of appreciation of its beauty. But often enough the valued experience is found in the creation and/or active appreciation of some *work* of significant and satisfying form.

E SOCIABILITY (FRIENDSHIP)

Fifthly, there is the value of that sociability which in its weakest form is realised by a minimum of peace and harmony amongst men, and which ranges through the forms of human community to its strongest form in the flowering of full friendship. Some of the collaboration between one person and another is no more than instrumental to the realisation by each of his own individual purposes. But friendship involves acting for the sake of one's friends' purposes, one's friends' well-being. To be in a relationship of friendship with at least one other person is a fundamental form of good, is it not? ...

F PRACTICAL REASONABLENESS

Sixthly, there is the basic good of being able to bring one's own intelligence to bear effectively (in practical reasoning that issues in action) on the problems of choosing one's actions and lifestyle and shaping one's own character. Negatively, this involves that one has a measure of effective freedom; positively, it involves that one seeks to bring an intelligent and reasonable order into one's own actions and habits and practical attitudes. This order in turn has (i) an internal aspect, as when one strives to bring one's emotions and dispositions into the harmony of an inner peace of mind that is not merely the product of drugs or indoctrination nor merely passive in its orientation; and (ii) an external aspect, as when one strives to make one's actions (which are external in that they change states of affairs in the world and often enough affect the relations between persons) authentic, that is to say, genuine realisations of one's own freely ordered evaluations, preferences, hopes, and self-determination. This value is thus complex, involving freedom and reason, integrity and authenticity. But it has a sufficient unity to be treated as one; and for a label I choose 'practical reasonableness' ...

G 'RELIGION'

Seventhly, and finally in this list, there is the value of what, since Cicero, we summarily and lamely call 'religion'. For, as there is the order of means to ends, and the pursuit of life, truth, play, and aesthetic experience in some individually selected order of priorities and patterns of specialisation, and the order that can be brought into human relations through collaboration, community, and friendship, and the order that is to be brought into one's character and activity through inner integrity and outer authenticity, so, finally there arise such questions as (a) How are all these orders, which have their immediate origin in human initiative and pass away in death, related to the lasting order of the whole cosmos and to the origin, if any, of that order? (b) Is it not perhaps the case that human freedom, in which one rises above the determinism of instinct and impulse to an intelligent grasp of worthwhile forms of good, and through which one shapes and masters one's environment but also one's own character, is itself somehow subordinate to something which makes that human freedom, human intelligence, and human mastery possible (not just 'originally' but from moment to moment) and which is free, intelligent and sovereign in a way (and over a range) no human being can be?

Misgivings may be aroused by the notion that one of the basic human values is the establishment and maintenance of proper relationships between oneself (and the orders one can create and maintain) and the divine. For there are, always, those who doubt or deny that the universal order-of-things has any origin beyond the 'origins' known to the natural sciences, and who answer question (b) negatively. But is it reasonable to deny that it is, at any rate, peculiarly important to have thought reasonably and (where possible) correctly about these questions of the origins of cosmic order and of human freedom and reason – whatever the answer to those questions turns out to be, and even if the answers have to be agnostic or negative? And does not that importance in large part consist in this: that if there is a transcendent origin of the universal order-of-things and of human freedom and reason, then one's life and actions are in fundamental disorder if they are not brought, as best one can, into some sort of harmony with whatever can be known or surmised about that transcendent other and its lasting order? More important for us than the ubiquity of expressions of religious concerns, in all human cultures, is the question: Does not one's own sense of 'responsibility', in choosing what one is to be and do, amount to a concern that is not reducible to the concern to live, play, procreate, relate to others, and be intelligent? Does not even a Sartre, taking as his point de départ that God does not exist (and that therefore 'everything is permitted'), nonetheless appreciate that he is 'responsible' – obliged to act with freedom and authenticity, and to will the liberty of other persons equally with his own – in choosing what he is to be; and all this, because, *prior to* any choice of his, 'man' is and is-to-be free? And is this not a recognition (however residual) of, and concern about, an order of things 'beyond' each and every man? And so, without wishing to beg any question, may we not for convenience call that concern, which is concern for a good consisting in an irreducibly distinct form of order, 'religious'? ...

AN EXHAUSTIVE LIST?

Now besides life, knowledge, play, aesthetic experience, friendship, practical reasonableness and religion, there are countless objectives and forms of good. But I suggest that these other objectives and forms of good will be found, on analysis, to be ways or combinations of ways of pursuing (not always sensibly) and realising (not always successfully) one of the seven basic forms of good, or some combination of them.

Moreover, there are countless aspects of human self-determination and self-realisation besides the seven basic aspects which I have listed. But these other aspects, such as courage, generosity, moderation, gentleness, and so on, are not themselves basic values; rather, they are ways (not means, but modes) of pursuing the basic values, and fit (or are deemed by some individual, or group, or culture, to fit) a man for their pursuit.

. . .

Again, though the pursuit of the basic values is made psychologically possible by the corresponding inclinations and urges of one's nature, still there are many inclinations and urges that do not correspond to or support any basic value: for example, the inclination to take more than one's share, or the urge to gratuitous cruelty. There is no need to consider whether these urges are more, or less, 'natural' (in terms of frequency, universality, intensity, etc) than those urges which correspond to the basic values. For I am not trying to justify our recognition and pursuit of basic values by deducing from, or even by pointing to, any set of inclinations. The point, rather, is that selfishness, cruelty, and the like, simply do not stand to something self-evidently good as the urge to self-preservation stands to the self-evident good of human life. Selfishness, cruelty, etc, stand in need of some explanation, in a way that curiosity, friendliness, etc, do not. ...

But are there just seven basic values, no more and no less? And what is meant by calling them basic? ...

ALL EQUALLY FUNDAMENTAL

... First, each is equally self-evidently a form of good. Secondly, none can be analytically reduced to being merely an aspect of any of the others, or to being merely instrumental in the pursuit of any of the others. Thirdly, each one, when we focus on it, can reasonably be regarded as the most important. Hence there is no objective hierarchy amongst them. Let me amplify this third point, which includes the other two.

If one focuses on the value of speculative truth, it can reasonably be regarded as more important than anything; knowledge can be regarded as the most important thing to acquire; life can be regarded as merely a pre-condition, of lesser or no intrinsic value; play can be regarded as frivolous: one's concern about 'religious' questions can seem just an aspect of the struggle against error, superstition, and ignorance; friendship can seem worth forgoing, or be found exclusively in sharing and enhancing knowledge; and so on. But one can shift one's focus. If one is drowning, or, again, if one is thinking about one's child who died soon after birth, one is inclined to shift one's focus to the value of life simply as such. The life will not be regarded as a mere pre-condition of anything else; rather, play and knowledge and religion will seem secondary, even rather optional extras. But one can shift one's focus, in this way, one-by-one right round the circle of basic values that constitute the horizon of our opportunities. We can focus on play, and reflect that we spend most of our time working simply in order to afford leisure; play is performances enjoyed for their own sake as performances and thus can seem to be the point of everything; knowledge and religion and friendship can seem pointless unless they issue in the playful mastery of wisdom, or participation in the play of the divine puppetmaster (as Plato said), or in the playful intercourse of mind or body that friends can most enjoy ...

Of course, each one of us can reasonably *choose* to treat one or some of the values as of more importance in *his* life. A scholar chooses to dedicate himself to the pursuit of knowledge, and thus gives its demands priority, to a greater or lesser degree (and perhaps for a whole lifetime), over the friendships, the worship, the games, the art and beauty that he might otherwise enjoy. He might have been out saving lives through medicine or famine relief, but he chooses not to. But he may change his priorities; he may risk his life to save a drowning man, or give up his career to nurse a sick wife or to fight for his community. The change is not in the relation between the basic values as that relation might reasonably have seemed to him before he chose his life-plan (and as it should always seem to him when he is considering human opportunity and flourishing in general); rather, the change is in his chosen life-plan. That chosen plan *made* truth more important and fundamental for him. His new choice changes the status of that value *for him*; the change is in him. Each of us has a subjective order of priority amongst the basic values; this ranking is no doubt partly shifting and partly stable, but it is in any case essential if we are to act at all to some purpose. But one's reasons for choosing the particular ranking that one does choose are reasons that properly relate to one's temperament, upbringing, capacities, and opportunities, not to differences of rank of intrinsic value between the basic values.

Thomas Aquinas, in his formal discussion of the basic forms of good and self-evident primary principles of practical reasoning – which he calls the first principles and most general precepts of natural law – sets a questionable example. For he arranges the precepts in a threefold order: (i) human life is a good to be sustained, and what threatens it is to be prevented; (ii) the coupling of man and woman, and the education of their young, etc, is to be favoured, and what opposes it is to be avoided; (iii) knowledge (especially of the truth about God), sociable life, and practical reasonableness are goods, and ignorance, offence to others, and practical unreasonableness are to be avoided. And his rationale for this threefold ordering (which all too easily is interpreted as a ranking) is that the self-preservative inclinations corresponding to the first category are common not just to all men but to all things which have a definite nature; that the sexual-reproductive inclinations corresponding to the second category of goods are shared by human beings with all other animate life; and that the inclinations corresponding to the third category are peculiar to mankind. Now all this is no doubt true, and quite pertinent in a metaphysical meditation on the continuity of human order with the universal order-of-things (of which human nature is a microcosmos, incorporating all levels of being; inorganic, organic. ... mental ...). But is it relevant to a meditation on the *value* of the various basic aspects of human well-being? Are not speculative considerations intruding into a reconstruction of principles that are practical and that, being primary, indemonstrable, and self-evident, are not derivable (nor sought by Aquinas to be derived) from any speculative considerations? ...

A DEFINITION OF LAW

Throughout this chapter, the term 'law' has been used with a focal meaning so as to refer primarily to rules made, in accordance with regulative legal rules, by a determinate and effective authority (itself identified and, standardly, constituted as an institution by legal rules) for a 'complete' community, and buttressed by sanctions in accordance with the rule-guided stipulations of adjudicative institutions, this ensemble of rules and institutions being directed to reasonably resolving any of the community's co-ordination problems (and to ratifying, tolerating, regulating, or overriding co-ordination solutions from any other institutions or sources of norms) for the common good of that community, according to a manner and form itself adapted to that common good by features of specificity, minimisation of arbitrariness and maintenance of a quality of reciprocity between the subjects of the law both amongst themselves and in their relations with the lawful authorities.

This multi-faceted conception of law has been reflectively constructed by tracing the implications of certain requirements of practical reason, given certain basic values and certain empirical features of persons and their communities. The intention has not been lexicographical; but the construction lies well within the boundaries of common use of 'law' and its equivalents in other languages. The intention has not been to describe existing social orders; but the construction corresponds closely to many existing social phenomena that typically are regarded as central cases of law, legal system, Rule of Law, etc. Above all, the meaning has been constructed as a *focal* meaning, not as an appropriation of the term 'law' in a univocal sense that would exclude from the reference of the term anything that failed to have all the characteristics (and to their full extent) of the central case. And, equally important, it has been fully recognised that each of the terms used to express the elements in the conception (eg 'making', 'determinate', 'effective', 'a community', 'sanctioned', 'rule-guided', 'reasonable', 'non-discriminatory', 'reciprocal', etc) has itself a focal meaning and a primary reference, and therefore extends to analogous and secondary instances which lack something of the central instance. ... Law, in the focal sense of the term, is *fully* instantiated only when each of these component terms is fully instantiated.

If one wishes to stress the empirical/historical importance, or the practical/rational desirability, of sanctions, one may say, dramatically, that an unsanctioned set of laws is 'not really law', If one wishes to stress the empirical/historical importance, or the practical/rational desirability of determinate legislative and/or adjudicative institutions, one may say, dramatically, that a community without such institutions 'lacks a real legal system' or 'cannot really be said to have "a legal system".' If one wishes to stress the empirical/historical importance, or the practical/rational desirability, of rules authorising or regulating private or public change in the rules or their incidence, one may say, dramatically, that a set of rules which includes no such rules 'is not a legal system'. All these things have often been said, and can reasonably be said provided that one is seeking to draw attention to a feature of the central case of law and not to banish the other non-central cases to some other discipline.

H L A HART
The Concept of Law [3]
(1961)

We shall take Legal Positivism to mean the simple contention that it is in no sense a necessary truth that laws reproduce or satisfy certain demands of morality, though in fact they have often done so. But just because those who have taken this view have either been silent or differed very much concerning the nature of morality, it is necessary to consider two very different forms in which Legal Positivism has been rejected. One of these is expressed most clearly in the classical theories of Natural Law: that there are certain principles of human conduct, awaiting discovery by human reason, with which man-made law must conform if it is to be valid. The other takes a different, less rationalist view of morality, and offers a different account of the ways in which legal validity is connected with moral value. We shall consider the first of these in this section and the next.

In the vast literature from Plato to the present day which is dedicated to the assertion, and also to the denial, of the proposition that the ways in which men ought to behave may be discovered by human reason, the disputants on one side seem to say to those on the other, 'You are blind if you cannot see this' only to receive in reply, 'You have been dreaming.' This is so, because the claim that there are true principles of right conduct, rationally discoverable, has not usually been advanced as a separate doctrine but was originally presented, and for long defended, as part of a general conception of nature, inanimate and living. This outlook is, in many ways, antiethetic to the general conception of nature which constitutes the framework of modern secular thought. Hence it is that, to its critics, Natural Law theory has seemed to spring from deep and old confusions from which modern thought has triumphantly freed itself; while to its advocates, the critics appear merely to insist on surface trivialities, ignoring profounder truths.

Thus many modern critics have thought that the claim that laws of proper conduct may be discovered by human reason rested on a simple ambiguity of the word 'law', and that when this ambiguity was exposed Natural Law received its

[3] Hart, H L A (1961) *The Concept of Law*. Oxford University Press, Oxford, pp113-115.

death-blow. It is in this way that John Stuart Mill dealt with Montesquieu, who in the first chapter of the *Esprit des Lois* naively inquires why it is that, while inanimate things such as the stars and also animals obey 'the law of their nature', man does not do so but falls into sin. This, Mill thought, revealed the perennial confusion between laws which formulate the course or regularities of nature, and laws which require men to behave in certain ways. The former, which can be discovered by observation and reasoning, may be called 'descriptive' and it is for the scientist thus to discover them; the latter cannot be so established, for they are not statements or descriptions of facts, but are 'prescriptions' or demands that men shall behave in certain ways. The answer therefore to Montesquieu's question is simple: prescriptive laws may be broken and yet remain laws, because that merely means that human beings do not do what they are told to do; but it is meaningless to say of the laws of nature, discovered by science, either that they can or cannot be broken. If the stars behave in ways contrary to the scientific laws which purport to describe their regular movements, these are not broken but they lose their title to be called 'laws' and must be reformulated. To these differences in the sense of 'law', there correspond systematic differences in the associated vocabulary of words like 'must', 'bound to', 'ought', and 'should'. So, on this view, belief in Natural Law is reducible to a very simple fallacy: a failure to perceive the very different senses which those law-impregnated words can bear. It is as if the believer had failed to perceive the very different meaning of such words in 'You are bound to report for military service' and 'It is bound to freeze if the wind goes round to the north'.

Critics like Bentham and Mill, who most fiercely attacked Natural Law, often attributed their opponents' confusion between these distinct senses of law, to the survival of the belief that the observed regularities of nature were prescribed or decreed by a Divine Governor of the Universe. On such a theocratic view, the only difference between the law of gravity and the Ten Commandments – God's law for Man – was, as Blackstone asserted, the relatively minor one that men, alone of created things, were endowed with reason and free will; and so unlike things, could discover and disobey the divine prescriptions. Natural Law has, however, not always been associated with belief in a Divine Governor or Lawgiver of the universe, and even where it has been, its characteristic tenets have not been logically dependent on that belief. Both the relevant sense of the word 'natural', which enters into Natural Law, and its general outlook minimizing the difference, so obvious and so important to modern minds, between prescriptive and descriptive laws, have their roots in Greek thought which was, for this purpose, quite secular. Indeed, the continued reassertion of some form of Natural Law doctrine is due in part to the fact that its appeal is independent of both divine and human authority, and to the fact that despite a terminology, and much metaphysics, which few could now accept, it contains certain elementary truths of importance for the understanding of both morality and law. These we shall endeavour to disentangle from their metaphysical setting and restate here in simpler terms.

. . .

The doctrine of Natural Law is part of an older conception of nature in which the observable world is not merely a scene of such regularities, and knowledge of nature is not merely a knowledge of them. Instead, on this older outlook every nameable kind of existing thing, human, animate, and inanimate, is conceived not only as tending to maintain itself in existence but as proceeding towards a definite optimum state which is the specific good – or the end appropriate for it.

. . .

This mode of thinking about nature seems strange when stated abstractly. It may appear less fantastic if we recall some of the ways in which even now we refer at least to living things, for a teleological view is still reflected in common ways of describing their developments. Thus in the case of an acorn, growth into an oak is something which is not only regularly achieved by acorns, but is distinguished unlike its decay (which is also regular) as an optimum state of maturity in the light of which the intermediate stages are both explained and judged as good or bad, and the 'functions' of its various parts and structural changes identified. The normal growth of leaves is required if it is to obtain the moisture necessary for 'full' or 'proper' development, and it is the 'function' of leaves to supply this. Hence we think and speak of this growth as what 'ought naturally to occur'. In the case of the action or movements of inanimate things, such ways of talking seem much less plausible unless they are artefacts designed by human beings for a purpose. The notion that a stone on falling to the ground is realizing some appropriate 'end' or returning to its 'proper place', like a horse galloping home to a stable, is now somewhat comic.

Indeed, one of the difficulties in understanding a teleological view of nature is that just as it minimized the differences between statements of what regularly happens and statements of what ought to happen, so too it minimizes the difference, so important to modern thought, between human beings *with* a purpose of their own which they consciously strive to realize and other living or inanimate things. For in the teleological view of the world, man, like other things, is thought of as tending towards a specific optimum state or end which is set for him and the fact, that he, unlike other things, may do this consciously, is not conceived as a radical difference between him and the rest of nature. This specific human end or good is in part, like that of other living things, a condition of biological maturity and developed physical powers; but it also includes, as its distinctively human element, a development and excellent of mind and character manifested in thought and conduct. Unlike other things, man is able by reasoning and reflection to discover what the attainment of this excellence of mind and character involves and to desire it. Yet even so, on this teleological view, this optimum state is not man's good or end because it desires it; rather he desires it because it is already his natural end.

. . .

These crude examples designed to illustrate teleological elements still alive in ordinary thought about human action, are drawn from the lowly sphere of biological fact which man shares with other animals. It will be rightly observed that what makes sense of this mode of thought and expression is something entirely obvious: it is the tacit assumption that the proper end of human activity is survival, and this rests on the simple contingent fact that most men most of the time wish to continue in existence. The actions which we speak of as those which are naturally good to do, are those which are required for survival; the notions of a human need, of harm, and of the *function* of bodily organs or changes rests on the same simple fact. Certainly if we stop here, we shall have only a very attenuated version of Natural Law: for the classical exponents of this outlook conceived of survival (*perseverare in esse suo*) as merely the lowest stratum in a much more complex and far more debatable concept of the human end or good for man. Aristotle included in it the disinterested cultivation of the human intellect, and Aquinas the knowledge of God, and both these represent values which may be and have been challenged. Yet other thinkers, Hobbes and Hume among them, have been willing to lower their sights: they have seen in the modest aim of survival the central indisputable element which gives empirical good sense to the terminology of Natural Law. 'Human nature cannot by any means subsist without the association of individuals: and that association never could have place were no regard paid to the laws of equity and justice.'[4]

. . .

There are, however, simpler, less philosophical, considerations than these which show acceptance of survival as an aim to be necessary, in a sense more directly relevant to the discussion of human law and morals. We are committed to it as something presupposed by the terms of the discussion; for our concern is with social arrangements for continued existence, not with those of a suicide club. We wish to know whether, among these social arrangements, there are some which may illuminatingly be ranked as natural laws discoverable by reason, and what their relation is to human law and morality. To raise this or any other question concerning *how* men should live together, we must assume that their aim, generally speaking, is to live. From this point the argument is a simple one. Reflection on some very obvious generalizations – indeed truisms – concerning human nature and the world in which men live, show that as long as these hold good, there are certain rules of conduct which any social organization must contain if it is to be viable. Such rules do in fact constitute a common element in the law and conventional morality of all societies which have progressed to the point where these are distinguished as different forms of social control. With them are found, both in law and morals, much that is peculiar to a particular society and much that may seem arbitrary or a mere matter of choice. Such universally recognized principles of conduct which have a basis in elementary truths concerning human beings, their natural environment, and aims, may be considered the *minimum content* of Natural Law, in contrast with the more grandiose and more challengeable constructions

[4] Hume 'Of Justice and Injustice' *Treatise of Human Nature*, III, ii.

which have often been proffered under that name. In the next section we shall consider, in the form of five truisms, the salient characteristics of human nature upon which this modest but important minimum rests.

THE MINIMUM CONTENT OF NATURAL LAW

In considering the simple truisms which we set forth here, and their connexion with law and morals, it is important to observe that in each case the facts mentioned afford a *reason* why, given survival as an aim, law and morals should include a specific content. The general form of the argument is simply that without such a content laws and morals could not forward the minimum purpose of survival which men have in associating with each other. In the absence of this content men, as they are, would have no reason for obeying voluntarily any rules; and without a minimum of co-operation given voluntarily by those who find that it is in their interest to submit to and maintain the rules, coercion of others who would not voluntarily conform would be impossible. It is important to stress the distinctively rational connexion between natural facts and the content of legal and moral rules in this approach, because it is both possible and important to inquire into quite different forms of connexion between natural facts and legal or moral rules. Thus, the still young sciences of psychology and sociology may discover or may even have discovered that, unless certain physical, psychological, or economic conditions are satisfied, eg unless young children are fed and nurtured in certain ways within the family, no system of laws or code of morals can be established, or that only those laws can function successfully which conform to a certain type. Connexions of this sort between natural conditions and systems of rules are not mediated by *reasons*; for they do not relate the existence of certain rules to the conscious aims or purpose of those whose rules they are. Being fed in infancy in a certain way may well be shown to be a necessary condition or even a *cause* of a population developing or maintaining a moral or legal code, but it is not a *reason* for their doing so. Such causal connexions do not of course conflict with the connexions which rest on purposes or conscious aims; they may indeed be considered more important or fundamental than the latter, since they may actually explain why human beings have those conscious aims or purposes which Natural Law takes as its starting-points. Causal explanations of this type do not rest on truisms nor are they mediated by conscious aims or purposes: they are for sociology or psychology like other sciences to establish by the methods of generalization and theory, resting on observation and, where possible, on experiment. Such connexions therefore are of a different kind from those which relate the content of certain legal and moral rules to the facts stated in the following truisms.

Human vulnerability

The common requirements of law and morality consist for the most part not of active services to be rendered but of forbearances, which are usually formulated in negative form as prohibitions. Of these the most important for social life are those that restrict the use of violence in killing or inflicting bodily harm. The basic character of such rules may be brought out in a question: If there were not these rules what point could there be for beings such as ourselves in having rules of *any* other kind? The force of this rhetorical question rests on the fact that men are both occasionally prone to, and normally vulnerable to, bodily attack. Yet though this is a truism it is not a necessary truth; for things might have been, and might one day be, otherwise. There are species of animals whose physical structure (including exoskeletons or a carpace) renders them virtually immune from attack by other members of their species and animals who have no organs enabling them to attack. If men were to lose their vulnerability to each other there would vanish one obvious reason for the most characteristic provision of law and morals: *Thou shalt not kill.*

Approximate equality

Men differ from each other in physical strength, agility, and even more in intellectual capacity. Nonetheless it is a fact of quite major importance for the understanding of different forms of law and morality, that no individual is so much more powerful than others, that he is able, without co-operation, to dominate or subdue them for more than a short period. Even the strongest must sleep at times and, when asleep, loses temporarily his superiority. This fact of approximate equality, more than any other, makes obvious the necessity for a system of mutual forbearance and compromise which is the base of both legal and moral obligations. Social life with its rules requiring such forbearances is irksome at times; but it is at any rate less nasty, less brutish, and less short than unrestrained aggression for beings thus approximately equal. It is, of course, entirely consistent with this and an equal truism that when such a system of forbearance is established there will always be some who will wish to exploit it, by simultaneously living within its shelter and breaking its restrictions. This, indeed is, as we later show, one of the natural facts which makes the step from merely moral to organized, legal forms of control a necessary one. Again, things might have been otherwise. Instead of being approximately equal there might have been some men immensely stronger than others and better able to dispense with rest, either because some were in these ways far above the present average, or because most were far below it. Such exceptional men might have much to gain by aggression and little to gain from mutual forbearance or compromise with others. But we need not have recourse to the fantasy of giants among pygmies to see the cardinal importance of the fact of approximate equality: for it is illustrated better by the facts of international life, where there are (or were) vast disparities in strength and vulnerability between the states. This inequality, as we shall later see, between the units of international law is one of the things that has imported to it a character so different from municipal law and limited the extent to which it is capable of operating as an organized coercive system.

Limited altruism

Men are not devils dominated by a wish to exterminate each other, and the demonstration that, given only the modest aim of survival, the basic rules of law and morals are necessities, must not be identified with the false view that men are predominantly selfish and have no disinterested interest in the survival and welfare of their fellows. But if men are not devils, neither are they angels; and the fact that they are a mean between these two extremes is something which makes a system of mutual forbearances both necessary and possible. With angels, never tempted to harm others, rules requiring forbearances would not be necessary. With devils prepared to destroy, reckless of the cost to themselves, they would be impossible. As things are, human altruism is limited in range and intermittent, and the tendencies to aggression are frequent enough to be fatal to social life if not controlled.

Limited resources

It is a merely contingent fact that human beings need food, clothes, and shelter; that these do not exist at hand in limitless abundance; but are scarce, have to be grown or won from nature, or have to be constructed by human toil. These facts alone make indispensable some minimal form of the institution of property (though not necessarily individual property), and the distinctive kind of rule which requires respect for it. The simplest forms of property are to be seen in rules excluding persons generally other than the 'owner' from entry on, or the use of land, or from taking or using material things. If crops are to grow, land must be secure from indiscriminate entry, and food must, in the intervals between its growth or capture and consumption, be secure from being taken by others. At all times and places life itself depends on these minimal forbearances. Again, in this respect, things might have been otherwise than they are. The human organism might have been constructed like plants, capable of extracting food from air, or what it needs might have grown without cultivation in limitless abundance.

Limited understanding and strength of will

The facts that make rules respecting persons, property, and promises necessary in social life are simple and their mutual benefits are obvious. Most men are capable of seeing them and of sacrificing the immediate short-term interests which conformity to such rules demands. They may indeed obey, from a variety of motives: some from prudential calculation that the sacrifices are worth the gains, some from a disinterested interest in the welfare of others, and some because they look upon the rules as worthy of respect in themselves and find their ideals in devotion to them. On the other hand, neither understanding of long-term interest, nor the strength or goodness of will, upon which the efficacy of these different motives towards obedience depends, are shared by all men alike. All are tempted at times to prefer their own immediate interests and, in the absence of a special organization for their detection and punishment, many would succumb to the temptation. No doubt the advantages of mutual forbearance are so palpable that the number and strength of those who would co-operate voluntarily in a coercive system will normally be greater than any likely combination of malefactors. Yet, except in very small closely-knit societies, submission to the system of restraints would be folly if there were no organization for the coercion of those who would then try to obtain the advantages of the system without submitting to its obligations. 'Sanctions' are therefore required not as the normal motive for obedience, but as a *guarantee* that those who would voluntarily obey shall not be sacrificed to those who would not. To obey, without this, would be to risk going to the wall. Given this standing danger, what reason demands is *voluntarily* co-operation in a *coercive* system.

. . .

It is to be observed that the same natural fact of approximate equality between men is of crucial importance in the efficacy of organized sanctions. If some men were vastly more powerful than others, and so not dependent on their forbearance, the strength of the malefactors might exceed that of the supporters of law and order. Given such inequalities, the use of sanctions could not be successful and would involve dangers at least as great as those which they were designed to suppress. In these circumstances instead of social life being based on a system of mutual forbearances, with force used only intermittently against a minority of malefactors, the only viable system would be one in which the weak submitted to the strong on the best terms they could make and lived under their 'protection'. This, because of the scarcity of resources, would lead to a number of conflicting power centres, each grouped round its 'strong man': these might intermittently war with each other, though the natural sanction, never negligible, of the risk of defeat might ensure an uneasy peace. Rules of a sort might then be accepted for the regulation of issues over which the 'powers' were unwilling to fight. Again we need not think in fanciful terms of pygmies and giants in order to understand the simple logistics of approximate equality and its importance for law. The international scene, where the units concerned have differed vastly in strength, affords illustration enough. For centuries the disparities between states have resulted in a system where organized sanctions have been impossible, and law has been confined to matters which did not affect 'vital' issues. How far atomic weapons, when available to all, will redress the balance of unequal power, and bring forms of control more closely resembling municipal criminal law, remains to be seen.

The simple truisms we have discussed not only disclose the core of good sense in the doctrine of Natural Law. They are of vital importance for the understanding of law and morals, and they explain why the definition of the basic forms of these in purely formal terms, without reference to any specific content or social needs, has proved so inadequate. Perhaps the major benefit to jurisprudence from this outlook is the escape it affords from certain misleading dichotomies which often obscure the discussion of the characteristics of law. Thus, for example, the traditional question whether every legal system must provide for sanctions can be presented in a fresh and clever light, when we command the view of things presented by this simple version of Natural Law. We shall no longer have to choose between two unsuitable alternatives which are often taken as exhaustive: on the one hand that of saying that this is required by 'the' meaning of the words 'law' or 'legal system', and on the other that of saying that it is 'just a fact' that most legal systems do provide for sanctions. Neither of these alternatives is satisfactory. There are no settled principles forbidding the use of the word 'law' of systems where there are no centrally organized sanctions, and there is good reason (though no compulsion) for using the expression 'international law' of a system, which has none. On the other hand we do need to distinguish the place that sanctions must have within a municipal system, if it is to serve the minimum purposes of beings constituted as men are. We can say, given the setting of natural facts and aims, which make sanctions both possible and necessary in a municipal system, that this is a natural necessity; and some such phrase is needed also to convey the status of the minimum forms of protection for persons, property, and promises which are similarly indispensible features of municipal law. It is in this form that we should reply to the positivist thesis that 'law may have any content'. For it is a truth of some importance that for the adequate description not only of law but of many other social institutions, a place must be reserved, besides definitions and ordinary statements of fact, for a third category of statements: those the truth of which is contingent on human beings and the world they live in retaining the salient characteristics which they have.

Legal and Social Theory

11. SOCIOLOGICAL JURISPRUDENCE

R POUND
Contemporary Juristic Theory [1]
(1940)

A MEASURE OF VALUES

Since Jhering showed us the difference between the legal institution we set up to secure a recognized claim or demand and the claim or demand itself, as it exists apart from the law, we have known the claim or demand by the name of interest. The term has occasioned some confusion because it has easily been confused with an idea of advantage; the more so since Jhering's social utilitarianism made social advantage the criterion of value and treated it as something given, as something we know exactly as we know that a certain claim or demand exists de facto and is pressed upon lawmakers and courts for recognition. Everyone has an interest in, that is, makes a claim to the satisfaction of his desires. They are his interests as he sees it, and his view of the matter cannot be ignored by telling him it is not to his advantage to want what he feels he wants and insists he ought to have. Very likely we can't give him what he claims or all that he claims, but it is because we have to consider the conflicting or overlapping claims of others, not because we decide he does not want it. We must, therefore, as I have said, begin by ascertaining what are the claims or demands which press upon lawmakers and judges and administrative agencies for recognition and securing.

In the inventory with which we must begin it is convenient to classify the interests of which the legal order must take account as individual or public or social. All interests are those of individual human beings asserted by individuals. But some are claims or demands or desires involved in the individual life and asserted in title of that life. Others are claims or demands or desires involved in life in the politically organized society and asserted in title of that society. Others or the same in other aspects are claims or demands or desires involved in social life in civilized society and asserted in title of that life. Every claim does not necessarily go once and for all in one of these categories. The same claim may be asserted and may have to be looked at from different standpoints; it may be asserted in title of more than one

[1] Pound, R (1940) *Contemporary Justice Theory*. Ward Ritchie Press, pp610–613.

aspect of life. Thus my claim to my watch may be asserted as an individual interest of substance when I sue someone, who walks off with it without my consent, either to recover possession of it or to obtain the money value as damages for converting it. But it may be looked at also as a social interest in the security of acquisitions and asserted as such when I persuade the district attorney to prosecute for larceny someone who has stolen it from me.

A mere sketch in broad lines of the scheme of interests which have pressed upon the legal order in the past will suffice for our purposes. Individual interests are interests of personality or interests in the domestic relations or interests of substance. Interests of personality are those involved in the individual physical and spiritual existence; in one's body and life, ie security of his physical person and his bodily health, in free exertion of one's will, ie freedom from coercion, and from deception as to what one is tricked into doing by false representations, in free choice of location, in one's reputation, in freedom to contract and of entering into relations with others, in free industry, ie in freely employing himself or gaining employment in any occupation or activity for which he is or is considered qualified, and in free individual belief and opinion. It is enough to point out in passing that the interests in freedom of contract and in freedom of industry overlap or come into competition with claims of labouring men asserted through trade unions and have raised typically difficult questions for the courts for a generation.

Like difficult questions are raised by individual interests in the domestic relations. It is obvious that husband and wife have each a claim or demand which they make against the whole world that outsiders shall not interfere with the relation. Yet on a weighing of all the interests involved California and many other states have been impelled to abrogate the action for alienation of affections by which that interest had been secured. The interest is still recognized but effective security is now denied. It is obvious too that the relation involves reciprocal claims or demands which each asserts against the other. The claims of the husband to the society of the wife and to her services for the benefit of the household, formerly well secured, are now deprived of all substantial security on a weighing in comparison with the individual interest of the wife in individual free self-assertion. But the claim or demand of the wife for support and maintenance is not only recognized but is secured in a variety of ways which make it one of the best secured interests known to the law. So it is with the interests involved in the relation of parent and child. Formerly the claims of the parent were given effect by privileges of correction, by control of the child's earnings, and by a wide authority of shaping the training and bringing up of the child in every phase. Everywhere today individual interests of the child and a social interest in dependents have been weighed against the claims of parents, and juvenile courts, courts of domestic relations, and family courts in our large cities have greatly changed the balance of these interests.

By interests of substance we mean the claims or demands asserted by individuals in title of the individual economic existence. Claims with respect to property involve too many questions to make it worth while to do more than mention them in the present connection. It will be more useful for our immediate purpose to look at a group of interests in economically advantageous relations with others. Such relations may be social or domestic or official or contractual. If a man is wrongfully and maliciously expelled from a social club and injury to his social standing in the community may have a serious economic effect upon him. Yet other claims have to be considered and the courts cannot compel the members of the club to associate with him if they persist in refusing to do so. In one case where the courts ordered the expelled member restored to membership the club reinstated him and then dissolved and formed a new club, leaving him out. We have noted already how claims of the husband to the services of the wife in the household are no longer effectively secured either against outside interference with the relation or against the wife's refusal to perform. As to official relations, public interests have to be weighed and the older conception of property in a profitable office has been given up. But the most significant questions have arisen with respect to contractual relations. If A has a contract with B he makes a claim against the whole world that third persons shall not interfere to induce B to break the contract. Yet the third person may assert claims which have to be taken account of in this connection, and some of the hardest questions in labour law have turned on recognition of claims of labour organizations to induce breaking of contracts of employment and what should be regarded as giving a privilege to interfere with such contracts.

As to public interests, it will be enough to instance one type of question where difficult problems of weighing have arisen. How far is the dignity of the political organization of society an interest to be taken into account? When the political organization was struggling with kin organization and religious organization for the primacy in social control, the dignity of the state was a very serious matter. Hence it was settled that the state could not be sued without its consent, that its debts could not be set off against its claims, that it was not estopped by what was done by its officials, and that its claims were not lost by official neglect to assert them nor barred by limitation. Other public interests, eg a claim to unimpaired efficiency of the political organization, entered into the reckoning. But the extent to which the rules just mentioned secure no more than the dignity of the state and the weight to be given to that interest today are controversial subject in public law.

One could devote a whole lecture to a catalogue of social interests. First we may put the general security, including claims to peace and order, the first social interest to obtain legal recognition, the general safety, long recognized under the maxim that the public safety is the highest law, the general health, the security of acquisitions and the security of transactions. The two last afford an excellent example of the overlapping and conflict of recognized interests. From the standpoint of the security of acquisitions a thief or one who wrongfully holds another's property should not be able to transfer to a third person a better title than he has. But from the standpoint of the security of transactions, people generally who have no knowledge or notice of the owner's claim and, acting in good faith, part with value in a business transaction with one in possession of the property ought to be protected. Possession ought to give a power of business transactions as to the thing possessed and apparently owned. This question as to the limits of what is called negotiability has been coming up all over the world and recent legislation has been giving greater effect to the security of transactions in comparison with the security of acquisitions. Closely related, and scarcely less important is the social interest in the security of social institutions, domestic, religious, political, and economic. According as one gives the chief weight to the individual claims of husband and wife or to the social interest in marriage as a social institution, he arrives at different results on the vexed questions of divorce legislation. According as he gives more weight to individual interests in free belief and opinion or to the social interest in the security of political institutions, he will reach different results as to legislation against and prosecutions for sedition. Other important social interests are an interest in the general morals, an interest in the use and conservation of social resources, and an interest in general progress, social, political, economic and cultural. Finally and by no means least there is the social interest in the individual life, the claim or demand asserted in title of social life in civilized society that each individual be secure in his freedom, have secured to him opportunities, political, social and economic, and be able to live at least a reasonably minimum human life in society. Here again all manner of overlappings and conflicts are continually encountered. But perhaps enough has been said to bring out that every item in the catalogue requires to be weighed with many others and that no one can be admitted to its full extent without impairing the scheme as a whole.

J STONE
Law and the Social Sciences [2]
(1966)

... Sociological jurisprudence, like any other outcropping of human thought, was itself a creature of a time and place, and its earlier scope and tenor were in part conditioned by this. Before World War I, when its work developed in the United States, the beginnings of social legislation and of a positive federal attitude towards economic institutions and their stability and progress were still struggling for legitimation in face of various social and economic ideologies, traditional common-law hostility to statutes, jealousy for states' rights, and the conceptualism and logicism shared with the followers of Austin in England and of the Pandectists on the European continent. The social evils to which statutes held unconstitutional were often a serious response, accelerated with accelerating industrial and economic change; so did the invocations of the federal commerce power against economic ills and abuses.

[2] Stone, J (1966) *Law and the Social Sciences.* University of Minnesota Press, Minneapolis, pp637-638.

Stating the matter more generally, the maladjustment and inadequacies of the law for its contemporary tasks gave to early sociological jurisprudence an overwhelmingly activist drive which, even when it expressed itself in general terms, was in fact directed at ad hoc remedies for all the particular defaults of the legal order. A great deal of the work in this area even to the present day is still of this nature. And, of course, thus regarded such a program is inexhaustible, and its non-fulfillment even in a century of work is certain. In this sense the program was over-ambitious, and was thus still open to the charge of failure even after it had contributed to massive changes in the law and in attitudes towards it. As with engineers of other kinds, and especially the traffic engineer of a modern city, Pound's 'social engineer' was certain to be a busy man, far behind in his work, however many and mighty the projects already completed.

Finally, it seems clearer now that it was in 1946 that movements of thought and action touching the relations of law and society, insofar as they move into more fruitful contact with other social sciences, must come to place more stress on the importance of cognition of the social and economic order in its complex unity. And this even when they are bent upon an approach to diagnosis and remedy of specific evils through legal action. Economic thought has come to approach the problems of human distress due to economic fluctuations through control of key points in an understood economic ordering, itself institutionally framed within the more comprehensive social order. Contemporary sociological thought, well illustrated ... in the aspirations of Parsons' later thought, seeks a framework of thought receptive of social data which will allow us to see 'the social system' as an integrated equilibration of the multitude of operative systems of values and institutions embraced within it. Whatever the difficulties of the Parsonian efforts in this direction, we believe that some corresponding change of horizons is likely in sociological jurisprudence, as many of the more elementary and glaring legal maladjustments which provoked the activism of its initial program become corrected.

The change may indeed already have begun. We are, for example, no longer perplexed by the question of interfering with liberty of contract, when gross inequality of bargaining power makes abuse of liberty likely. It has been handled in an ad hoc way by legislating for specific relations like landlord and tenant or lender and borrower. We are, on the other hand, increasingly perplexed by such comparatively new and diffuse problems as that of the use of trade union pressure against non-members, pressure of capital concentrations against competitors and consumers, the steady growth of juvenile and urban delinquency, the creeping paralysis of traffic congestion in the spreading metropolis, chronic delays in the administration of justice, the adjustment of capital-labour relations and of habits of leisure and systems of education to the age of automation.

These are the more characteristic kinds of areas demanding legal action for the future of the Western democracies. No doubt some problems will continue to be thrown up, for which the ad hoc approach of early sociological jurisprudence, making direct assault on the points where legal maladjustment is immediately manifest, is apt. But the sociological jurist of the future will also have to approach his characteristic problems through a vast effort at understanding the wider social context, seeking by the light of available social knowledge the key points of the systems of action from which adjustment can be effectively made. Nor indeed, is this likely development at too great odds with some aspects of the past aspirations of sociological jurisprudence. For a number of these, such as the demand that the necessary expertise for pre-legislative tasks be made available on a stable institutionalised base, are as relevant to the broad tasks of cognition as they are to the ad hoc tasks of legal activism. So is the search, which has already produced crisis after crisis in the tasks of practitioners and courts, for more basic and meaningful categories of thought, for instance, in the laws of damages for personal injuries, of liability for dangerous chattels and operations, of anti-trust law, of the law of economic association, and a score of others. And the impressive contemporary work of Willard Hurst in social and economic legal history is in important part a search for categories of thought, drawn from empirical historical data, which will serve to put into the order of reason the interplay of legal and non-legal phenomena in the dimension of time ...

R COTTERRELL
The Sociology of Law: An Introduction [3]
(1984)

Whatever the wider significance of law in society, perhaps the most obvious characteristic of law as a cluster of institutions and professional practices in Western societies is its apparent isolation. A most tangible experience of this air of isolation of the world of law is to walk from the noise and bustle of London streets through the gates of the Inns of Court, into the leafy squares with their neat lawns where the barristers who serve the Royal Courts of Justice have their chambers and where the life of the law, in this narrow professional sense, goes on with a tranquility far removed from anything happening beyond the walls that surround the Inns.

To many people law seems separate from other aspects of life. It appears as an arcane world of professionalism centred on a body of esoteric knowledge which is intimidating to the uninitiated in its bulk and obscurity. Laymen usually seek to avoid it. Few actually want to be involved in litigation. Few people other than lawyers discover the mysteries contained in the thousands of volumes of law reports and legal treatises. Legal experience is thought to exist in a different realm from social experience. Judges in England are popularly if often erroneously assumed to be as remarkable for their limited knowledge of life beyond the courtroom as for their mastery of what goes on within it.

[3] Cotterrell, R (1984) *The Sociology of Law: An Introduction*. Butterworths, London, pp17-19.

This apparent isolation is closely related to and in part sustained by the professional autonomy of lawyers which varies in character and degree in different Western societies and has many ramifications. One consequence of it is that lawyers' typical conceptions of law, shaped and refined in their professional environment, have long had a self sufficiency and comprehensiveness which have made them extremely resistant to different and perhaps opposed views of the nature and functions of law arising outside legal professional circles. The concern of this chapter is to outline some basic sociological assumptions involved in these typical conceptions of law and to suggest some of the important sociological questions to which they give rise but which they do not answer.

One of the most important characteristics of law seen from this professional standpoint has been its intellectual isolation. Law has been envisaged in such a way that as doctrine and professional practice it can be analysed and understood in terms of its own internal categories and without reference to the social environment within which it develops. It is specifically in the modern Western societies with which this book is concerned that this remarkable conception of law has been most fully developed. As noted in the Introduction, it has been founded on the assumed rational doctrinal structure of law and underpinned by a positivist conception of legal science. In earlier times, the idea of law as an arcane field of special knowledge was blended with an assertion (considered to be without need of empirical demonstration or theoretical examination) of the roots of legal ideas in general culture. Law was seen as a craft handed down by tradition and consisting of technical mysteries accessible only through the practical experience of apprenticeship. In fact, in the Anglo-American legal world this earlier craft conception of law has not entirely disappeared but rather been overlaid with modern professional conceptions.

Anglo-American legal thinking still remains strongly influenced by the traditions of the English common law – that is, of law developed pragmatically case by case through judicial decisions rather than being elaborated from a priori general concepts or legislated in the form of codes or statutes. In the common law conception law grows like coral, through the slow accumulation of minutiae over the centuries, the encrustation of precedent. The rational strength of the law comes not from any systematic overall structure but from the accumulated wisdom of the judges preserved in the thousands of recorded cases which make up this coral kingdom. In a modern era when legislation created by elected assemblies constitutes by far the most important source of new law in Western societies, this older conception of law can hardly dominate. Yet in the Anglo-American legal world it expresses itself in lawyers' tendency to see judges as at the heart of the legal system, to view legislation with some reserve, and to laud the virtues of case law. Common law still remains a subsidiary source of new law in these jurisdictions and, more importantly, the concepts developed in common law remain a general foundation of legal reasoning within them. For this reason they remain known as common law systems in contrast to the civil law code-based systems of continental Europe.

Perhaps because lawyers' claims about the intellectual autonomy of law have, in general, been so tenaciously maintained without regard to developments in social science they are difficult to confront directly using modern sociological literature which adopts standpoints radically different from these orthodox professional conceptions. A more useful strategy, then, is to consider some relatively early sociological perspectives on law which, because of the intellectual environment of their time, engage orthodox or traditional lawyers' conceptions on their own ground, bringing to light tensions or ambiguities in legal professional thoughtways, at the same time as they elaborate sociological assumptions contained within them.

FOLKWAYS AND MORES

In his classic work *Folkways* (1906), the American sociologist William Graham Sumner indirectly provides a convenient sociological commentary on assumptions typical of common law thinking. Sumner sets out on what has been for many theorists the basic sociological quest: to explain the forces of social cohesion, the elements that contribute order and unity in societies. The boundless ambition of the book – to generalise about all societies and all human history – locates it firmly in a late nineteenth–century tradition. Certainly it draws on a vast range of ethnographic material from numerous societies. Sumner writes, 'If we put together all we have learnt from anthropology and ethnography about primitive men and primitive society we perceive that the first task of life is to live (ie to survive) ... Need was the first experience and it was followed by some blundering effort to satisfy it' (Sumner 1906: 17-18). The basic method for early man in attempting to solve the problems of survival was trial and error, a blundering utilitarianism. The ability to distinguish pleasure and pain is 'the only psychical power is to be assumed' (1906: 18). The experience of pleasure and pain provided the test of success. But the historical struggle for survival went on in groups so that many seeking the same aim tended to come to similar opinions as to what was best, more productive of pleasure than pain. 'Each profited by the other's experience; hence there was concurrence towards that which proved to be most expedient. All at last adopted the same way for the same purpose; hence the ways turned into customs and became mass phenomena. Instincts were developed in connection with them. In this way folkways arise' (1906: 18).

R F V HEUSTON
Judicial Prosopography [4]
(1986)

According to the Oxford English Dictionary Second Supplement, prosopography has as one of its meanings 'collective biography.' The more specialised meaning has its

[4] Heuston, R F V 'Judicial Prosopography' (1986) 102 *Law Quarterly Review* 90.

origin in the work of ancient historians, which stresses that something of value may be learned from studying a group of persons in the context of their family and political backgrounds. So the word is more novel than the idea or concept. Within the past decade the word has been used to describe the result of researches in the legal history of the sixteenth and of the nineteenth centuries.[5] It can I hope be used to describe my project to publish *Lives of the Lord Chancellors: 1940–1970*. I was myself ignorant of the word when I published the first volume in 1964. Now, like Monsieur Jourdain, it is delightful to discover that my labours can be graced by so dignified a word.

Is there still any room for judicial biography? The question must be asked after reading a careful article in the *British Journal of Sociology* which under the title 'Research on the English Judicial Process'[6] provides a survey of all the literature on the structure and function of the courts – but does not cite a single biography or autobiography. There have certainly been many sociological studies of the legal profession and legal services within the past two decades. This is indeed a growth industry, as Mr D R Harris has noted.[7] None of these studies seem to be interested in prosopography. On the other hand each of the three major scholarly works which have been devoted to the House of Lords in the past 15 years – namely those by Blom-Cooper and Drewry, Stevens, and Paterson contain considerable biographical material.

Academics certainly continue to be fascinated by the judgments in appellate tribunals and by the work of those who produce them. There has been a remarkable increase in the 'literature of judicial activism,' as it has been called. This interest or fascination in judgments is often not shared by their authors. So of the six Lord Chancellors in my forthcoming book, two had apparently an intense dislike for the judicial side of their work. Lord Kilmuir and Lord Gardiner were on the Woolsack for a total of nearly 14 years – just under half the period covered by my whole study. Yet Lord Kilmuir delivered only 24 judgments during his chancellorship – an average of three per year. Lord Gardiner delivered only three judgments in six years – an average of one every two years. After his retirement Lord Kilmuir surrendered his pension and so was not obliged to sit judicially, and he did not do so. Lord Gardiner in his retirement delivered only one judgment. Each of these of course had made substantial contributions in other directions to the English legal system. My tentative conclusion is that there is still room for the biographical study of those who produce judgments (or opinions, as those in the House of Lords are now properly called). Once labelled speeches, they are now opinions, as the speeches go unspoken, but are made available for a fee to the public shortly after they have been notionally delivered in the Appellate Committee.

Perhaps I could here draw attention to another use of the word opinion which seems to me to be a neglected source of literature for the legal profession. I refer to

---

[5] See the two books by Dan Duman, *The Judicial Bench in England* (1982), and *English & Colonial Bars* (1983); and Baker (1984) *Criminal Law Journal* 180.
[6] Baum (1977) *British Journal of Sociology* 511.
[7] Harris 'Socio-Legal Studies in the United Kingdom' (1983) 3 *Legal Studies* 315, 320.

the opinion of the barrister. Yet is it not an interesting institution deserving of study? It is well known to be one means by which solicitors safeguard themselves from actions for professional negligence; at a high level it may be a means whereby clients, personal or corporate, can plan for the future. My impression is that the involvement of the legal profession in this sort of long-term planning has much increased. Perhaps I could provide one example from the career of Lord Jowitt. In 1955 Jowitt, by then an ex-Lord Chancellor, had become interested in the interpretation of the Dangerous Drugs Act 1951. The statute gave power to the Home Secretary to control the use of heroin: could this be construed so as to authorise the Home Secretary to prohibit its use? This is what the Home Secretary had in fact done by a ministerial regulation. Jowitt thought that the Home Secretary had acted beyond his powers, but he also though that the Lord Chancellor, Lord Kilmuir, might not be willing to accept without argument the opinion of one of his predecessors. So Jowitt obtained counsel's opinion from Mr Brian MacKenna, QC as he then was. Lord Kilmuir was deeply impressed, and a subsequent debate in the House of Lords[8] gave Jowitt such support that the Government refused to stand over what the Home Secretary had done. Another neglected source of law is the reported arguments of counsel. These are fortunately still published in the Law Reports. They often display great scholarly research. The argument for the losing side will show, as sharply as any dissenting judgment, how far the decision of the majority has gone.

My eye was caught by a sentence in something published by Sir Otto Kahn-Freund, the second Blackstone Lecturer, in a volume published over 25 years ago entitled *Law and Opinion in England in the Twentieth Century*. Sir Otto, after dealing with *Allen* v *Flood*[9] which, he asserted, displayed a liberal, non-interventionist policy on the part of the judiciary towards trade unions, wrote (and the sentence was repeated 20 years later in his *Selected Writings*): 'In 1901, however, the composition of the House of Lords had changed and a regulative policy prevailed.' This, of course, referred to *Quinn* v *Leathem*.[10] Opposite the words 'the composition of the House of Lords had changed,' I had pencilled 'No.' I remember wondering that such an error should have been made by one who 'combined high speculative power with exact and comprehensive knowledge of detail,' to use Warden Fisher's happy phrase about F W Maitland.[11] Indeed Kahn-Freund is perhaps the only jurist since Maitland of whom this could be properly said.

There are certainly many examples in the history of scholarship of the errors of great men being copied by their successors. Something like this may have happened here. Recently two much respected publications on labour law stated clearly that the tribunal which decided *Quinn* v *Leathem* was differently composed from that which decided *Allen* v *Flood*.[12]

---

[8]   195 H L Deb, col 20.
[9]   [1898] AC 1.
[10] [1901] AC 495.
[11] *Constitutional History*, p vi.
[12] *Rookes* v *Barnard* [1964] AC 1229, 1216.

Quinn v *Leathem is* of course a very difficult case. Over 20 years ago Lord Devlin doubted whether 'even today, it is possible to say with certainty what *Quinn* v *Leathem* decided.'[13] The statement is also true of *Allen* v *Flood*. But I am not concerned with rules or doctrines or principles, rather with the process whereby the rule or doctrine or principle has been produced. In other words with the question: who decided the case? So let me blow the cobwebs off some people's copies of the Law Reports. As every law student knows, in December 1897 nine Law Lords delivered judgment allowing by a majority of six to three the appeal of the trade union official Allen in an action brought against him by Flood and Taylor.

. . .

It may be worth considering the 21 judges under five different headings:

1) Age
2) Educational background
3) Ethnic background
4) Legal background
5) Political background

Some social historians, working on prime facie assumptions, would say that those who decided for the plaintiffs and against the defendant trade union official would have been older, Chancery lawyers, English, from a privileged social or educational background, and having sat in the House of commons – of course as Tories or Liberal Unionists. In contrast, those who decided in favour of the defendant union official might have been thought to be younger, common lawyers, from a minority racial and social background, and pure lawyers uncontaminated by political experience. On four out of these five headings a social historian would be wrong. On age alone do the facts give him some support. Only three of these 21 judges had been born in the reign of Victoria (Herschell, Wright and Kennedy). The other 18 were not Victorians. Two had been born in the reign of George III; nine in that of George IV, and seven in that of William IV. Of the 21 judges only two (Wright and Kennedy) were under the age of 60 at the date of the hearing in December 1897. By contrast 30 years earlier in *Rylands* v *Fletcher*, of the 11 judges who delivered judgments, only one (Cranworth) was over the age of 60 at the date of the judgment. The average age of the six judges in the Court of Exchequer chamber was 59. Furthermore, three of these had been appointed when very young – Willes and Blackburn in their early 40's.

It is clear that the older judges were against the Boilermakers' Union – this was certainly true of Esher, born in the year of Waterloo, Hawkins, born in 1817, and Halsbury, born in 1823. Although at the date of the appeal Halsbury was a mere 74, he was to go on to sit at the age of 93 in 1916 – a record which has so far remained unbeaten. In the Court of Appeal the average age was 70 and in the House of Lords

---

[13] See Heydon (1978) *Economic Torts*, p51; Davies and Freedland, *Labour Law*, (2nd edn), p148
Rookes v *Barnard* [1964] AC 1129, 1216.

the average age of the three Law Lords in favour of upholding the Court of Appeal was 68 – exactly the same as that of the six High Court judges who also voted for the plaintiff.

On the other hand the average age of the six Law Lords in favour of the boilermakers was only 66 – the same age as that of Mr Justice Mathew, while Mr Justice Wright was a mere 58.

Secondly, what deductions can be made from the educational background of the 21 judges? (In pre-1914 England this would have been almost equivalent to their social background.) To my surprise, I found that no fewer than four of the 21 judges had been undergraduates at Trinity College, Dublin; Oxford had five; Cambridge, Edinburgh and London had two each. The other six had not been to any university. Of those who were graduates none had taken a degree in law. Nearly all the judges came from the professional middle classes to which the exhaustive researches of the late Dan Duman have attributed the vast bulk of the Victorian judges. But there were two exceptions at opposite ends of the spectrum – Lord Herschell and Lord Macnaghten. Lord Herschell alone came from a disadvantaged background. His father was an immigrant Polish Jew, and like Arthur Cohen, he had to go to University College, London, rather than to Oxford or Cambridge. As Gladstone's Solicitor General he was offered the Woolsack in 1886 when the senior law officer refused it on grounds of conscience. Herschell, like Arthur Cohen, would have had no difficulty in sympathising with a minority; he strongly supported Home Rule, and as has been seen fervently supported the rights of the trade union official. As for Lords Morris and Ashbourne, it would be pleasant to record that these two graduates of Trinity College, Dublin, enjoyed a good reputation as jurists. But they did not. Morris was distinguished by the fact that he was the only judge on the Irish bench in the late nineteenth century who never received a threatening letter. Ashbourne, who held the Great Seal of Ireland for the record period of 17 years, was recorded by Halsbury's successor, Lord Loreburn, as 'useless or worse – I have to struggle to keep him away from the House of Lords.' But this biographer mentions that 'he was shrewd, and he looked wise' – not bad qualities for a trial judge.

The third category (ethnic background) follows on logically from the second. The Celtic fringe, if they may be so described, were divided. Lords Morris and Ashbourne were for the shipwrights. Lord Macnaghten and Watson and Shand were for the boilermakers. So also was Mr Justice Mathew, one of the High Court judges summoned to advise.

W H DAVIES
The Inquest [14]
(1871–1940)

I took my oath I would inquire,
Without affection, hate, or wrath,
Into the death of Ada Wright –
So help me God! I took that oath.

When I went out to see the corpse,
The four months' babe that died so young,
I judged it was seven pounds in weight,
And little more than one foot long.

One eye, that had a yellow lid,
Was shut – so was the mouth, that smiled;
The left eye open, shining bright –
It seemed a knowing little child.

For as I looked at that one eye,
It seemed to laugh, and say with glee:
'What caused my death you'll never know –
Perhaps my mother murdered me.'

When I went into court again,
To hear the mother's evidence –
It was a love-child, she explained.
And smiled, for our intelligence.

'Now, Gentlemen of the Jury,' said
The coroner – 'this woman's child
By misadventure met its death.'
'Aye, aye,' said we. The mother smiled.

And I could see that child's one eye
Which seemed to laugh, and say with glee:
'What caused my death you'll never know –
Perhaps my mother murdered me.'

[14] Davies, W H (1940) 'The Inquest'. In *Collected Poems*. Reprinted (1962) in *Georgian Poetry*, ed Reeves, Penguin, London.

12. AMERICAN REALISM

O W HOLMES
The Common Law [1]
(1881)

The life of the law has not been logic: it has been experience. The felt necessities of the time, the prevalent moral and political theories, intuitions of public policy, avowed or unconscious, even the prejudices which judges share with their fellow-men, have had a good deal more to do than the syllogism in determining the rules by which men should be governed. The law embodies the story of a nation's development through many centuries, and it cannot be dealt with as if it contained only the axioms and corollaries of a book of mathematics. In order to know what it is, we must know what it has been, and what it tends to become. We must alternately consult history and existing theories of legislation. But the most difficult labour will be to understand the combination of the two into new products at every stage. The substance of the law at any given time pretty nearly corresponds, so far as it goes, with what is then understood to be convenient; but its form and machinery, and the degree to which it is able to work out desired results, depend very much upon its past.

O W HOLMES
The Path of the Law [2]
(1897)

Take the fundamental question. What constitutes the law? You will find some text writers telling you that it is something different from what is decided by the courts of Massachusetts or England, that it is a system of reason, that it is a deduction from principles of ethics or admitted axioms or what not, which may or may not coincide with the decisions. But if we take the view of our friend the bad man we shall find that he does not care two straws for the axioms or deductions, but that he

---

[1] Holmes, O W (1881) *The Common Law*. Harvard University Press, Massachussetts, p1.
[2] Holmes, O W 'The Path of the Law' (1897) *10 Harvard Law Review 457*.

does want to know what the Massachusetts or English courts are likely to do in fact. I am much of his mind. The prophecies of what the courts will do in fact, and nothing more pretentious, are what I mean by the law.

J FRANK
Law and the Modern Mind [3]
(English ed 1949)

Actually, these so-called realists have but one common bond, a negative characteristic already noted: scepticism as to some of the conventional legal theories, a scepticism stimulated by a zeal to reform, in the interest of justice, some courthouse ways. Despite the lack of any homogeneity in their positive views, these 'constructive sceptics,' roughly speaking, do divide into two groups; however, there are marked differences, ignored by the critics, between the two groups.

The first group, of whom Llewellyn is perhaps the outstanding representative, I would call 'rule sceptics.' They aim at greater legal certainty. That is, they consider it socially desirable that lawyers should be able to predict to their clients the decisions in most lawsuits not yet commenced. They feel that, in too many instances, the layman cannot act with assurance as to how, if his acts become involved in a suit, the court will decide. As these sceptics see it, the trouble is that the formal legal rules enunciated in courts' opinions – sometimes called 'paper rules' – too often prove unreliable as guides in the prediction of decisions. They believe that they can discover, behind the 'paper rules,' some 'real rules' descriptive of uniformities or regularities in actual judicial behaviour, and that those 'real rules' will serve as more reliable prediction-instruments, yielding a large measure of workable predictability of the outcome of future suits. In this undertaking, the rule sceptics concentrate almost exclusively on upper-court opinions. They do not ask themselves whether their own or any other prediction-device will render it possible for a lawyer or layman to prophesy, before an ordinary suit is instituted or comes to trial in a trial court, how it will be decided. In other words, these rule sceptics seek means for making accurate guesses, not about decisions of trial courts, but about decisions of upper courts when trial-court decisions are appealed. These sceptics cold-shoulder the trial courts. Yet, in most instances, these sceptics do not inform their readers that they are writing chiefly of upper courts.

The second group I would call 'fact sceptics.' They, too, engaging in 'rule scepticism,' peer behind the 'paper rules.' Together with the rule sceptics, they have stimulated interest in factors, influencing upper-court decisions, of which, often, the opinions of those courts give no hint. But the fact sceptics go much further. Their

[3] Frank J (1949) *Law and the Modern Mind*, English edn Stevens and Sons Ltd, London, pp732-736.

primary interest is in the trial courts. No matter how precise or definite may be the formal legal rules, say these fact sceptics, no matter what the discoverable uniformities behind these formal rules, nevertheless it is impossible, and will always be impossible, because of the elusiveness of the facts on which decisions turn, to predict future decisions in most (not all) lawsuits, not yet begun or not yet tried. The fact sceptics, thinking that therefore the pursuit of greatly increased legal certainty is, for the most part, futile – and that its pursuit, indeed may well work injustice – aim rather at increased judicial justice. This group of fact sceptics includes, among others, Dean Leon Green, Max Radin, Thurman Arnold, William O Douglas (now Mr Justice Douglas), and perhaps E M Morgan.

Within each of these groups there is diversity of opinion as to many ideas. But I think it can be said that, generally, most of the rule sceptics, restricting themselves to the upper-court level, live in an artificial two dimensional legal world, while the legal world of the fact sceptics is three-dimensional. Obviously, many events occurring in the fact sceptics' three-dimensional cosmos are out of sight, and therefore out of mind, in the rule sceptics' cosmos.

The critical anti-sceptics also live in the artificial upper-court world. Naturally, they have found less fault with the rule sceptics than with the fact sceptics. The critics, for instance, said that Llewellyn was a bit wild yet not wholly unsound, but the men like Dean Green grossly exaggerated the extent of legal uncertainty (ie the unpredictability of decisions). To my mind, the critics shoe the wrong foot: Both the rule sceptics and the critics grossly exaggerate the extent of legal certainty, because their own writings deal only with the prediction of upper-court decisions. The rule sceptics are, indeed, but the left-wing adherents of a tradition. It is from the tradition itself that the fact sceptics revolted.

As a reading of this book will disclose, I am one of the fact sceptics. The point there made may be summarized thus: If one accepts as correct the conventional description of how courts reach their decisions, then a decision of any lawsuit results from the application of a legal rule or rules to the facts of the suit. That sounds rather simple, and apparently renders it fairly easy to prophesy the decision, even of a case not yet commenced or tried, especially when as often happens, the applicable rule is definite and precise (for instance, the rule about driving on the right side of the road). But particularly when pivotal testimony at the trial is oral and conflicting, as it is in most lawsuits, the trial court's 'finding' of the facts involves a multitude of elusive factors: First, the trial judge in a non-jury trial or the jury in a jury trial must learn about the facts from the witnesses; and witnesses, being humanly fallible, frequently make mistakes in observation of what they saw and heard, or in their recollections of what they observed, or in their court-room reports of those recollections. Second, the trial judges or juries, also human, may have prejudices – often unconscious unknown even to themselves – for or against some of the witnesses, or the parties to the suit, or the lawyers.

Those prejudices, when they are racial, religious, political, or economic, may sometimes be surmised by others. But there are some hidden, unconscious biases of trial judges or jurors – such as, for example, plus or minus reactions to women, or unmarried women, or red-haired women, or brunettes, or men with deep voices or high-pitched voices, or fidgety men, or men who wear thick eyeglasses, or those who have pronounced gestures or nervous tics – biases of which no one can be aware. Concealed and highly idiosyncratic, such biases – peculiar to each individual judge or juror – cannot be formulated as uniformities or squeezed into regularized 'behaviour patterns.' In that respect, neither judges nor jurors are standardized.

The chief obstacle to prophesying a trial-court decision is, then, the inability, thanks to these inscrutable factors, to foresee what a particular trial judge or jury will believe to be the facts. Consider, particularly, the perplexity of a lawyer asked to guess the outcome of a suit not yet commenced: He must guess whether some of the witnesses will persuasively lie, or will honestly but persuasively give inaccurate testimony; as, usually, he does not even know the trial judge or jury who will try the case, he must also guess the reactions – to the witnesses, the parties and the lawyers – of an unknown trial judge or jury.

These difficulties have been overlooked by most of those (the rule sceptics included) who write on the subject of legal certainty or the prediction of decisions. They often call their writings 'jurisprudence'; but, as they almost never consider juries and jury trials, one might chide them for forgetting 'jurisprudence.'

Moreover, most of them overlook another feature, not revealed in the conventional description of how courts decide cases, a feature unusually baffling: According to the conventional description, judging in a trial court is made up of two components which, initially distinct, are logically combined to produce a decision. Those components, it is said, are (1) the determination of the facts and (2) the determination of what rules should be applied to those facts. In reality, however, those components often are not distinct but intertwine in the thought processes of the trial judge or jury. The decision is frequently an undifferentiated composite which precedes any analysis or breakdown into facts and rules. Many a time, for all anyone can tell, a trial judge makes no such analysis or breakdown when rendering his decision unaccompanied by an explanation. But even when he publishes an explanation, it may be misdescriptive of the way in which the decision was reached.

Shutting their eyes to the actualities of trials, most of the lawyers who write for other lawyers or for laymen about the courts are victims of the Upper-Court Myth. They have deluded themselves and, alas, many non-lawyers, with two correlated false beliefs: (1) They believe that the major cause of legal uncertainty is uncertainty in the rules, so that if the legal rules – or the 'real rules' behind the 'paper rules' – are entirely clear and crisp, the doubts about future decisions largely vanish. (2) They believe that, on appeals, most mistakes made by trial courts can be rectified by the upper courts. In truth, as noted above, the major cause of legal uncertainty is fact-uncertainty – the unknowability, before the decision, of what the trial court will 'find' as the facts, and the unknowability after the decision of the way in which it 'found' those facts. If a trial court mistakenly takes as true the oral testimony of an honest but inaccurate witness or a lying witness, seldom can an upper court detect this mistake; it therefore usually adopts the facts as found by the trial court. It does so because the trial court saw and heard the witnesses testify, while the upper court has before it only a lifeless printed report of the testimony, a report that does not contain the witnesses' demeanor, which is often significantly revealing. ...

With this perspective, we get new light on the doctrine of following the precedents. ... That doctrine ... may have less practical importance to the ordinary man than its more ardent advocates accord it. Yet no sane informed person will deny that, within appropriate limits, judicial adherence to precedents possesses such great value that to abandon it would be unthinkable. ...

However, even when properly and conscientiously utilized, the practice of following the precedents cannot guarantee the stability and certainty it seems to promise to some of those who confine their scrutiny to upper-court decisions. For, in an upper court, ordinarily no fact finding problem exists, as the facts are beyond dispute, having already been found by the trial court. The usual questions for the upper court are, then, these: Do the facts of the case now before the court sufficiently resemble those of an earlier case so that the rule of that case is applicable? If there is such a resemblance, should that rule now be applied or should it be modified or abandoned? Although able lawyers cannot always guess how an upper court will answer those questions, the educated guesses of those lawyers are good in the majority of instances. When, in a trial court, the parties to a suit agree on the facts, so that the facts are undisputed, that court faces only those same questions; and again, usually, able lawyers can guess the answers.

But, to repeat, in most cases in the trial courts the parties do dispute about the facts, and the testimony concerning the facts is oral and conflicting. In any such case, what does it mean to say that the facts of a case are substantially similar to those of an earlier case? It means, at most, merely that the trial court regards the facts of the two cases as about the same. Since, however, no one knows what the trial court will find as the facts, no one can guess what precedent ought to be or will be followed either by the trial court or, if an appeal occurs, by the upper court. This weakness of the precedent doctrine becomes more obvious when one takes into account the 'composite' factor, the intertwining of rules and facts in the trial court's decision.

This weakness will also infect any substitute precedent system, based on 'real rules' which the rule sceptics may discover, by way of anthropology – ie the mores, customs, folkways – or psychology, or statistics, or studies of the political, economic, and social backgrounds of judges, or otherwise. For no rule can be hermetically sealed against the intrusion of false or inaccurate oral testimony which the trial judge or jury may believe.

J FRANK
Courts on Trial [4]
(1949)

... I have raised doubts about the adequacy of several assumptions of traditional legal thinking, pointing out that, unless so qualified by exceptions as to be all but meaningless, they are out of line with courtroom happenings. I have also smoked out some concealed assumptions, and have attempted to disclose inconsistencies between them and those that are acknowledged. Here is a list of some of the old 'axioms' ...

1) The 'personal element' in the judicial process should not and usually does not have much effect on either legal rights or court decisions. Even if we admit that the 'personalities' of witnesses, lawyers, jurors and judges do have considerable effect, we must disregard all elements of those 'personalities' which are not fairly uniform.
2) The legal rules are the dominant factor in decision-making.
3) When those rules are precise, they ordinarily prevent litigation; and, if litigation does occur, it will be easy to predict the decisions.
4) Trial judges and juries have only the limited discretion conferred by the legal rules; they have no discretion when those rules are precise.
5) Decisions result from the application of legal rules to the actual facts involved in law-suits.
6) If the actual facts of two cases are the same, usually the decisions in those cases will be identical.
7) Trial courts usually discover the actual facts of cases; usually 'the truth will out'; innocent men are hardly ever convicted; seldom does a man lose his property or his means of livelihood because of a court's mistaken notion of the facts.
8) The intense fighting method of conducting trials is the best aid in discovering those facts.
9) Effective criticism of most decisions is easy.
10) Upper courts can, and do, correct most of the mistakes of trial courts.
11) Upper courts are far more important than trial courts.
12) Less attention need be paid to the selection of trial judges than to that of upper court judges.
13) Almost any man licensed to practice as a lawyer is qualified to be a trial judge.
14) Juries are better fact-finders than judges.
15) Juries are better at rule-making and rule-revising than judges.
16) It is desirable that juries should ignore any legal rules they deem undesirable.

[4] Frank, J N (1949) *Courts on Trial*. Princeton University Press, pp736-737.

17) In lawsuits (whether or not tried by juries) legal rules relating to property and commercial transactions are precise and usually lead to predictable decisions.

18) Individualization of cases, if desirable, should be accomplished surreptitiously, not openly.

19) The method of following precedents, if properly used, ensures certainty and stability, supplies rules on which men can safely rely.

20) Trial courts, in fact finding, have little to do with the interpretation of statutes.

21) Non-lawyers should be deceived into believing that the results of the judicial process are more certain, regular, uniform and just than in truth they are or can be.

22) Law students should not be persuaded to observe at first-hand what goes on in trial and law offices.

23) The attempt to obtain legal certainty (ie predictability of decisions) is more important than the attempt to obtain just decisions of specific law suits.

I suggest that the reader ask himself which the opposite of each of those old assumptions will not, directly or indirectly, click better with what can be observed in the legal realm, and, in some instances, call attention to ignored aspects of courthouse doings.

One major defect of the traditional legal assumptions is that those who use them mix up two attitudes: (a) 'This is true.' (b) 'This should be true.' The users, without knowing it, slide back and forth between saying, 'This is what now happens in courts.' and 'This is what I would like to have happen in courts,' between a description of the existent and a program for the future.

LEE LOEVINGER
Jurimetrics – The Next Step Forward [5]
(1949)

It is one of the greatest anomalies of modern times that the law, which exists as a public guide to conduct, has become such a recondite mystery that it is incomprehensible to the public and scarcely intelligible to its own votaries. The rules which are supposed to be the guides to action of men living in society have become the secret cult of a group of priestly professionals. The mystic ritual of this cult is announced to the public, if at all, only in a bewildering jargon. Daily the law becomes more complex, citizens become more confused, and society becomes less cohesive. Of Course, people do not respect that which they can neither understand nor see in effective operation. So the lawmongers bemoan the lack of respect for law. Now the lawyers are even bewailing the lack of respect for lawyers.

Many remedies are proposed: We must have better law enforcement – that is, more policemen to make the people obey the laws they do not understand. We must

[5] From 33 *Minnesotta Law Review* 455.

have a great moral renascence – presumably some sort of mystical process which will enable people intuitively to apprehend the mysteries of law. We need better education – catch 'em young, and teach them to respect the law while they're still credulous and uncritical. We ought to pass a new law to make people respect the old laws – ignorance of the law is no excuse, even for lawyers. We need better 'public relations' between the lawyers and the public – which simply means that the lawyers want to advertise like everybody else. There is a school of support for every proposal except the one that it is the law itself which needs to be changed. ...

Because jurisprudence has set the pattern for legal thinking, and because jurisprudence has been concerned with trying to answer meaningless questions by futile speculation, the law has proceeded very largely on a priori grounds and has adapted itself to social needs only under great pressure and very slowly. The lawyers have, in fact, so bemused themselves with words and theories that they have not even yet developed anything like a rational system for performing their principal function of deciding particular controversies. Most decisions are presented behind a verbal facade that is cast in the syllogistic form. But it requires little sophistication to demonstrate that the logical form has little to do with judicial decisions.

The terms which apply to [a] case are selected only after the result has been decided. But the choice of legal terms to describe an act is certainly not a 'logical' operation. Where it is not purely arbitrary, it is, at most, intuitive. Thus, by present methods, the determination of every genuine legal issue is made at the sub-verbal (and usually sub-conscious) level, where formal 'logic' can neither exist nor exert influence.

Recognition of the fact that lawsuits are not decided by logic is not new. Bentham suggested as much, and Holmes said it. More recently, Frank, Arnold and others have elaborated the point. But here the modern movement has bogged down. Frank insists that uncertainty is inherent in the legal process, and that the grasping for certainty in general principles is simply an expression of infantile emotional attitudes which have persisted into adulthood. Arnold finds the explanation of the inconsistencies and absurdities of the law in the fact that all our social institutions are mere symbols of our dreams and aspirations. But all this is merely a continuation of the ancient quest for the philosopher's stone. The new school seeks it in some scientific, rather than some moral, explanation or principle, but the fallacy is the same. This is simply a new jurisprudence with a new vocabulary. The argument seeks to substitute a modern analysis for an ancient one, but the traditional techniques are still in use. It is all armchair speculation.

... The only important area of human activity which has developed no significant new methods in the last twenty centuries is law.

... If we would increase our knowledge and have some chance of arriving at an intelligent solution to our problems, it is essential that we adopt scientific methods of inquiry. ...

13. SCANDINAVIAN REALISM

KARL OLIVECRONA
Law as Fact [1]
(1971)

FINDING A STARTING POINT

The purpose of this book is to explain the nature of what we call the law of a human community. The interest is focused on the situation typically prevailing in modern Western society. So-called international law is, on the whole, left outside the scope of the investigation. Ancient forms of law are only occasionally considered.

A difficulty immediately appears when we propose to elucidate the nature of the law. That is how to avoid circularity.

The object of inquiry is said to be 'the law' of a modern community. But does not this imply some knowledge of what the law is? How else could any object of inquiry be designated by this expression? But then the inquiry seems to presuppose previous knowledge of its object.

We are apparently caught in a dilemma. One seems to be unable to define the object of investigation without already being familiar with it.

Not surprisingly, therefore, works on the nature of the law often begin with a definition of the concept of law. If a definition is not proffered, a concept of law is usually presupposed as a necessary starting point.

The dilemma has not escaped observation. It has been noted and accepted as unavoidable. This, for instance, is the position of the German jurist-philosopher Ernst Bierling. He expressly says that a definition of the law must be part of the introduction to a treatise on the principles of jurisprudence though it can only be the result of a whole series of investigations.[2] You must know beforehand what you can only know on the basis of your studies.

If such were really the case, the science of the nature of the law would be in an awkward position. It would of necessity have to move in a circle. What purpose could it then serve? And if different authors start from different suppositions concerning the law, as they actually do, how could it be ascertained which view, if

---

[1] Olivecrona, Karl (1971) *Law as Fact*, 2nd edn. Stevens, London, pp1-6, 217-219, 220-221, 253-254.
[2] *Juristitsche Prinzipienlehre* (1894-1917, reprinted in 1961) 19.

any, would be the correct one? The science of the nature of the law would seem to be lost in a quagmire.

Such a defeatist view is not warranted. It should be possible here, as well as in other branches of science, to define the object of inquiry without anticipating the result. This means framing the questions without making any assumption concerning the answer.

In raising a scientific question one always starts from something which is supposed to be known. The question is called forth by an unpleasant feeling of having a gap in our knowledge. It is an incitement to make a search in order to fill the gap. The investigator is like an explorer standing on the frontier of new country, never trod by human feet. He assumes that the earth does not abruptly cease at the horizon but stretches forth with plains or hills or water as it may be. He sets his course by means of the compass and goes to see what is to be found there.

Let us take an example from natural science. When the investigation of lightning began, before the time of Benjamin Franklin, the situation can be supposed to have been of roughly the following kind.

A certain celestial phenomenon called lightning was well known. People had many times seen a flash in the skies followed by thunder; this was called lightning. When some curiosity concerning the nature of this phenomenon began to be felt, one could first ask whether it usually appears under special atmospheric conditions, at certain times of the year, at localities with peculiar geological properties, and so on. What was known from the start was the celestial spectacle as it appeared to the eye. Its relationship to some other known phenomena such as changes in the weather and the composition of the soil was the first object of investigation. No assumption concerning the result had to be made.

Curiosity was further extended to the causes of the flash of light and the thunder. The general advance of natural science made it possible to relate the celestial occurrences to other known phenomena, especially to the newly discovered manifestations of electricity, and to the laws of light and sound. Hypotheses were formed and tried experimentally. This did not mean that any results of the inquiries were anticipated. A working hypothesis is a guess concerning the unknown made on the basis of some known facts with the intention of its being verified or falsified by experiments. Like the explorer's compass, a hypothesis serves to indicate the direction of the investigation and to give it a systematic character. As the science of lightning and natural science in general proceeded, new hypotheses could be formed on a broader basis of known facts.

An assumption concerning the causes of the light and the thunder was made when these phenomena were ascribed to the action of a god who threw a thunderbolt in anger to punish human beings. This was no working hypothesis. It was an assertion concerning reality based on pure speculation, and it could lead nowhere. As long as it was held to include the explanation of lightning, no progress in knowledge could be made.

When we propose to investigate the nature of 'the law' we cannot start from some visual impressions as happened with the study of lightning. A 'law' is not to be seen, nor is a 'right' or an 'obligation'. But we know that people talk of laws and rights and obligations.

The man in the street may lack pretensions to any particular knowledge of 'the law'. Nevertheless, his mind is stocked with a considerable supply of 'legal' or 'juristic' notions, and he makes use of many 'legal' terms in his daily life. He holds that he is a 'citizen' of a 'country' (a 'kingdom' or a 'republic') with its own 'government' and 'parliament' or 'diet'. He knows that certain texts called 'laws' are issued by these authorities. How this is done he probably does not know in detail; his ideas on the subject may be very dim. But when the papers announce that some new 'law' affecting his trade has been brought into being, he takes it for granted that everything has been done in the right way. He takes care to make himself acquainted with the new law; for he knows that everyone has to obey it; unpleasant consequences are likely to occur if the law is disregarded.

Furthermore, our man is firmly convinced that he has a number of 'rights' and 'duties'. He 'owns' a house where he lives with his family; but he has a 'loan' from the 'bank' on which he must pay 'interest'. He is obliged to pay 'taxes', to send his children to school, and to do a lot of other things. He has the right to 'vote' at the 'elections', to be 'paid' for his work, to get his old age 'pension', and so on. In case of a dispute with another man about his own right and the other man's duty, he can go to a 'court' to have the matter settled by a 'judgment'.

The legal notions are not of importance for the day's activities only. In the evening, when the citizen listens to the radio or looks at his TV, he will not be able to understand the news unless he is familiar with the existence of other countries which have their respective governments and 'boundaries'. Even when he bids good night to his 'wife' a legal notion is involved.

The common language and the content of the common mind may serve as a starting point for our investigation. We have some immediate knowledge of these things just as people had some immediate knowledge of the celestial phenomena from which the study of lightning once began. We therefore have the necessary factual basis from which the inquiry may proceed.

The course of the inquiry may be set in different directions. One possibility is to study the common mind itself by analysing its notions and tracing their history. This could lead to a more extended knowledge of our ideas concerning 'the law' and the language used to express them. The object of the inquiry could be described as legal ideology.

Another possible course is to go beyond the common mind and ask what empirical realities we find where the legal notions are applied. This inquiry is not concerned with ideology but with objective facts.

We can ask, for instance, what we find where people say that a 'frontier' exists between two countries. On the map a line is drawn; the land on the one side is called country A, the land on the other side country B. If we proceed to the localities corresponding to the map, we may find different things: some heaps of stones at regular intervals, a clearing in the forest, a stretch of barbed wire, a road block. We are told that these different things are supposed to mark out the border-line on the ground. As the arrangements are obviously not made for fun, we ask what purpose they serve. The answer is that the frontier has to be made perceptible to people because it is of importance in many ways: one must not cross the frontier without a passport, a sum of money must be paid for certain goods brought from the one country to the other, the 'police' and other 'authorities' are different on both sides of the frontier, and above all there are different military establishments on each side. One can go on to ask how the frontier has come to be drawn in this way. It appears to be the result of a 'peace treaty'. Furthermore, we may ask why the proclamation of a 'frontier' in that way can have such effects as have been described. The treaty was made by the 'representatives' of two 'states' and was supposed to end a 'war'. For some reasons which have to be studied the conclusion of the treaty has exerted a profound influence on the behaviour of people. Furthermore, we are told that the significance of the frontier is regulated by 'legislation'. Now a great many questions emerge: what happens where people talk of legislation, what exists where we speak of a state, and so on. One question leads to another without end.

In a corresponding way we can start the investigation from another point. We may ask, for instance, what actual situation we find in the case where somebody is said to be the 'owner' of an object, what situation we find when somebody is held to have a 'monetary claim' against somebody else, what a 'court of justice' is, or what a 'judgment' by such a court is. Whatever point of departure is chosen, we are soon led to the same questions about the 'state', its 'representatives', its 'legislation', and so on. New facts are collected and related to previously known facts. Thus the range of our knowledge is successively enlarged. The investigation proceeds step by step from known facts. No assumption is made concerning what is not yet known.

A third course of inquiry would be to begin with the theories about the nature of 'the law' and try to ascertain their content of truth. This would eventually lead us to the same questions as were just mentioned.

One feature is common to all three courses of inquiry. At the beginning, current notions and current language about the state and legislation, about rights and obligations, are taken as facts. From these the search is started. We do not pretend to have any previous knowledge as to what the state is, what legislation means, or what a right or an obligation is. What we know is the way people talk about these things. Therefore no circularity occurs.

Of the three courses of inquiry the last one offers certain advantages. It is better to start with the more precise ideas of acute and learned jurists and philosophers than with the more vague notions of the common mind. The point of departure will then be the present position of legal theory.

The theories of law are usually divided into two groups which carry the names of natural law theory and legal positivism. For the most part this classification is taken to be exhaustive; every theory of law is put into the one group or the other.

The term natural law theory is usually applied to every theory in which a 'law of nature' is supposed to exist and which is concerned with the elucidation of this law. Such theories have been known from Antiquity to our time. The theories collected under the name of legal positivism have in common the rejection of the notion of a natural law. They are of comparatively recent origin. If we disregard certain precursory views in Antiquity, legal positivism began to appear in the eighteenth century and gained strength during the nineteenth century. It largely superseded natural law theory and was for a long time widely regarded as *the* scientific theory of law. During recent decades, however, a remarkable renaissance of natural law theory has taken place.

A common characteristic of the theories reckoned as belonging to legal positivism is the tendency to realism. It seems suitable, therefore, to begin the investigation with a scrutiny of legal positivism. But legal positivism emerged in opposition to natural law theory. It has to be seen against the background of the idea of a 'natural' law as the basis of 'positive' law.

. . .

LEGAL PERFORMATIVES

It has long been recognised that besides sentences expressing statements there are sentences expressing questions, exclamations, commands, wishes, or concessions. ... There are other possibilities of interpreting such statements. To overlook these possibilities is usually called the 'descriptive' fallacy.

These reflections are not least applicable to legal language. We use a great many 'apparently descriptive statements' ostensibly indicating some 'odd additional feature in the reality reported'. Statements about rights are a case in point. ... Indeed, all talk about law is of this nature: governments, legislation, administration, offices in the state organisation, marriage, guardianship, juridical persons, etc. It pervades common discourse as well as the technical language of jurists.

Ostensibly to bring about these 'additional features' a peculiar form of speech is being employed. ... Making use of the term 'performatives' ('performative utterances') the expressions characteristic of this language, were called 'performatory imperatives'; ... The study of the expressions in question is essential for understanding legal language.

Performatives as imperatives

As an example of a performative utterance the case of a person appointed to name a ship pronouncing the phrase 'I name this ship the *Queen Elizabeth*' when smashing a bottle of champagne against the bows. Another example is taken from the marriage ceremony: 'I take this woman to be my lawful wedded wife'. A third example is the sentence occurring in a will: 'I give and bequeath my watch to my brother'.

Grammatically, these utterances are in the indicative. But the form of language is misleading. The meaning of the utterances is not to state a fact. What the person naming the ship wants to say is: 'the name of this ship shall be the *Queen Elizabeth*!' In the marriage ceremony the sense of the formula used by the bridegroom is: 'this woman shall be my lawful wedded wife!' The testator means to say: 'the right of property to my watch shall be transferred to my brother!'

Thus the meaning of the sentences is that something shall be brought about: the ship shall get a name, the bridegroom a wife, and the brother the right of property to a watch. The sentences are veiled imperatives. ...

But if they are really imperatives, these imperatives seem to be of a strange nature. They are not addressed to another person: nobody is commanded to do, or forbear from doing something when it is said that a particular word shall be the name of the ship, that the woman shall be the wife of the bridegroom, or that the watch shall be the property of the brother. The imperatives are intended to call forth the effects that the ship is to carry the name of ..., the woman to be the wife of the man, and the watch to belong to the brother. These effects are supposed to follow from the pronunciation of the imperatives in question provided this is done in the right circumstances: and as it seems, the imperatives would make no sense if the effects could not take place.

Two questions arise with regard to these imperatives. (i) Can there be an imperative without an addressee? (ii) Can any other effect than a psychological one be called forth through an imperative?

IMPERATIVES WITHOUT AN ADDRESSEE

It is only a preconception that an imperative must enjoin some behaviour on an addressee. The language abounds with imperatives of other kinds. There are, for instance, imperatives imposing a feeling on an addressee, such as: 'Love thy neighbour!' But here we are concerned only with imperatives which lack an addressee.

We find such an imperative in the first chapter of Genesis. In the beginning God said: 'Let there be light; and there was light.' The Creator did not address any human being; there was none to be addressed. Nevertheless he used the imperative form of speech. 'Let there be light' means: there shall be light. This imperative has no addressee; and it enjoins no action. The imperative is directed towards the coming into being of light.

The use of imperatives without an addressee has not been reserved for the creator of the world. They are employed in many connections; and they are especially common in legal language.

The old Roman laws contain many examples. The authority of a father over his son (the *patria potestas*) included that the father could sell the services of the son for a limited period (probably not more than five years). But when a father has sold a son thrice, the law of the XII Tables says (table IV), the son shall be free from the father. (*Si pater filium ter venum duuit, filius a patre liber esto.*) This is clearly an imperative. But it is addressed neither to the father, nor to the son or to anybody else. The imperative is directed towards a change in the status of the son: he shall be a free man! Its meaning is that a change in his status shall take place.

With regard to a patronus who has acted deceitfully towards a client (a dependent person) table VIII says that he shall be sacer. (*Patronus si clienti fraudem fecerit, sacer esto*.) There is no addressee to this imperative. Its meaning is to bring about that the deceitful *patronus* becomes *sacer*.

At the solemn act of a sale called *mancipatio*, certain conditions could be added by a pronouncement. With respect to this case table VI says that the pronouncement shall have legal force. (*Cum nexum faciet mancipiumque, uti lingua nuncupassit, ita ius esto*.) This is no command to the parties of the transactions. The provision of the law is intended to endow the pronouncement with legal validity.

According to Gaius (Inst 2, 117) a correct expression to be used in a testament was to say: Titius shall be my heir! (Titius heres esto!) The meaning is not to issue a command to anybody but to institute Titius as heir.

To take an example from my own country, we have an ancient record from the thirteenth century of the 'making' of a king. An essential element in the ceremony, performed on a meadow near Uppsala, was that the 'lawmen' of the different provinces, each in his turn, stepped forward and recited a formula saying: 'I pronounce thee to be king, I pronounce thee to possess the crown and the kingdom, to rule the land and the realm, to give strength to the law and to keep the peace.' Until recently this procedure was held to constitute the election of a king; but it is now generally recognised that this was a mistake: the ceremony represents no election. Beforehand it had been determined (in what way, we do not know) who was to be king. The ceremony was an act of investiture. When a lawman said: 'I pronounce thee to be king' this meant: 'I lay the name of a king upon thee' or: 'you shall have the name of a king!' The formula was an imperative endowing the chosen man with the name and properties of a king.

Imperatives bestowing on persons rights, powers, privileges, and legal qualities have always been used in legislation. It has seemed quite natural to employ this form of language in laying down rules and also to use it in concrete acts of investiture.

In the constitution of the USA there are many examples. Article 1, section 1, says: 'All legislative Powers herein granted shall be vested in a Congress of the United States, which shall consist of a Senate and a House of Representatives.' Article II, section 1, provides: 'The executive Power shall be vested in a President of the United States of America.'

These imperatives do not contain any orders for the behaviour of the citizens of the USA. They allocate certain powers to Congress and the President respectively.

Countless examples of similar imperatives could be gathered from all kinds of legislation. Such imperatives are also used, for instance, in nominating people to offices. Suppose a man is appointed to be a judge. This is done through a declaration of the competent authority saying, whatever words are employed: X shall be a judge. These performative imperatives are indeed so common and well known that it would be superfluous to mention further examples in support of the contention that they form part of our language.

THE EFFECT OF THE IMPERATIVES

In Genesis, the words of the Creator took effect according to their literal sense: 'Let there be light; and there was light.' The light came into being because He commanded so; and everything else on earth was created in the same way: by the commands of God.

In these cases the effects of the performatory imperatives were physical. The almighty Creator was supposed to be capable of bringing about light, and the herbs, the animals, etc, through His words.

The effects of the performatory imperatives with which we are concerned are not physical. They are 'legal' effects.

. . .

Legal language is not a descriptive language. It is a directive, influential language serving as an instrument of social control. The 'hollow' words are like sign-posts with which people have been taught to associate ideas concerning their own behaviour and that of others.

To serve as an instrument of social control legal language is, and must be, a regularised and repetitive language. The hollow words can function as sign-posts only if they are in some way 'authoritatively' established as such and used in accordance with some rules. Many words are used in a similar way outside the 'legal' sphere. The ship is named by a lady on whom 'authority' to do so has been conferred in conformity with custom; the rule that the ship should be spoken of under the name given by her is generally known and applied; everybody repeats the name when there is occasion to do so; and the ship is supposed to 'have' that name. A man is appointed judge by somebody 'empowered' according to the constitution to do so; he is then universally spoken of as being a judge; and the legal and social rules attached to the office of a judge are regularly applied with regard to him. The use of language for social control is not confined to the legal sphere; it plays an important role in most kinds of human relations.

Language may seem to be a frail instrument of social control. No wonder its efficiency in this respect was originally connected with the belief in mysterious forces that were manipulated by means of ritual phrases. Such beliefs have probably lingered for a long time. What remains of them today is difficult to say and cannot be discussed here.

With the emergence of the state the use of legal language became connected with the regularised use of organised power. Social history includes a process in which magical beliefs have slowly withered away while the supernatural sanctions have been replaced by hard and fast ones inflicted by the organs of the state.

But many more factors than magical beliefs and the use of sanctions must, of course, be taken into consideration in explaining how language serves as a means of social control. Upbringing, indoctrination, habits of thought and behaviour taken over by every new generation from the preceding one, propaganda of different kinds, etc, play their part.

Despite its apparent frailty, language is amazingly powerful as an instrument of social control – depending on the setting in which it is employed. In establishing a division of property, a monetary system, an interchange of goods on a vast scale, corporations for business and other purposes, an orderly government, etc, legal language plays a vital role. It is an instrument for keeping the peace, as well as for sending men to death on the battlefield in time of war.

14. HISTORICAL JURISPRUDENCE

F K von SAVIGNY
System of the Modern Roman Law [1]
(1840)

In the general consciousness of a people lives positive law and hence we have to call
it people's law (*Volksrecht*). It is by no means to be thought that it was the particular
members of the people by whose arbitrary will, law was brought forth; in that case
the will of individuals might perhaps have selected the same law, perhaps however
and more probably very varied laws. Rather it is the spirit of a people (Volksgeist)
living and working in common in all the individuals, which gives birth to positive
law, which therefore is to the consciousness of each individual not accidentally but
necessarily one and the same. Since therefore we acknowledge an invisible origin of
positive law we must as to that origin, renounce documentary proof: but this defect
is common to our and every other view of that origin, since we discover in all
peoples who have ever presented themselves within the limits of authentic history an
already existing positive law of which the original generation must lie beyond those
limits. There are not wanting proofs of another sort and suitable to the special
nature of the subject-matter. Such a proof lies in the universal, uniform recognition
of positive law and in the feeling of inner necessity with which its conception is
accompanied. This feeling expresses itself most definitely in the primeval assertion
of the divine origin of law or statutes; a more manifest opposition to the idea of its
arising from accident or the human will is not to be conceived. A second proof lies
in the analogy of other peculiarities of peoples which have in like manner an origin
invisible and reaching beyond authentic history, for example, social life and above all
speech. In this is found the same independence of accident and free individual
choice, the same generation from the activity of the spirit of the people working in
common in each individual; in speech too from its sensible nature, all this is more
evident and recognizable than in law. Indeed the individual nature of a particular
people is determined and recognised solely by those common directions and
activities of which speech as the most evident obtains the first place.

The form however in which law lives in the common consciousness of a people is
not that of abstract rules but as the living intuition of the institutions of law in their

[1] Von Savigny, F K (1840) 'System of the Modern Roman Law.' In *Savigny's System of Modern Roman Law,
Book II*. Translated by W H Rattigan (1884) Wildy and Sons, London, pp890-893.

organic connexion, so that whenever the necessity arises for the rules to be conceived in its logical form, this must be first formed by a scientific procedure from that total intuition. That form reveals itself in the symbolical acts which display in visible shape and essence of the jural relation and in which the primitive laws express themselves more intelligibly and thoroughly than in written laws.

In this view of the origin of positive law, we have at present kept out of sight the progress of the life of a people in time. If we now look also at this operation upon law we must above all ascribe to it an establishing force. The longer the convictions of law live in a people, the more deeply they become rooted in it. Moreover law will develop itself by use and what originally was present as a mere germ will by practice assume a definite shape to the consciousness. However in this way the changing of law is also generated. For as in the life of single men, no glimpse of complete passiveness can be perceived, but a continual organic development, so is it with the life of peoples and with each single element of which that concrete life is composed. Thus we find in speech a constant gradual shaping and development and in like manner in law. This gradual formation is subject to the same law of generation from inner power and necessity, independent of accident and individual will, as its original arising was. But the people experiences in this natural process of development, not merely a change in general, but it experiences it in a settled, regular series of events and of these each has its peculiar relation to the expression of the spirit of the people in which the law is generated. This appears in the clearest and strongest manner in the youth of a people for then the connexion is more intimate, the consciousness of it is more generally diffused and is less obscured by the variety of individual cultivation. Moreover in the same degree in which the cultivation of individuals becomes heterogeneous and predominant and in which a sharper division of employments, of acquirements, and of ranks produced by these, enters, the generation of law which rests upon the common consciousness becomes more difficult; and this mode of generation would disappear altogether if new organs for that purpose were not formed by the influence of these self-same new circumstances; these organs are legislation and the science of law of which the nature will be immediately explained.

This new development of law may have an entirely different relation to the originally existing law. New institutions of law may be generated by it, the existing law transformed or it may be entirely swept away if it has become foreign to the thought and need of the age.

The generation of law has been preliminarily posited in the people as the active, personal subject. The nature of this subject will now be more accurately defined. If in the examination of the jural relation, we remove by abstraction, all its special content, there remains over as a common nature, the united life of a plurality of men, regulated in a defined manner. We might naturally be led to stop short at this abstract conception of a plurality and regard law as its discovery, without which the external freedom of no individual could subsist, but such an accidental meeting of an indefined multitude is a conception both arbitrary and entirely wanting in truth: and even if they found themselves so met together, the capacity for producing law would be entirely wanting since with a need the power of at once supplying it, is not given. In fact we find so far as history informs us upon the matter, that wherever men live together, they stand in an intellectual communion which reveals as well as establishes and develops itself by the use of speech. In this natural whole is the seat of the generation of law and in the common intelligence of the nation penetrating individuals, is found the power of satisfying the necessity above recognised.

The boundaries however of individual nations are certainly undefined and wavering and this state of doubt also shows itself in the unity or variety of the law engendered in them. Thus as to kindred races it may appear uncertain whether they are to be regarded as one people or as several; in like manner we also frequently find in their law not an entire consonance, probably however an affinity.

Even where the unity of a people is doubted, within its limits are often found inner circles which are included in a special connexion side by side with the general union of the people, as cities and villages, guilds and corporations of every sort which altogether form popular divisions of the whole. In these circles again a special generation of law may have its seat as particular law, side by side with the general law of the nation which by that particular law is on many sides completed or altered.

When we regard the people as a natural unity and merely as the subject of positive law, we ought not to think only of the individuals comprised in that people at any particular time; that unity rather runs through generations constantly replacing one another, and thus it unites the present with the past and the future. This constant preservation of law is effected by tradition and this is conditioned by, and based upon, the not sudden but ever gradual change of generations. The independence of the life of individuals, here asserted of law, appertains first to the unchanged continuation of the rules of law: it is secondly too the foundation of the gradual formation of law and in this connexion we must ascribe to it a special importance.

This view in which the individual people is regarded as the generator and subject of positive or practical law may appear too confined to some who might be inclined to ascribe that generation rather to the general spirit of humanity than to that of a particular people. On closer examination these two views do not appear conflicting. What works in an individual people is merely the general human spirit which reveals itself in that people in a particular manner. The generation of law is a fact and one common to the whole. This is conceivable only of those, between whom a communion of thought and action is not only possible but actual. Since then such a communion exists only within the limits of an individual people so here also can practical law alone be created, although in its production, the expression of a generative principle common to men in general, is perceived, but not the peculiar will of individual peoples, of which perhaps no single trace might be found in other peoples. For this product of the people's mind is sometimes entirely peculiar to a single people, though sometimes equally present in several peoples.

SIR HENRY MAINE
Ancient Law [2]
(1930)

The movement of the progressive societies has been uniform in one respect. Through all its course it has been distinguished by the gradual dissolution of family dependency, and the growth of individual obligation in its place. The Individual is steadily substituted for the Family, as the unit of which civil laws take account. The advance has been accomplished at varying rates of celerity, and there are societies not absolutely stationary in which the collapse of the ancient organisation can only be perceived by careful study of the phenomena they present. But, whatever its pace, the change has not been subject to reaction or recoil, and apparent retardations will be found to have been occasioned through the absorption of archaic ideas and customs from some entirely foreign source. Nor is it difficult to see what is the tie between man and man which replaces by degrees those forms of reciprocity in rights and duties which have their origin in the Family. It is Contract. Starting, as from one terminus of history, from a condition of society in which all the relations of Persons are summed up in the relations of Family, we seem to have steadily moved towards a phase of social order in which all these relations arise from the free agreement of Individuals. ...

The word Status may be usefully employed to construct a formula expressing the law of progress thus indicated, which, whatever be its values, seems to me to be sufficiently ascertained. All the forms of Status taken notice of in the Law of Persons were derived from, and to some extent are still coloured by, the powers and privileges anciently residing in the Family. If then we employ Status, agreeably with the usage of the best writers, to signify these personal conditions only, and avoid applying the term to such conditions as are the immediate or remote result of agreement, we may say that the movement of the progressive societies has hitherto been a movement from *Status to Contract*.

[2] Maine, Sir Henry (1930). In *Ancient Law*, ed F Pollock. John Murray, London.

15. ANTHROPOLOGICAL JURISPRUDENCE

E A HOEBEL
Law of Primitive Man [1]
(1954)

Law performs certain functions essential to the maintenance of all but the most simple societies.

The first is to define relationships among the members of a society, to assert what activities are permitted and what are ruled out, so as to maintain at least minimal integration between the activities of individuals and groups within the society.

The second is derived from the necessity of taming naked force and directing force to the maintenance of order. It is the allocation of authority and the determination of who may exercise physical coercion as a socially recognised privilege-right, along with the selection of the most effective forms of physical sanction to achieve the social ends that the law serves.

The third is the disposition of trouble cases as they arise.

The fourth is to redefine relations between individuals and groups as the conditions of life change. It is to maintain adaptability.

Purposive definition of personal relations is the primary law-job. Other aspects of culture likewise work to this end, and, indeed, the law derives its working principles (jural postulates) previously developed in the nonlegal spheres of action. However, the law's important contribution to the basic organisation of society as a whole is that the law specifically and explicitly defines relations. It sets the expectancies of man to man and group to group so that each knows the focus and the limitations of its demand-rights on others, its duties to others, its privilege-rights and powers as against others, and its immunities and liabilities to the contemplated or attempted acts of others. This is the 'bare-bones job', as Karl Llewellyn likes to call it. It is the ordering of the fundamentals of living together.

No culture has a specific starting point in time; yet in the operation of the first function it is as though men were getting together and saying to each other, 'Look here! Let's have a little organisation here or we'll never get anywhere with this mess! Let's have a clear understanding of who's who, what we are to do, and how we are going to do it!' In its essence it is what the social-contract theorists recognised as the foundation of social order.

[1] Hoebel, E A (1954) *Law of Primitive Man*. Harvard University Press, Boston.

191

The second function of the law – the allocation of authority to exercise coercive physical force – is something almost peculiar to things legal.

Custom has regularity, and so does law. Custom defines relationships, and so does law. Custom is sanctioned, and so is law. But the sanctions of law may involve physical coercion. Law is distinguished from mere custom in that it endows certain selected individuals with the privilege-right of applying the sanction of physical coercion, if need be. The legal, let it be repeated, has teeth that can bite. But the biting, if it is to be legal and not mere gangsterism, can be done only by those persons to whom the law has allocated the privilege-right for the affair at hand.

We have seen that in primitive law authority is a shifting, temporary thing. Authority to enforce a norm resides (for private wrongs) with the wronged individual and his immediate kinsmen – but only for the duration of time necessary to follow through the procedural steps that lead to redress or punishment of the culprit. In primitive law the tendency is to allocate authority to the party who is directly injured. This is done in part out of convenience, for it is easier to let the wronged party assume the responsibility of legal action. It is also done because the primitive kinship group, having a more vital sense of entity, is naturally charged with a heavier emotional effect. In any event, when the community qua community acknowledges the exercise of force by a wronged person or his kinship group as correct and proper in a given situation, and so restrains the wrongdoer from striking back, then law prevails and order triumphs over violence.

We have also found in our studies of primitive societies that in a limited number of situations authority is directly exercised by the community on its own behalf. It takes the form of lynch law in some instances where clear procedures have not been set up in advance, as in the Comanche treatment of excessive sorcery and Shoshone treatment in cannibalism. Lynch law among primitives, however, is not a backsliding from, or detouring around, established formal law as it is with us. It is a first fitful step towards the emergence of criminal law in a situation in which the exercise of legal power has not yet been refined and allocated to specific persons. It is a blunt crude tool wielded by the gang hand of an outraged public.

Yet lynch law is rare among primitives. Even the simplest of them have crystallised standards as to what constitutes criminal behaviour, and the exercise of public authority is delegated to official functionaries – the chieftain, the council of chiefs, and the council of elders.

Power may sometimes be personal, as is the power of the bully in the society of small boys, and as was to some extent the power of William the Conqueror. But personal tyranny is a rare thing among primitives. Brute force of the individual does not prevail. Chiefs must have followers. Followers always impose limitations on their leaders. Enduring power is always institutionalised power. It is *transpersonalised*. It resides in the office, in the social status, rather than in the man. The constitutional structures of the several tribes examined in this book have all clearly revealed how political and legal authority are in each instance delimited and circumscribed.

This point is emphasised only to dispel any residue of the hoary political philosophies that assumed without basis in fact that primitive societies existed under the rule of fang and claw.

However, the personal still obtrudes. An 'office' although culturally defined is, after all, exercised by an individual. And who that individual is at any moment certainly makes a difference. There is leeway in the exercise or non-exercise of power just as there are limits. A man may be skilled in finding the evidence and the truth in the cases he must judge and in formulating the norms to fit the case in hand – or he may be all thumbs. He may be one who thirsts for power and who will wield all he can while grasping for more. Or he may shrink from it. Power defined through allocation of legal authority is by its nature trans-personalised, yet by the nature of men it can never be wholly depersonalised. A Franklin Roosevelt is not a Warren Harding.

The third function of law calls for little additional comment ... Some trouble cases pose absolutely new problems for solution. In these cases the first and second functions may predominate. Yet this is not the situation in the instance of most legal clashes in which the problem is not the formulation of law to cover a new situation but rather the application of pre-existing law. These cases are disposed of in accordance with legal norms already set before the issue in question arises. The job is to clean the case up, to suppress or penalise the illegal behaviour and to bring the relations of the disputants back into balance, so that life may resume its normal course. This type of law-work has frequently been compared to work of the medical practitioner. It is family doctor stuff, essential to keeping the social body on its feet. In more homely terms, Llewellyn has called it, 'garage-repair work on the general order of the group when that general order misses fire, or grinds gears, or even threatens a total breakdown'. It is not ordinarily concerned with grand design, as is the first law-job. Nor is it concerned with redesign as is the fourth. It works to clear up all the little social messes (and the occasional big ones) that recurrently arise between the members of the society from day to day.

Most of the trouble cases do not, in a civilised society, of themselves loom large on the social scene, although in a small community even one can lead directly to a social explosion if not successfully cleaned up. Indeed, in a primitive society the individual case always holds the threat of a little civil war if procedure breaks down, for from its inception it sets kin group against kin group – and if it comes to fighting, the number of kinsmen who will be involved is almost always immediately enlarged. The first may engulf a large part of the tribe in internecine throat-cutting. Relatively speaking, each run-of-the-mill trouble case in primitive law imposes a more pressing demand for settlement upon the legal system than is the case with us.

While system and integration are essential, flexibility and constant revision are no less so. Law is a dynamic process in which few solutions can be permanent. Hence, the fourth function of law: the redefinition of relations and the reorientation of expectancies.

Initiative with scope to work means new problems for the law. New inventions, new ideas, new behaviours keep creeping in. Especially do new behaviours creep in, nay, sweep in, when two unlike societies come newly into close contact. Then the law is called upon to decide what principles shall be applied to conflicts of claim rooted in disparate cultures. Do the new claims fit comfortably to the old postulates?' Must the newly realised ways of behaving be wholly rejected and legally suppressed because they are out of harmony with the old values? Or can they be modified here and altered there to gain legal acceptance? Or can the more difficult operation of altering or even junking old postulates to accommodate a new way be faced? Or can fictions be framed that can lull the mind into acceptance of the disparate new without the wrench of acknowledged junking of the old? What *is* it that is wanted? The known and habitual, or the promise of the new and untested? Men may neglect to turn the law to the answer of such questions. But they do not for long. Trouble cases generated by the new keep marching in. And the fourth law-job presses for attention.

Recapitulation of just one Cheyenne case will throw the process into focus. The acquisition of horses greatly altered all Plains Indian culture. One important Cheyenne basic postulate ran, 'Except for land and tribal fetishes, all material goods are private property, but they should be generously shared with others.' When it comes to horses, this led some men to expect that they could freely borrow horses without even the courtesy of asking. For horse owners this got to the point of becoming a serious nuisance, as in the case of Pawnee and Wolf Lies Down. Wolf Lies Down put his trouble case to the members of the Elk Soldier Society. They got his horse back from him with a handsome free-will offering of additional 'damages' from the defendant to boot. The trouble case was neatly disposed of. But the Elk Soldiers did not stop there. There was some preventive channeling of future behaviour to be done. Hence the 'Now we shall make a new rule.[2] There shall be no more borrowing of horses without asking. If any man takes another's goods without asking, we will go over and get them back for him. More than that, if the taker tries to keep them, we will give him a whipping.' Here was the fourth function of law being performed. The lines for future conduct re horses were made clear.[2]

Work under Function IV represents social planning brought into focus by the case of the instant and with an eye to the future.

The problem of reorienting conduct and redirecting it through the law when new issues emerge is always tied to the bare-bones demand of basic organisation and the minimal maintenance of order and regularity. It may also shade over into work coloured by a greater or lesser desire to achieve more than a minimum of smoothness in social relations. When this becomes an important aspect of law-work, a special aspect of law-ways activity may be recognised: the creation of techniques that efficiently and effectively solve the problems posed to all the other law-jobs so that the basic values of the society are realised through the law and not frustrated by it.

The doing of it has been by Llewellyn 'Juristic Method'. It is the method not only of getting the law-jobs done but doing them with a sure touch for the net effect that results in smoothness in the doing and a harmonious wedding of what is aspired

[2] Llewellyn and Hoebel (1941) *The Cheyenne Way*, p128

to by men and what is achieved through the law. It is the work not just the craftsman but of the master craftsman ...

L L FULLER
Human Interaction and the Law [3]
(1969)

This neglect of the phenomenon called customary law has, I think, done great damage to our thinking about law generally. Even if we accept the rather casual analysis of the subject offered by the treatises, it still remains true that a proper understanding of customary law is of capital importance in the world of today. In the first place, much of international law, and perhaps the most vital part of it, is essentially customary law. Upon the successful functioning of that body of law world peace may depend. In the second place, much of the world today is still governed internally by customary law. The newly emerging nations (notably in India, Africa, and the Pacific) are now engaged in a hazardous transition from systems of customary law to systems of enacted law. The stakes in this transition – for them and for us – are very high indeed. So the mere fact that we do not see ourselves as regulating our conduct toward fellow countrymen by customary law does not mean that it is of no importance to us as world citizens.

The thesis I am going to advance here is, however, something more radical than a mere insistence that customary law is still of considerable importance in the world of today. I am going to argue that we cannot understand 'ordinary' law (that is, officially declared or enacted law) unless we first obtain an understanding of what is called customary law.

In preparing my exposition I have to confess that at this point I encountered a great frustration. This arises from the term 'customary law' itself. This is the term found in the titles and the indices, and if you want to compare what I have to say with what others have said, this is the heading you will have to look under. At the same time the expression 'customary law' is a most unfortunate one that obscures, almost beyond redemption, the nature of the phenomenon it purports to designate. Instead of serving as a neutral pointer, it prejudges its subject; it asserts that the force and meaning of what we call 'customary law' lie in mere habit or usage.

Against this view I shall argue that the phenomenon called customary law can best be described as a *language of interaction*. To interact meaningfully men require a social setting in which the moves of the participating players will fall generally within some predictable pattern. To engage in effective social behaviour men need the support of intermeshing anticipations that will let them know what their opposite numbers will do, or that will at least enable them to gauge the general

---

[3] Fuller, L L 'Human Interaction and the Law' (1969) *American Journal of Jurisprudence*, 14, p1.

scope of the repertory from which responses to their actions will be drawn. We sometimes speak of customary law as offering an unwritten 'code of conduct'. The word 'code' is appropriate here because what is involved is not simply a negation, a prohibition of certain disapproved actions, but also the obverse side of this negation, the meaning it confers on foreseeable and approved actions, which then furnish a point of orientation for ongoing interactive responses. Professors Parsons and Shils have spoken of the function, in social action, of 'complementary expectations'; the term 'complementary expectations' indicates accurately the function I am here ascribing to the law that develops out of human interaction, a form of law that we are forced – by the dictionaries and title headings – to call 'customary law'. ...

The first of these objections is that customary law in primitive societies may lay down rules that have nothing to do with human interaction. There may be offenses against deities and spirits; a man may be punished, even by death for an act committed out of the presence of other persons where that act violates some taboo. The answer to this is, I suggest, that animistic views of nature may vastly extend the significance one man's acts may have for his fellows. ... The extent to which one man's beliefs and acts will be seen as affecting his fellows will depend upon the degree to which men see themselves as parts, one of another, and upon their beliefs about the intangible forces that unite them. Within the extended family the distinction between other-regarding and self-regarding acts will assume an aspect very different from what it has in our own society, composed, as that society is, largely to strangers with a strong disbelief in the supernatural.

A further objection to the conception of customary law as a language of interaction may be stated in these terms: Any such conception is much too rationalistic and attributes to customary law a functional aptness, a neatness of purpose, that is far from the realities of primitive practice. Customary law is filled with ritualistic routines and pointless ceremonies; these may cater to a certain instinct for drama, but they can hardly be said to serve effective communication or the development of stable expectations that will organise and facilitate interaction.

In answer I would assert, on the contrary, that a significant function of ritual is precisely that of communication, of labelling acts so that there can be no mistake as to their meaning. ... Certainly among a people who have no state-kept official records to show who is married to whom, the elaborate wedding ceremonies found in some customary systems can be said to serve a purpose of communication and clarification.

To illustrate the points I have been making with regard to ritualism, and, more generally, with regard to the communicative function of customary practices, I should like to refer briefly to a development that appears to be occurring in the diplomatic relations of Russia and the United States. Here we may be witnessing something like customary law in the making. Between these two countries there seems to have arisen a kind of reciprocity with respect to the forced withdrawal of diplomatic representatives. The American government, for example, believes that a member of the Russian embassy is engaged in espionage, or, perhaps I should say, it believes him to be *over*engaged in espionage; it declares him persona non grata and requires his departure from this country. The expected response, based on past experience, is that Russia will acquiesce in this demand, but will at once counter with a demand for the withdrawal from Russia of an American diplomatic agent of equal rank. Conversely, if the Russians expel an American emissary, the United States will react by shipping back one of Russia's envoys.

Here we have, for the time being at least, a quite stable set of interactional expectancies; within the field covered by this practice each country is able to anticipate with considerable confidence the reactions of its opposite number. This means that its decisions can be guided by a tolerably accurate advance estimate of costs. We know that if we throw one of their men out, they will throw out one of ours.

It should be noticed that the practice is routinised and contains (at least latently) ritualistic and symbolic qualities. Suppose, for example, that the American authorities were confronted with this dilemma: the Russians have declared persona non grata a high-ranking member of the American embassy in Moscow, and it turns out to be difficult to find an appropriate counterpart for return to Russia. We may suppose, for example, that the Soviet representatives of equal rank with the expelled American are persons Washington would like very much to see remain in this country. In this predicament it could cross the minds of those responsible for the decision that they might, in order to preserve a proper balance, return to Russia five men of a lower rank than the expelled American, or perhaps even that the expulsion of ten filing clerks would be the most apt response.

Now I suggest that any responsible public official would reflect a long time before embracing such an alternative. Its danger would lie in the damage it would inflict on the neat symbolism of a one-to-one ratio, in the confusion it might introduce into the accepted meaning of the acts involved. This is a case where both sides would probably be well-advised to stick with the familiar ritual since a departure from it might forfeit the achieved gains of a stable interactional pattern.

The illustration just discussed may seem badly chosen because it represents, one might say, a very impoverished kind of customary law, a law that confers, not a reciprocity of benefits, but a reciprocity in expressions of hostility. But much of the customary law of primitive peoples, it should be recalled, serves exactly the same function. Open and unrestricted hostilities between tribes often become in time subject to tacit and formalised restraints and may, in the end, survive only as a ritualistic mock battle. Furthermore, in the diplomatic practice I have described here there may be present a richer reciprocity than appears on the surface. At the time of the *Pueblo* incident it was suggested that Russia and the United States may share an interest in being moderately and discreetly spied on by one another. We don't want the Russians to pry out our military secrets, but we want them to know, on the basis of information they will trust, that we are not planning to mount a surprise attack on them. This shared interest may furnish part of the background of the ritualistic and patterned exchange of diplomatic discourtesies that seems to be developing between the two countries.

... How much of what is called customary law really deserves the epithet 'law'? Anthropologists have devoted some attention to this question and have arrived at divergent responses to it, including one which asserts that the question is itself misconceived, since you cannot apply a conception interwoven with notions of explicit enactment to a social context where rules of conduct come into existence without the aid of a lawmaker. Among those who take the question seriously the answer proposed by Hoebel has perhaps attracted the most attention; it will repay us to consider it for a moment. Hoebel suggests that in dealing with stateless or primitive societies

... law may be defined in these terms: A social norm is legal if its neglect or infraction is regularly met, in threat or in fact, by the application of physical force by an individual or group possessing the socially recognised privilege of so acting.

16. THE ORIGINS OF MARXISM AND ITS APPLICATION IN REAL SOCIETIES

ROBERT FREEDMAN
Marx on Economics [1]
(1969)

Karl Heinrich Marx was born at Trier in Germany in 1801. He studied law at the University of Bonn, and then proceeded to Berlin University, where he studied literature, law, history and finally philosophy. He received his PhD at Jena in 1842. He worked as a journalist in Cologne and then in Paris, where he met Friedrich Engels with whom he formed a close friendship. Although much influenced by the work of Hengel, Marx in a sense reversed it by adopting a doctrine of materialism. He began to relate the state of society to its economic foundations and means of production and recommended armed revolution on the part of the proletariat. He was expelled from France in 1845 and taught economics in Belgium for three years. He and Engels prepared the *Communist Manifesto* (1848) as a statement of the Communist League's policy. After revisiting France and Germany briefly during 1848 he sought permanent asylum in England in 1849 and lived in London until his death in 1883. Supported by the generosity of Engels, Marx and his family nevertheless lived in great poverty. After years of research, much of which he carried out at the British Museum, he published in 1867 the first volume of his great work, *Das Kapital.* Two posthumous volumes were later completed from the mass of notes and manuscripts he left. Karl Marx's other writings included *Poverty of Philosophy, Contribution to the Critique of Political Economy, Theories of Surplus Value*, and *German Ideology.*

[1] Freedman, Robert (1969) *Marx on Economics*. Pelican Books, London.

KARL MARX and FRIEDRICH ENGELS
The Communist Manifesto [2]
(1858)

The history of all hitherto existing society is the history of class struggles.

Freeman and slave, patrician and plebian, lord and serf, guild-master and journeyman, in a word, oppressor and oppressed, stood in constant opposition to one another, carried on an uninterrupted fight, now hidden, now open, a fight that each time ended either in a revolutionary reconstitution of society at large or in the common ruin of the contending classes.

In the earlier epochs of history, we find almost everywhere a complicated arrangement of society into various orders, a manifold gradation of social rank. In ancient Rome we have patricians, knights, plebians, slaves; in the Middle Ages feudal lords, vassals, guild-masters, journeymen, apprentices, serfs; in almost all of these classes, again, subordinate gradations.

The modern bourgeois society that has sprouted from the ruins of feudal society has not done away with class antagonisms. It has but established new classes, new conditions of oppression, new forms of struggle in place of the old ones.

Our epoch, the epoch of the bourgeoisie, however, possesses this distinctive feature: it has simplified the class antagonisms.

KARL MARX
A Critique of the Gotha Programme [3]
(1875)

The right of the producers is proportional to the labour they supply; the equality consists in the fact that measurement is made with an *equal standard*, labour.

But one man is superior to another physically or mentally, and so supplies more labour in the same time, or can labour for a longer time; and labour, to serve as a measure, must be defined by its duration or intensity, otherwise it ceases to be a standard of measurement. This *equal* right is an unequal right for unequal labour. It recognises no class differences, because everyone is only a worker like everyone else; but it tacitly recognises unequal individual endowment, and thus productive capacity, as natural privileges. *It is therefore a right of inequality in its content, like every right*. Right by its very nature can only consist in the application of an equal

[2] Marx, K and Engels, F (1955) *The Manifesto of the Communist Party (1858)*. Foreign Languages Publishing House, London.
[3] Marx, K (1875) *A Critique of the Gotha Programme*. Reprinted from Freedman, R (1969) *Marx on Economics*. Pelican Books, London.

standard; but unequal individuals (and they would not be different individuals if they were not unequal) are only measurable by an equal standard in so far as they are brought under an equal point of view, are taken from one *definite* side only, eg in the present case are regarded *only as workers*, and nothing more seen in them, everything else being ignored. Further, one worker is married, another not; one has an equal output, and hence an equal share in the social consumption fund, one will in fact receive more than another, one will be richer than another, and so on. To avoid all these defects, right instead of being equal would have to be unequal.

But these defects are inevitable in the first phase of communist society, as it is when it has just emerged after prolonged birthpangs from capitalist society. Right can never be higher than the economic structure of society and the cultural development thereby determined.

In a higher phase of communist society, after the enslaving subordination of individuals under division of labour, and therewith also the antithesis between mental and physical labour, has vanished; after labour, from a mere means of life, has itself become a prime necessity of life; after the productive forces have also increased with the all-round development of the individual, and all the springs of cooperation wealth flow more abundantly – only then can the narrow horizon of bourgeois right be fully left behind, and society inscribe on its banners 'From each according to his ability, to each according to his needs!'

17. CONTEMPORARY MARXISM

E PASHUKANIS
Law and Marxism [1]
(1978)

The withering away of certain categories of bourgeois law (the categories as such, not this or that precept) in no way implies their replacement by new categories of proletarian law, just as the withering away of the categories of value, capital, profit and so forth in the transition to fully-developed socialism will not mean the emergence of new proletarian categories of value, capital and so on.

The withering away of the categories of bourgeois law will, under these conditions, mean the withering away of law altogether, that is to say the disappearance of the juridical factor from social relations.

The transition period – as Marx showed in his 'Critique of the Gotha Programme' – is characterised by the fact that social relations will, for a time, necessarily continue to be constrained by the 'narrow horizon of bourgeois right'. It is interesting to analyse what constitutes, in Marx's view, this narrow horizon of bourgeois right (*Recht*). Marx presupposes a social order in which the means of production are socially owned and in which the producers do not exchange their products. Consequently, he assumes a higher stage of development than the 'new economic policy' which we are presently experiencing.[2] He sees the market as having been already replaced by an organised framework, such that in no way

'... does the labour employed on the products appear here as *the value* of these products, as a material quality possessed by them, since now, in contrast to capitalist society, individual labour no longer exists in an indirect fashion but directly as a component part of the total labour.'

Nevertheless, Marx says, even when the market and market exchange have been completely abolished, the new communist society will of necessity be

'... in every respect, economically, morally and intellectually, still stamped with the birth marks of the old society from whose womb it emerges.'

This becomes evident in the principle of distribution as well, according to which

'... the individual producer receives back from society – after the deductions have been made – exactly what he gives to it.'

---

[1] Pashukanis, E (1978) *Law and Marxism*. Translated from the German by B Einhorn. Inks Links Ltd, London, pp1073-1075.

[2] That is 'New Economic Policy'. The NEP was introduced in 1921 and established a mixed economy with a free market. It ended in 1928 with the establishment of the first Five Year Plan.

Marx stresses that in spite of the radical transformation of form and content

> '... the same principle prevails as that which regulates the exchange of commodities, as far as this is exchange of equal values ... a given amount of labour in one form is exchanged for an equal amount of labour in another form.'

To the extent that the relation of the individual producer to society still retains the form of the exchange of equivalents, it also retains the form of law (*Recht*), for 'right' (Recht) by its very nature can consist only in the application of an equal standard.' However, as this makes no allowance for the natural inequality of individual talent, it is 'a right of inequality, in its content, like every right.' Marx does not mention that there must be a state authority which guarantees the enforcement of these norms of 'unequal' right by its coercion, thus retaining its 'bourgeois limit', but that goes without saying. Lenin concludes:

> 'Of course, bourgeois right in regard to the distribution of *consumer* goods inevitably presupposes the existence of the *bourgeois state*, for right is nothing without an apparatus capable of enforcing the observance of the standards of right.
> It follows that under communism there remains for a time not only bourgeois right, but even the bourgeois state, without the bourgeoisie!'

Once the form of equivalent exchange is given then the form of law – the form of public, or state authority – is also given, and consequently this form persists even after the class structure has ceased to exist. The withering away of law, and with it, of the state, ensues, in Marx's view, only after 'labour has become not only a means of life but life's prime want,' when the productive forces grow together with the all-round development of the individual, when everyone works spontaneously according to their abilities. ...

Thus Marx conceives of the transition to developed communism not as a transition to new forms of law, but as a withering away of the legal form as such, as a liberation from that heritage of the bourgeois epoch which is fated to outlive the bourgeoisie itself.

At the same time, Marx reveals that the fundamental condition of existence of the legal form is rooted in the very economic organisation of society. In other words, the existence of the legal form is contingent upon the integration of the different products of labour according to the principle of equivalent exchange. In so doing, he exposes the deep interconnection between the legal form and the commodity form. Any society which is constrained, by the level of development of its productive forces, to retain an equivalent relation between expenditure and compensation of labour, in a form which even remotely suggests the exchange of commodity values, will be compelled to retain the legal form as well. Only by starting from this fundamental aspect can one understand why a whole series of other social relations assume legal form. To draw the inference from this, however, that there must always be laws and courts, since not even with the greatest possible economic provision would there be an end to all offences against the person, would simply mean taking secondary, minor aspects for the main, fundamental ones. Even progressive bourgeois criminology has become convinced that the prevention of crime may properly be viewed as a medical–educational problem. To solve this problem, jurists, with their 'evidence', their codes, their concepts of 'guilt', and of 'full or diminished responsibility', or their fine distinctions between complicity, aiding and abetting, instigation and so on, are entirely superfluous. And the only reason this theoretical conviction has not yet laid to the abolition of penal codes and criminal courts is, of course, that the overthrow of the legal form is dependent, not only on transcending the framework of bourgeois society, but also on a radical emancipation from all its remnants.

The critique of bourgeois jurisprudence from the standpoint of scientific socialism must follow the example of Marx's critique of bourgeois political economy. For that purpose, this critique must, above all, venture into enemy territory. It should not throw aside the generalisations and abstractions elaborated by bourgeois jurists, whose starting point was the need of their class and of their times. Rather, by analysing these abstract categories, it should demonstrate their true significance and lay bare the historically limited nature of the legal form.

E P THOMPSON
Whigs and Hunters [3]
(1975)

So we are back, once again, with that law: the institutionalised procedures of the ruling class. This, no doubt, is worth no more of our theoretical attention; we can see it as an instrument of class power tout court. But we must take even this formulation, and see whether its crystalline clarity will survive immersion in scepticism. To be sure, we can stand no longer on that traditional ground of liberal academicism, which offers the eighteenth century as a society of consensus, ruled within the parameters of paternalism and deference, and governed by a 'rule of law' which attained (however imperfectly) towards impartiality. That is not the society which we have been examining; we have not observed a society of consensus; and we have seen the law being devised and employed, directly and instrumentally, in the imposition of class power. Nor can we accept a sociological refinement of the old view, which stresses the imperfections and partiality of the law, and its subordination to the functional requirements of socio–economic interest groups. For what we have observed is something more than the law as a pliant medium to be twisted this way and that by whichever interests already possess effective power. Eighteenth-century law was more substantial than that. Over and above its pliant, instrumental functions it existed in its own right, as ideology; as an ideology which not only served, in most respects, but which also legitimised class power. The

[3] Thompson, E P (1975) *Whigs and Hunters*. Penguin Books, Isleworth, Middlesex, p1056.

hegemony of the eighteenth-century gentry and aristocracy was expressed, above all, not in military force, not in the mystification of a priesthood or of the press, not even in economic coercion, but in the rituals of the study of the Justices of the Peace, in the quarter-sessions, in the pomp of Assizes and in the theatre of Tyburn.

Thus the law (we agree) may be seen instrumentally as mediating and reinforcing existent class relations and, ideologically, as offering to these a legitimation. But we must press our definitions a little further. For if we say that existent class relations were mediated by the law, this is not the same thing as saying that the law was no more than those relations translated into other terms, which masked or mystified the reality. This may, quite often, be true but it is not the whole truth. For class relations were expressed, not in any way one likes, but *through the forms of law*; and the law, like other institutions which from time to time can be seen as mediating (and masking) existent class relations (such as the Church or the media of communication), has its own characteristics, its own independent history and logic of evolution.

Moreover, people are not as stupid as some structuralist philosophers suppose them to be. They will not be mystified by the first man who puts on a wig. It is inherent in the especial character of law, as a body of rules and procedures, that it shall apply logical criteria with reference to standards of universality and equity. It is true that certain categories of person may be excluded from this logic (as children or slaves), that other categories may be debarred from access to parts of the logic (as women or, for many forms of eighteenth-century law, those without certain kinds of property), and that the poor may often be excluded, through penury, from the law's costly procedures. All this, and more, is true. But if too much of this is true, then the consequences are plainly counterproductive. Most men have a strong sense of justice, at least with regard to their own interests. If the law is evidently partial and unjust, then it will mask nothing, legitimise nothing, contribute nothing to any class's hegemony. The essential precondition for the effectiveness of law, in its function as ideology, is that it shall display an independence from gross manipulation and shall seem to be just.

18. FEMINIST JURISPRUDENCE

Gillick v West Norfolk and Wisbech Area Health Authority and Department of Health and Social Security [1985] 3 WLR 830

The Department of Health and Social Security issued to area health authorities a memorandum of guidance on family planning services ('the guidance') which contained a section dealing with contraceptive advice and treatment for young people. It stated that clinic sessions should be available for people of all ages, that in order not to undermine parental responsibility and family stability the department hoped that attempts would always be made to persuade children under the age of 16 who attended clinics to involve their parent or guardian at the earliest stage of consultation, and that it would be most unusual to provide contraceptive advice to such children without parental consent. It went on to state that to abandon the principle of confidentiality between doctor and patient in respect of children under 16 years might cause some not to seek professional advice at all, thus exposing them to risks such as pregnancy and sexually transmitted diseases, and that in exceptional cases it was for a doctor exercising his clinical judgment to decide whether to prescribe contraception. The plaintiff, who was the mother of five girls under the age of 16 years, wrote to her local area health authority seeking an assurance from them that no contraceptive advice or treatment would be given to any of her daughters while under 16 years of age without her knowledge and consent. The area health authority refused to give such an assurance and stated that in accordance with the guidance the final decision must be for the doctor's clinical judgment. The plaintiff began an action by writ for, inter alia, a declaration that the guidance gave advice which was unlawful and wrong and which adversely affected parental rights and duties. Woolf J held that in order to obtain the relief sought the plaintiff had to establish that adherence to the advice contained in the guidance would inevitably result in the commission of unlawful conduct, that the probabilities were that a doctor would not render himself liable to criminal proceedings by following the advice in the guidance, and that a girl under 16 was capable of consenting to medical treatment so that a lack of parental consent would not render the doctor's conduct unlawful. He concluded that the plaintiff was not entitled to the relief sought. The Court of Appeal allowed the plaintiff's appeal on the grounds, inter alia, that a girl under 16 was incapable either of consenting to medical treatment or of validly prohibiting a doctor from seeking the consent of her parents, and that the advice contained in the guidance was contrary to law in that any doctor who treated a girl under 16 without the consent of her parent or guardian would be infringing the inalienable and legally enforceable rights of parents relating to the custody and upbringing of their children which save in an emergency could not be overridden otherwise than by resort to a court exercising its jurisdiction to act in the best interests of the child.

On appeal by the department:

Held, allowing the appeal (Lord Brandon and Lord Templeman dissenting):

(1) That a girl under the age of 16 years had the legal capacity to consent to medical examination and treatment, including contraceptive treatment, if she had sufficient maturity and intelligence to understand the nature and implications of the proposed treatment.

(2) That the parental right to control a minor child deriving from parental duty was a dwindling right which existed only in so far as it was required for the child's benefit and protection; that the extent and duration of that right could not be ascertained by reference to a fixed age, but depended on the degree of intelligence and understanding of that particular child and a judgment of what was best for the welfare of the child; that the parents' right to determine whether a child under 16 should have medical treatment terminated when the child achieved sufficient intelligence and understanding to make that decision itself.

(3) That the bona fide exercise by a doctor of his clinical judgment as to what he honestly believed to be necessary for the physical, mental and emotional health of his patient was a complete negation of the guilty mind which was essential for the commission of a criminal offence ...

LORD SCARMAN: '... Victoria Gillick, mother of five daughters under the age of 16, challenges the lawfulness of a memorandum of guidance issued by the Department of Health and Social Security which she says encourages and in certain circumstances recommends health authorities, doctors, and others concerned in operating the department's family planning services to provide contraceptive advice and treatment to girls under the age of 16 without the knowledge or consent of a parent. Mrs Gillick is a wife and mother living in a united family with her husband and their children. The husband supports the action being taken, as they both see it, to protect their daughters. No further need be said of their family situation in deciding this appeal.

Mrs Gillick began her proceedings by the issue of a writ against two defendants, the health authority for the area in which she lives and the department. She claims in an ordinary civil action declaratory relief against both defendants that the guidance is unlawful, and against the area health authority alone a declaration that no doctor or other person in its employ may give contraception or abortion advice to Mrs Gillick's children under the age of 16 without her prior knowledge and consent. The area health authority has taken no part in the litigation, but the department has fought the case strenuously. The appeal to the House is that of the department: the health authority has not appealed and is not represented.

The written case submitted on Mrs Gillick's behalf to the House formulates three propositions of law, any one of which, if made good, would suffice to entitle her to relief. They are as follows:

"(i) parental rights should be protected from any invasion or interference neither authorised by a competent court nor expressly authorised by statute: [the parental rights case];

(ii) the provision of contraceptive treatment to girls under the age of 16 either constitutes criminal conduct in itself or is so closely analogous thereto as to be contrary to public policy: [the criminal law case];

(iii) a girl below the age of 16 is not capable in law of giving a valid consent to medical treatment and in the particular context of this case to contraceptive or abortion treatment:' [the age of consent point]."

... Before discussing the question, I put out of the way the two exceptions which I understand both parties to the appeal accept: namely the order of a competent court, and emergency. Nobody disputes the existence of the court exception, nor does the other situation call for more than a brief mention. ...

Mrs Gillick relies on both the statute law and the case law to establish her proposition that parental consent is in all other circumstances necessary. The only statutory provision directly in point is section 8 of the Family Law Reform Act 1969. Subsection (1) of the section provides that the consent of a minor who has attained the age of 16 to any surgical, mental, or dental treatment which in the absence of consent would constitute a trespass to his person shall be as effective as if he were of full age and that the consent of his parent or guardian need not be obtained. Subsection (3) of the section provides:

"Nothing in this section shall be construed as making ineffective any consent which would have been effective if this section had not been enacted."

I cannot accept the submission made on Mrs Gillick's behalf that subsection (1) necessarily implies that prior to its enactment the consent of a minor to medical treatment could not be effective in law. Subsection (3) leaves open the question whether the consent of a minor under 16 could be an effective consent. Like my noble and learned friend, Lord Fraser of Tullybelton, I read the section as clarifying the law without conveying any indication as to what the law was before it was enacted. So far as minors under 16 are concerned, the law today is as it was before the enactment of the section.

The law has, therefore, to be found by a search in the judge-made law for the true principle. The legal difficulty is that in our search we find ourselves in a field of medical practice where parental right and a doctor's duty may point us in different directions. This is not surprising. Three features have emerged in today's society which were not known to our predecessors: (1) contraception as a subject for medical advice and treatment; (2) the increasing independence of young people; and (3) the changed status of woman. In times past contraception was rarely a matter for the doctor: but with the development of the contraceptive pill for women it has become part and parcel of every-day medical practice, as is made clear by the department's *Handbook of Contraceptive Practice* (1984 revision), particularly para. 1.2. Family planning services are now available under statutory powers to all without any express limitation as to age or marital status. Young people, once they have attained the age of 16, are capable of consenting to contraceptive treatment, since it is medical treatment: and, however extensive be parental right in the care and upbringing of children, it cannot prevail so as to nullify the 16-year's old capacity to consent which is now conferred by statute. Furthermore, women have obtained by the availability of the pill a choice of life-style with a degree of independence and of opportunity undreamed of until this generation and greater, I would add, than any law of equal opportunity could by itself effect.

The law ignores these developments at its peril. The House's task, therefore, as the supreme court in a legal system largely based on rules of law evolved over the years by the judicial process is to search the overfull and cluttered shelves of the law reports for a principle, or set of principles recognised by the judges over the years but stripped of the detail which, however appropriate in their day, would, if applied today, lay the judges open to a justified criticism for failing to keep the law abreast of the society in which they live and work.

It is, of course, a judicial commonplace to proclaim the adaptability and flexibility of the judge-made common law. But this is more frequently proclaimed than acted upon. The mark of the great judge from Coke through Mansfield to our day has been the capacity and the will to search out principle, to discard the detail appropriate (perhaps) to earlier times, and to apply the principle in such a way as to satisfy the needs of his own time. If judge-made law is to survive as a living and relevant body of law, we must make the effort, however inadequately, to follow the lead of the great masters of the judicial art ...

> "... all law ought to stand upon principle; and unless decision has removed out of the way all argument and all principle, so as to make it impossible to apply them to the case before you, you must find out what is the principle upon which it must be decided." Lord Eldon quoted by Lord Campbell (1857) *Lives of the Lord Chancellors* 4th edn, vol. 10, ch 213, p244.

Approaching the earlier law in this way, one finds plenty of indications as to the principles governing the law's approach to parental right and the child's right to make his or her own decision. Parental rights clearly do exist, and they do not wholly disappear until the age of majority. Parental rights relate to both the person and the property of the child – custody, care and control of the person and guardianship of the property of the child. But the common law has never treated such rights as sovereign or beyond review and control. Nor has our law ever treated the child as other than a person with capacities and rights recognised by law. The principle of the law, as I shall endeavour to show, is that parental rights are derived from parental duty and exist only so long as they are needed for the protection of the person and property of the child. The principle has been subjected to certain age limits set by statute for certain purposes; and in some cases the courts have declared an age of discretion at which a child acquires before the age of majority the right to make his (or her) own decision. But these limitations in no way undermine the principle of the law, and should not be allowed to obscure it.

Let me make good, quite shortly, the proposition of principle ... When a court has before it a question as to the care and upbringing of a child it must treat the welfare of the child as the paramount consideration in determining the order to be made. There is here a principle which limits and governs the exercise of parental rights of custody, care, and control. It is a principle perfectly consistent with the law's recognition of the parent as the natural guardian of the child; but it is also a warning that parental right must be exercised in accordance with the welfare principle and can be challenged, even overridden, if it be not.

Secondly, there is the common law's understanding of the nature of parental right. We are not concerned in this appeal to catalogue all that is contained in what Sachs LJ has felicitously described as the "bundle of rights" (*Hewer v Bryant* [1970] 1 QB 357, 373) which together constitute the rights of custody, care and control. It is abundantly plain that the law recognises that there is a right and a duty of parents to determine whether or not to seek medical advice in respect of their child, and, having received advice, to give or withhold consent to medical treatment. The question in the appeal is as to the extent and duration of the right and the circumstances in which outside the two admitted exceptions to which I have earlier referred it can be overridden by the exercise of medical judgment. ...

The principle is that parental right or power of control of the person and property of his child exists primarily to enable the parent to discharge his duty of maintenance, protection, and education until he reaches such an age as to be able to look after himself and make his own decisions. Blackstone does suggest that there was a further justification for parental right, viz as a recompense for the faithful discharge of parental duty; but the right of the father to the exclusion of the mother and the reward element as one of the reasons for the existence of the right have been swept away by the guardianship of minors legislation to which I have already referred. He also accepts that by statute and by case law varying ages of discretion have been fixed for various purposes. But it is clear that this was done to achieve certainty where it was considered necessary and in no way limits the principle that parental right endures only so long as it is needed for the protection of the child.

Although statute has intervened in respect of a child's capacity to consent to medical treatment from the age of 16 onwards, neither statute nor the case law has ruled on the extent and duration of parental right in respect of children under the age of 16. More specifically, there is no rule yet applied to contraceptive treatment, which has special problems of its own and is a late-comer in medical practice. It is open, therefore, to the House to formulate a rule. The Court of Appeal favoured a fixed age limit of 16, basing themselves on a view of the statute law which I do not share and upon their view of the effect of the older case law which for the reasons already given I cannot accept. They sought to justify the limit by the public interest in the law being certain. Certainty is always an advantage in the law, and in some branches of the law it is a necessity. But it brings with it an inflexibility and a rigidity which in some branches of the law can obstruct justice, impede the law's development, and stamp upon the law the mark of obsolescence where what is needed is the capacity for development. The law relating to parent and child is concerned with the problems of growth and maturity of the human personality. If the law should impose upon the process of "growing up" fixed limits where nature knows only a continuous process, the price would be artificiality and a lack of realism in an area where the law must be sensitive to human development and social change. If certainty be thought desirable, it is better that the rigid demarcations necessary to achieve it should be laid down by legislation after a full consideration of all the relevant factors than by the courts confined as they are by the forensic process to the evidence adduced by the parties and to whatever may properly fall within the judicial notice of judges. Unless and until Parliament should think fit to intervene, the courts should establish a principle flexible enough to enable justice to be achieved by its application to the particular circumstances proved by the evidence placed before them.

The underlying principle of the law was exposed by Blackstone and can be seen to have been acknowledged in the case law. It is that parental right yields to the child's right to make his own decisions when he reaches a sufficient understanding and intelligence to be capable of making up his own mind on the matter requiring decision. Lord Denning MR captured the spirit and principle of the law when he said in *Hewer* v *Bryant* [1970] 1 QB 357, 369:

> "I would get rid of the rule in *In re Agar-Ellis* (1883) 24 Ch D 317 and of the suggested exceptions to it. That case was decided in the year 1883. It reflects the attitude of a Victorian parent towards his children. He expected unquestioning obedience to his commands. If a son disobeyed, his father would cut him off with a shilling. If a daughter had an illegitimate child, he would turn her out of the house. His power only ceased when the child became 21. I decline to accept a view so much out of date. The common law can, and should, keep pace with the times. It should declare in conformity with the recent Report of the Committee on the Age of Majority [Cmnd 3342, 1967], that the legal right of a parent to the custody of a child ends at the 18th birthday: and even up till then, it is a dwindling right which the courts will hesitate to enforce against the wishes of the child, and the more so the older he is. It starts with a right of control and ends with little more than advice."

... In the light of the foregoing I would hold that as a matter of law the parental right to determine whether or not their minor child below the age of 16 will have medical treatment terminates if and when the child achieves a sufficient understanding and intelligence to enable him or her to understand fully what is proposed. It will be a question of fact whether a child seeking advice has sufficient understanding of what is involved to give a consent valid in law. Until the child achieves the capacity to consent, the parental right to make the decisions continues save only in exceptional circumstances. Emergency, parental neglect, abandonment of the child, or inability to find the parent are examples of exceptional situations justifying the doctor proceeding to treat the child without parental knowledge and consent: but there will arise, no doubt, other exceptional situations in which it will be reasonable for the doctor to proceed without the parent's consent.

When applying these conclusions to contraceptive advice and treatment it has to be borne in mind that there is much that has to be understood by a girl under the age of 16 if she is to have legal capacity to consent to such treatment. It is not enough that she should understand the nature of the advice which is being given: she must also have a sufficient maturity to understand what is involved. There are moral and family questions, especially her relationship with her parents; long-term problems associated with the emotional impact of pregnancy and its termination; and there are the risks to health of sexual intercourse at her age, risks which contraception may diminish but cannot eliminate. It follows that a doctor will have to satisfy himself that she is able to appraise these factors before he can safely proceed upon the basis that she has at law capacity to consent to contraceptive treatment. And it further follows that ordinarily the proper course will be for him, as the guidance lays down, first to seek to persuade the girl to bring her parents into consultation, and if she refuses, not to prescribe contraceptive treatment unless she is satisfied that her circumstances are such that he ought to proceed without parental knowledge and consent ...

THE CRIMINAL LAW CASE

If this case should be made good, the discussion of parental rights is, of course, an irrelevance. If it be criminal or contrary to public policy to prescribe contraception for a girl under the age of 16 on the ground that sexual intercourse with her is unlawful and a crime on the part of her male partner, the fact that her parent knew and consented would not make it any less so. I confess that I find the submission based upon criminality or public policy surprising. So far as criminality is concerned, I am happy to rest on the judgment of Woolf J whose approach to the problem I believe to be correct. Clearly a doctor who gives a girl contraceptive advice or treatment not because in his clinical judgment the treatment is medically indicated for the maintenance or restoration of her health but with the intention of facilitating her having unlawful sexual intercourse may well be guilty of a criminal offence. It would depend, as my noble and learned friend, Lord Fraser of Tullybelton observes, upon the doctor's intention – a conclusion hardly to be wondered at in the field of the criminal law. The department's guidance avoids the trap of declaring that the decision to prescribe the treatment is wholly a matter of the doctor's discretion. He may prescribe only if she has the capacity to consent or if exceptional circumstances exist which justify him in exercising his clinical judgment without parental consent. The adjective "clinical" emphasises that it must be a medical judgment based upon what he honestly believes to be necessary for the physical, mental, and emotional health of his patient. The bona fide exercise by a doctor of his clinical judgment must be a complete negation of the guilty mind which is an essential ingredient of the criminal offence of aiding and abetting the commission of unlawful sexual intercourse.

The public policy point fails for the same reason. It cannot be said that there is anything necessarily contrary to public policy in medical contraceptive treatment if it be medically indicated as in the interest of the patient's health: for the provision of such treatment is recognised as legitimate by Parliament: section 5 of the National Health Service Act 1977. If it should be prescribed for a girl under 16 the fact that it may eliminate a health risk in the event of the girl having unlawful sexual intercourse is an irrelevance unless the doctor intends to encourage her to have that intercourse. If the prescription is the bone fide exercise of his clinical judgment as to what is best for his patient's health, he has nothing to fear from the criminal law or from any public policy based on the criminality of a man having sexual intercourse with her.

It can be said by way of criticism of this view of the law that it will result in uncertainty and leave the law in the hands of the doctors. The uncertainty is the price which has to be paid to keep the law in line with social experience, which is that many girls are fully able to make sensible decisions about many matters before they reach the age of 16. I accept that great responsibilities will lie on the medical profession. It is, however, a learned and highly trained profession regulated by statute and governed by a strict ethical code which is vigorously enforced. Abuse of the power to prescribe contraceptive treatment for girls under the age of 16 would render a doctor liable to severe professional penalty. The truth may well be that the rights of parents and children in this sensitive area are better protected by the professional standards of the medical profession than by "a priori" legal lines of division between capacity and lack of capacity to consent since any such general dividing line is sure to produce in some cases injustice, hardship, and injury to health.

For these reasons I would allow the department's appeal, and set aside the declaration that the guidance is unlawful. I would add that, since the second declaration granted by the Court of Appeal, which concerns only the area health authority, was based on the same reasoning as the first, it must be held to have been wrongly granted. The Court of Appeal's decision to grant it should be, in my opinion, overruled as erroneous in law.'

Justice

19. ARGUMENTS ABOUT JUSTICE

Waddington v Miah
[1974] 2 All ER 377 House of Lords

Miah, a non-patrial and probably a native of Bangladesh, who entered this country at Heathrow Airport, was charged with being an illegal immigrant and with possessing a false passport, contrary to sections 24 and 26 of the Immigration Act 1971. The Act was passed on 28 October 1971, the date on which Miah entered, but the relevant sections did not come into force until 1 January 1973. The indictment referred to dates before the relevant sections came into operation.

LORD REID: 'My Lords, the defendant was tried in the Crown Court at Grimsby on an indictment which contained two counts. Count 1 stated the offence charged as "illegal immigrant, contrary to section 24 of the Immigration Act 1971" and count 2 stated the offence as "Possession of false passport, contrary to section 26 of the Immigration Act 1971". That Act was passed on 28 October 1971, but the greater part of it, including sections 24 and 26, did not come into force until 1 January 1973. But the particulars given under count 1 were that the defendant "on a day unknown between the 22nd day of October 1970 and the 29th day of September 1972, being a person who was not patrial within the meaning of the Immigration Act 1971, knowingly entered the United Kingdom without leave." And the particulars given under count 2 were that the defendant "on the 29th day of September 1972, had in his possession for the purposes of the Immigration Act 1971, a passport No AC386290 which he had reasonable cause to believe to be false."

Despite objection that the Act is not retrospective the defendant was convicted. His conviction was quashed by the Court of Appeal. That court in granting leave to the prosecution to appeal certified the following question: "Whether the defendant could be convicted of offences against the Immigration Act 1971, in respect of things done by him before the Act came into force, and in particular offences against sections 24(1)(a) and 26(1)(d) of the Act."

... there has for a very long time been a strong feeling against making legislation, and particularly criminal legislation, retrospective.

It is also I think important to bear in mind that the Declaration of Human Rights of the United Nations (1949 Cmd 7662), provides in article 11(2) "No one shall be held guilty of any penal offence on account of any act or omission which did not constitute a penal offence, under national or international law, at the time when it was committed. Nor shall a heavier penalty be imposed than the one that was applicable at the time the penal offence was committed."

And the Convention for the Protection of Human Rights and Fundamental Freedoms (1953 Cmd 8969), ratified by the United Kingdom in 1951, provides by article 7:

> "(1) No one shall be held guilty of any criminal offence on account of any act or omission which did not constitute a criminal offence under national or international law at the time when it was committed ...
>
> (2) This article shall not prejudice the trial and punishment of any person for any act or omission which, at the time when it was committed, was criminal according to the general principles of law recognised by civilised nations."

This is a very clear case. I do not think it necessary to examine the details of the counts in this indictment.

I would dismiss the appeal. Costs are not usually awarded in cases of this kind but in view of the circumstances I would award to the defendant his costs in the House.'

20. RAWLS

J RAWLS
A Theory of Justice [1]
(1972)

In working out the conception of justice as fairness one main task clearly is to determine which principles of justice would be chosen in the original position. To do this we must describe this situation in some detail and formulate with care the problem of choice which it presents ... It may be observed, however, that once the principles of justice are thought of as arising from an original agreement in a situation of equality, it is an open question whether the principle of utility would be acknowledged. Offhand it hardly seems likely that persons who view themselves as equals, entitled to press their claims upon one another, would agree to a principle which may require lesser life prospects for some simply for the sake of a greater sum of advantages enjoyed by others. Since each desire to protect his interests, his capacity to advance his conception of the good, no one has a reason to acquiesce in an enduring loss for himself in order to bring about a greater net balance of satisfaction. In the absence of strong and lasting benevolent impulses, a rational man would not accept a basic structure merely because it maximised the algebraic sum of advantages irrespective of its permanent effect on its own basic rights and interests. Thus it seems that the principle of utility is incompatible with the conception of social cooperation among equals for mutual advantage. It appears to be inconsistent with the idea of reciprocity implicit in the notion of a well-ordered society. ...

I shall maintain instead that the persons in the initial situation would choose two rather different principles: the first requires equality in the assignment of basic rights and duties, while the second holds that social and economic inequalities, for example inequalities of wealth and authority, are just only if they result in compensating benefits for everyone, and in particular for the least advantaged members of society. These principles rule out justifying institutions on the grounds that the hardships of some are offset by a greater good in the aggregate. It may be expedient but it is not just that some should have less in order that others may prosper. But there is no injustice in the greater benefits earned by a few provided that the situation of persons not so fortunate is thereby improved. The intuitive idea is that since everyone's well-being depends upon a scheme of cooperation without which no one could have a satisfactory life, the division of advantages should be such as to draw forth the willing cooperation of everyone taking part in it, including

[1] Rawls, J (1972) *A Theory of Justice*. Oxford University Press, Oxford, pp526–529.

those less well suited. Yet this can be expected only if reasonable terms are proposed. The two principles mentioned seem to be a fair agreement on the basis of which those better endowed, or more fortunate in their social position, neither of which we can be said to deserve, could expect the willing cooperation of others when some workable scheme is a necessary condition of the welfare at all. ...

The problem of the choice of principles, however, is extremely difficult. I do not expect the answer I shall suggest to be convincing to everyone. It is, therefore, worth noting from the outset that justice as fairness, like other contract views, consists of two parts: (1) an interpretation of the initial situation and of the problem of choice posed there, and (2) a set of principles which, it is argued, would be agreed to. One may accept the first part of the theory (or some variant thereof), but not the other, and conversely. The concept of the initial contractual situation may seem reasonable although the particular principles proposed are rejected. To be sure, I want to maintain that the most appropriate conception of this situation does lead to principles of justice contrary to utilitarianism and perfectionism, and therefore that the contract doctrine provides an alternative to these views. Still, one may dispute this contention even though one grants that the contractarian method is a useful way of studying ethical theories and of setting forth their underlying assumptions.

Justice as fairness is an example of what I have called a contract theory. Now there may be an objection to the term 'contract' and related expressions, but I think it will serve reasonably well. Many words have misleading connotations which at first are likely to confuse. The terms 'utility' and 'utilitarianism' are surely no exception. They too have unfortunate suggestions which hostile critics have been willing to exploit; yet they are clear enough for those prepared to study utilitarian doctrine. The same should be true of the term 'contract' applied to moral theories. As I have mentioned, to understand it one has to keep in mind that it implies a certain level of abstraction. In particular, the content of the relevant agreement is not to enter a given society or to adopt a given form of government, but to accept certain moral principles. Moreover, the undertakings referred to are purely hypothetical: a contract view holds that certain principles would be acceptable in a well-defined initial situation.

The merit of the contract terminology is that it conveys the idea that principles of justice may be conceived as principles that would be chosen by rational persons, and that in this way conceptions of justice may be explained and justified. The theory of justice is a part, perhaps the most significant part of the theory of rational choice. ...

THE ORIGINAL POSITION AND JUSTIFICATION

I have said that the original position is the appropriate initial status quo which insures that the fundamental agreements reached in it are fair. This fact yields the name 'justice as fairness'. It is clear, then, that I want to say that one conception of justice is more reasonable than another, or justifiable with respect to it, if rational persons in the initial situation would choose its principles over those of the other for the role of justice. Conceptions of justice are to be ranked by their acceptability to persons so circumstanced. Understood in this way the question of justification is settled by working out a problem of deliberation: we have to ascertain which principles it would be rational to adopt given the contractual situation. This connects the theory of justice with the theory of rational choice.

If this view of the problem of justification is to succeed, we must, of course, describe in some detail the nature of this choice problem. A problem of rational decision has a definite answer only if we know the beliefs and interests of the parties, their relations with respect to one another, the alternatives between which they are to choose, the procedure whereby they make up their minds, and so on. As the circumstances are presented in different ways, correspondingly different principles are accepted. The concept of the original position, as I shall refer to it, is that of the most philosophically favoured interpretation of this initial choice situation for the purposes of the theory of justice.

But how are we to decide what is the most favoured interpretation? I assume, for one thing, that there is a broad measure of agreement that principles of justice should be chosen under certain conditions. To justify a particular description of the initial situation one shows that it incorporates those commonly shared presumptions. One argues from widely accepted but weak premises to more specific conclusions. Each of the presumptions should by itself be natural and plausible; some of them may seem innocuous or even trivial. The aim of the contract approach is to establish that taken together they impose significant bounds on acceptable principles of justice. The ideal outcome would be that these conditions determine a unique set of principles; but I shall be satisfied if they suffice to rank the main traditional conceptions of social justice.

One should not be misled, then, by the somewhat unusual conditions which characterise the original position. The idea here is simply to make vivid to ourselves the restrictions that it seems reasonable to impose on arguments for principles of justice, and therefore on these principles themselves. Thus it seems reasonable and generally acceptable that no one should be advantaged or disadvantaged by natural fortune or social circumstances in the choice of principles. It also seems widely agreed that it should be impossible to tailor principles to the circumstances of one's own case. We should insure further that particular inclinations and aspirations, and persons' conceptions of their good do not affect the principles adopted. The aim is to rule out those principles that it would be rational to propose for acceptance, however little the chance of success, only if one knew certain things that are irrelevant from the standpoint of justice. For example, if a man knew that he was wealthy, he might find it rational to advance the principle that various taxes for welfare measures be counted unjust; if he knew that he was poor, he would most likely propose the contrary principle. To represent the desired restrictions one imagines a situation in which everyone is deprived of this sort of information. One excludes the knowledge of those contingencies which sets men at odds and allows them to be guided by their prejudices. In this manner the veil of ignorance is arrived at in a natural way. This concept should cause no difficulty if we keep in mind the constraints on arguments that it is meant to express. At any time we can enter the original position, so to speak, simply by following a certain procedure, namely, by arguing for principles of justice in accordance with these restrictions.

It seems reasonable to suppose that the parties in the original position are equal. That is, all have the same rights in the procedure for choosing principles; each can make proposals, submit reasons for their acceptance and so on. Obviously the purpose of these conditions is to represent equality between human beings as moral persons, as creatures having a conception of their good and capable of a sense of justice. The basis of equality is taken to be similarity in these two respects. Systems of ends are not ranked in value; and each man is presumed to have the requisite ability to understand and to act upon whatever principles are adopted. Together with the veil of ignorance, these conditions define the principles of justice as those which rational persons concerned to advance their interests would consent to as equals when none are known to be advantaged or disadvantaged by social and natural contingencies.

. . .

I have emphasized that this original position is purely hypothetical. It is natural to ask why, if this agreement is never actually entered into, we should take any interest in these principles, moral or otherwise. The answer is that the conditions embodied in the description of the original position are ones that we do in fact accept. Or if we do not, then perhaps we can be persuaded to do so by philosophical reflection. Each aspect of the contractual situation can be given supporting grounds. ... On the other hand, this conception is also an intuitive notion that suggests its own elaboration, so that led on by it we are drawn to define more clearly the standpoint from which we can best interpret moral relationships. We need a conception that enables us to envision our objective from afar: the intuitive notion of the original position is to do this for us.

. . .

I shall now state in a provisional form the two principles of justice that I believe would be chosen in the original position. ... As we go on I shall run through several formulations and approximate step by step the final statement to be given much later. I believe that doing this allows the exposition to proceed in a natural way.

The first statement of the two principles reads as follows.
First: each person is to have an equal right to the most extensive basic liberty compatible with a similar liberty for others.

Second: social and economic inequalities are to be arranged so that they are both (a) reasonably expected to be to everyone's advantage, and (b) attached to positions and offices open to all. There are two ambiguous phrases in the second principle, namely 'everyone's advantage' and 'equally open to all'. Determining their sense more exactly will lead to a second formulation of the principle in s13. The final version of the two principles is given in s45, s39 considers the rendering of the first principle.

By way of general comment, these principles primarily apply, as I have said, to the basic structure of society. They are to govern the assignment of rights and duties and to regulate the distribution of social and economic advantages. As their formulation suggests, these principles presuppose that the social structure can be divided into two more or less distinct parts, the first principle applying to the one, the second to the other. They distinguish between those aspects of the social system that define and secure the equal liberties of citizenship and those that specify and establish social and economic inequalities. The basic liberties of citizens are, roughly speaking, political liberty (the right to vote and to be eligible for public office) together with freedom of speech and assembly; liberty of conscience and freedom of thought; freedom of the person along with the right to hold (personal) property; and freedom from arbitrary arrest and seizure as defined by the concept of the rule of law. These liberties are all required to be equal by the first principle, since citizens of a just society are to have the same basic rights.

The second principle applies, in the first approximation, to the distribution of income and wealth and to the design of organisations that make use of differences in authority and responsibility, or chains of command. While the distribution of wealth and income need not be equal, it must be to everyone's advantage, and at the same time, positions of authority and offices of command must be accessible to all. One applies the second principle by holding positions open, and then, subject to this constraint, arranges social and economic inequalities so that everyone benefits.

These principles are to be arranged in a serial order with the first principle prior to the second. This ordering means that a departure from the institutions of equal liberty required by the first principle cannot be justified by, or compensated for, by greater social and economic advantages. The distribution of wealth and income, and the hierarchies of authority, must be consistent with both the liberties of equal citizenship and equality of opportunity.

21. NOZICK

R NOZICK
Anarchy, State and Utopia [1]
(1974)

The fundamental question of political philosophy, one that precedes questions about how the state should be organized, is whether there should be any state at all. Why not have anarchy. Since anarchist theory, if tenable, undercuts the whole subject of *political* philosophy, it is appropriate to begin political philosophy with an examination of its major theoretical alternative. Those who consider anarchism not an unattractive doctrine will think it possible that political philosophy *ends* here as well. Others impatiently will await what is to come afterwards. Yet ... archists and anarchists alike, those who spring gingerly from the starting point as well as those reluctantly argued away from it, can agree that beginning the subject of political philosophy with state-of-nature theory has an *explanatory* purpose. (Such a purpose is absent when epistemology is begun with an attempt to refute the skeptic.) ...

More to the point, especially for deciding what goals one should try to achieve, would be to focus upon a nonstate situation in which people generally satisfy moral constraints and generally act as they ought. Such an assumption is not wildly optimistic; it does not assume that all people act exactly as they should. Yet this state–of–nature situation is the best anarchic situation one reasonably could hope for. Hence investigating its nature and defects is of crucial importance to deciding whether there should be a state rather than anarchy. If one could show that the state would be superior even to this most favored situation of anarchy, the best that realistically can be hoped for, or would arise by a process involving no morally impermissible steps, or would be an improvement if it arose, this would provide a rationale for the state's existence; it would justify the state.

The night-watchman state of classical liberal theory, limited to the functions of protecting all its citizens against violence, theft, and fraud, and to the enforcement of contracts, and so on, appears to be redistributive. We can image at least one social arrangement intermediate between the scheme of private protective associations and the night-watchman state. Since the night-watchman state is often called a minimal state, we shall call this other arrangement the *ultraminimal state*. An ultraminimal state maintains a monopoly over all use of force except that necessary in immediate self-defence, and so excludes private (or agency) retaliation for wrong and exaction

[1] Nozick, R (1985) 'Anarchy, State and Utopia (1974)'. In *Introduction to Jurisprudence*, 5th edn, eds Lord Lloyd and M D A Freeman. Stevens, London, pp538–541.

of compensation; but it provides protection and enforcement services *only* to those who purchase its protection and enforcement policies. People who don't buy a protection contract from the monopoly don't get protected. The minimal (night-watchman) state is equivalent to the ultraminimal state cojoined with a (clearly redistributive) Friedmanesque voucher plan, financed from tax revenues. Under this plan all people, or some (for example, those in need), are given tax-funded vouchers that can be used only for their purchase of a protection policy from the ultraminimal state.

Since the night-watchman state appears redistributive to the extent that it compels some people to pay for the protection of others, its proponents must explain why this redistributive function of the state is unique. If some redistribution is legitimate in order to protect everyone, why is redistribution not legitimate for other attractive and desirable purposes as well? What rational specifically selects protective services as the sole subject of legitimate redistributive activities?

A system of private protection, even when one protective agency is dominant in a geographical territory, appears to fall short of state. It apparently does not provide protection for everyone in its territory, as does a state, and it apparently does not possess or claim the sort of monopoly over the use of force necessary to a state. In our earlier terminology, it apparently does not constitute a minimal state, and it apparently does not constitute an ultraminimal state.

These very ways in which the dominant protective agency or association in a territory apparently falls short of being a state provide the focus of the individualist anarchist's complaint *against* the state. For he holds that when the state monopolizes the use of force in a territory and punishes others who violate its monopoly, and when the state provides protection for everyone by forcing some to purchase protection for others, it violates moral side constraints on how individuals may be treated. Hence, he concludes, the state itself is intrinsically immoral. The state grants that under some circumstances it is legitimate to punish persons who violate the rights of others, for it itself does so. How then does it arrogate to itself the right to forbid private exaction of justice by other nonaggressive individuals whose rights have been violated? *What* right does the private exacter of justice violate that is not violated also by the state when it punishes? When a group of persons constitute themselves as the state and begin to punish, *and forbid others from doing likewise,* is there some right these others would violate that they themselves do not? By what right, then, can the state and its officials claim a unique right (a privilege) with regard to force and enforce this monopoly? If the private exacter of justice violates no one's rights, then punishing him for his actions (actions state officials also perform) violates his rights and hence violates moral side constraints. Monopolizing the use of force then, on this view, is itself immoral, as is redistribution through the compulsory tax apparatus of the state. Peaceful individuals minding their own business are not violating the rights of others. It does not constitute a violation of someone's rights to refrain from purchasing something for him (that you have not entered specifically into an obligation to buy). Hence, so the argument continues, when the state threatens someone with punishment if he does not contribute to the protection of another, it violates (and its officials violate) his rights. In threatening him with something that would be a violation of his rights if done by a private citizen, they violate moral constraints.

To get something recognisable as a state we must show (1) how an ultraminimal state arises out of the system of private protective associations; and (2) how the ultraminimal state is transformed into the minimal state, how it gives rise to that 'redistribution' for the general provision of protective services that constitutes it as the minimal state. To show that the minimal state is morally legitimate, to show it is not immoral itself, we must show also that these transitions in (1) and (2) *each* are morally legitimate. In the rest of Part I of this work we show how each of these transitions occurs and is morally permissible. We argue that the first transition, from a system of private protective agencies to an ultraminimal state, will occur by an invisible-hand process in a morally permissible way that violates no one's rights. Secondly, we argue that the transition from an ultraminimal state to a minimal state morally must occur. It would be morally impermissible for persons to maintain the monopoly in the ultraminimal state without providing protective services for all, even if this requires specific 'redistribution'. The operators of the ultraminimal state are morally obliged to produce the minimal state ... We argue that no state *more* powerful or extensive than the minimal state is legitimate or justifiable; ...

The principle of compensation requires that people be compensated for having certain risky activities prohibited to them. It might be objected that either you have the right to forbid these people's risky activities or you don't. If you do, you needn't compensate the people for doing to them what you have a right to do; and if you don't, then rather than formulating a policy of compensating people for your unrightful forbidding, you ought simply to stop it. In neither case does the appropriate course seem to be to forbid and then compensate. But the dilemma, 'either you have a right to forbid it so you needn't compensate, or you don't have a right to forbid it so you should stop', is too short. It may be that you do have a right to forbid an action but only provided you compensate those to whom it is forbidden.

A protective agency dominant in a territory does satisfy the two crucial necessary conditions for being a state. It is the only generally effective enforcer of a prohibition on others using unreliable enforcement procedures (calling them as it sees them), and it over-sees these procedures. And the agency protects those nonclients in its territory whom it prohibits from using self-help enforcement procedures on its clients, in their dealings with its clients, even if such protection must be financed (in apparent redistributive fashion) by its clients. It is morally required to do this by the principle of compensation, which requires those who act in self-protection in order to increase their own security to compensate those they prohibit from doing risky acts which might actually have turned out to be harmless, for the disadvantages imposed upon them.

We noted ... that whether the provision of protective services for some by others was 'redistributive' would depend upon the reasons for it. We now see that such provision need not be redistributive since it can be justified on other than redistributive grounds, namely, those provided in the principle of compensation. (Recall that 'redistributive' applies to reasons for a practice or institution, and only elliptically and derivatively to the institution itself.) To sharpen this point, we can imagine that protective agencies offer two types of protection policies: those protecting clients against risky private enforcement of justice and those not doing so but protecting only against theft, assault, and so forth (provided these are not done in the course of private enforcement of justice). Since it is only with regard to those with the first type of policy that others are prohibited from privately enforcing justice, only they will be required to compensate the persons prohibited private enforcement for the disadvantages imposed upon them. The holders of only the second type of policy will not have to pay for the protection of others, there being nothing to have to compensate these others for. Since the reasons for wanting to be protected against private enforcement of justice are compelling, almost all who purchase protection will purchase this type of protection, despite its extra costs, and therefore will be involved in providing protection for the independents.

We have discharged our task of explaining how a state would arise from a state of nature without anyone's rights being violated. The moral objections of the individualist anarchist to the minimal state are overcome. It is not an unjust imposition of a monopoly; the *de facto* monopoly grows by an invisible-hand process and *by morally permissible means*, without anyone's rights being violated and without any claims being made to a special right that others do not possess. And requiring the clients of the *de facto* monopoly to pay for the protection of those they prohibit from self-help enforcement against them, far from being immoral, is morally required by the principle of compensation ...

What is the explanation of how a *minimal* state arises? The dominant protective association with the monopoly element is morally required to compensate for the disadvantages it imposes upon those it prohibits from self-help activities against its clients. However, it actually might fail to provide this compensation. Those operating an ultraminimal state are morally required to transform it into a minimal state, but they might choose not to do so. We have assumed that generally people will do what they are morally required to do. Explaining how a state could arise from a state of nature without violating anyone's rights refutes the principled objections of the anarchist. But one would feel more confidence if an explanation of how a state *would* arise from a state of nature also specified reasons why an ultraminimal state would be transformed into a minimal one, in addition to moral reasons, if it specified incentives for providing the compensation or the causes of its being provided in addition to people's desire to do what they ought. We should note that even in the event that no nonmoral incentives or causes are found to be sufficient for the transition from an ultraminimal to a minimal state, and the explanation continues to lean heavily upon people's moral motivations, it does not specify people's objective as that of establishing a state. Instead, persons view themselves as providing particular other persons with compensation for particular prohibitions they have imposed upon them. The explanation remains an invisible-hand one.

22. DWORKIN

RONALD DWORKIN
Taking Rights Seriously [1]
(1977)

JUSTICE AND RIGHTS

I trust that it is not necessary to describe John Rawls's famous idea of the original position in any great detail.[2] It imagines a group of men and women who come together to form a social contract. Thus far it resembles the imaginary congresses of the classical social contract theories. The original position differs, however, from these theories in its description of the parties. They are men and women with ordinary tastes, talents, ambitions, and convictions, but each is temporarily ignorant of these features of his own personality, and must agree upon a contract before his self-awareness returns.

Rawls tries to show that if these men and women are rational, and act only in their own self-interest, they will choose his two principles of justice. These provide, roughly, that every person must have the largest political liberty compatible with a like liberty for all, and that inequalities in power, wealth, income, and other resources must not exist except in so far as they work to the absolute benefit of the worst-off members of society. Many of Rawls's critics disagree that men and women in the original position would inevitably choose these two principles. The principles are conservative, and the critics believe they would be chosen only by men who were conservative by temperament, and not by men who were natural gamblers. I do not think this criticism is well-taken, but in this essay, at least, I mean to ignore the point. I am interested in a different issue.

Suppose that the critics are wrong, and that men and women in the original position would in fact choose Rawls's two principles as being in their own best interest. Rawls seems to think that the fact would provide an argument in favour of these two principles as a standard of justice against which to test actual political institutions. But it is not immediately plain why this should be so.

If a group contracted in advance that disputes among them would be settled in a particular way, the fact of that contract would be a powerful argument that such disputes should be settled in that way when they do arise. The contract would be in argument in itself, independent of the force of the reasons that might have led

[1] Dworkin, Ronald (1977) *Taking Rights Seriously*. Gerald Duckworth, London, pp150-151, 177-180.
[2] Rawls, John (1971) *A Theory of Justice* (infra).

different people to enter the contract. Ordinarily, for example, each of the parties supposes that a contract he signs is in his own interest; but if someone has made a mistake in calculating his self-interest, the fact that he did contract is a strong reason for the fairness of holding him nevertheless to the bargain.

Rawls does not suppose that any group ever entered into a social contract of the sort he describes. He argues only that if a group of rational men did find themselves in the predicament of the original position, they would contract for the two principles. His contract is hypothetical, and hypothetical contracts do not supply an independent argument for the fairness of enforcing their terms. A hypothetical contract is not simply a pale form of an actual contract; it is no contract at all.

. . .

I said that the use of a social contract, in the way that Rawls uses it, presupposes a deep theory that assumes natural rights. I want now to describe, in somewhat more detail, how the device of a contract applies that assumption. It capitalises on the idea, mentioned earlier, that some political arrangements might be said to be in the antecedent interest of every individual even though they are not, in the event, in his actual interest.

Everyone whose consent is necessary to a contract has a veto over the terms of that contract, but the worth of that veto, to him, is limited by the fact that his judgment may be one of antecedent rather than actual self-interest. He must commit himself, and so abandon his veto, at a time when his knowledge is sufficient only to allow him to estimate the best odds, not to be certain of his bet. So the contract situation is in one way structurally like the situation in which an individual with specific political rights confronts political decisions that may disadvantage him. He has a limited, political right to veto these, a veto limited by the scope of the rights he has. The contract can be used as a model for the political situation by shaping the degree or character of a party's ignorance in the contractual situation so that this ignorance has the same force on his decision as the limited nature of his rights would have in the political situation.

This shaping of ignorance to suit the limited character of political rights is most efficiently done simply by narrowing the individual goals that the parties to the contract know they wish to pursue. If we take Hobbes's deep theory, for example, to propose that men have a fundamental natural right to life, so that it is wrong to take their lives, even for social goals otherwise proper, we should expect a contract situation of the sort he describes. Hobbes's men and women, in Rawls's phrase, have lexically ordered security of life over all other individual goals; the same situation would result if they were simply ignorant of any other goals they might have and unable to speculate about the chances that they have about any particular one or set of these.

The ignorance of the parties in the original position might thus be seen as a kind of limiting case of the ignorance that can be found, in the form of a distorted or eccentric ranking of interests, in classical contract theories and that is natural to the contract device. The original position is a limiting case because Rawls's men are not simply ignorant of interests beyond a chosen few; they are ignorant of all the interests they have. It would be wrong to suppose that this makes them incapable of any judgments of self-interest. But the judgments they make must nevertheless be very abstract; they must allow for any combination of interests, without the benefit of any supposition that some of these are more likely than others.

The basic right of Rawls's deep theory, therefore, cannot be a right to any particular individual goal, like a right to security of life, or a right to lead a life according to a particular conception of the good. Such rights to individual goals may be produced by the deep theory, as rights that men in the original position would stipulate as being in their best interest. But the original position cannot itself be justified on the assumption of such a right, because the parties to the contract do not know that they have any such interest or rank it lexically ahead of others.

So the basic right of Rawls's deep theory must be an abstract right, that is, not a right to any particular individual goal. There are two candidates, within the familiar concepts of political theory, for this role. The first is the right to liberty, and it may strike many readers as both plausible and comforting to assume that Rawls's entire structure is based on the assumption of a fundamental natural right to liberty – plausible because the two principles that compose his theory of justice give liberty an important and dominant place, and comforting because the argument attempting to justify that place seems uncharacteristically incomplete.[3]

Nevertheless, the right to liberty cannot be taken as the fundamental right in Rawls's deep theory. Suppose we define general liberty as the overall minimum possible constraints, imposed by government or by other men, on what a man might want to do. We must then distinguish this general liberty from particular liberties, that is, freedom from such constraints on particular acts thought specially important, like participation in politics. The parties to the original position certainly have, and know that they have, an interest in general liberty, because general liberty will, pro tanto, improve their power to achieve any particular goals they later discover themselves to have. But the qualification is important, because they have no way of knowing that general liberty will in fact improve this power overall, and every reason to suspect that it will not. They know that they might have other interests, beyond general liberty, that can be protected only by political constraints on acts of others.

So if Rawlsian men must be supposed to have a right to liberty of some sort, which the contract situation is shaped to embody, it must be a right to particular liberties. Rawls does name a list of basic liberties, and it is these that his men do choose to protect through their lexically ordered first principle of justice. But Rawls plainly casts this principle as the product of the contract rather than as a condition of it. He argues that the parties to the original position would select these basic liberties to protect the basic goods they decide to value, like self-respect, rather than taking these liberties as goals in themselves. Of course they might, in fact, value the activities protected as basic liberties for their own sake, rather than as means to some other goal or interest. But they certainly do not know that they do.

---

[3] See Hart 'Rawls on Liberty and Its Priority' (1973) 40 *University of Chicago Law Review* 534.

The second familiar concept of political theory is even more abstract than liberty. This is equality, and in one way Rawlsian men and women cannot choose other than to protect it. The state of ignorance in the original position is so shaped that the antecedent interest of everyone must lie, as I said, in the same solution. The right of each man to be treated equally without regard to his person or character or tastes is enforced by the fact that no one else can secure a better position by virtue of being different in any such respect.

. . .

We may describe a right to equality of the second kind, which Rawls says is fundamental, in this way. We might say that individuals have a right to equal concern and respect in the design and administration of the political institutions that govern them. This is a highly abstract right. Someone might argue, for example, that it is satisfied by political arrangements that provide equal opportunity for office and position on the basis of merit. Someone else might argue, to the contrary, that it is satisfied only by a system that guarantees absolute equality of income and status, without regard to merit. A third man might argue that equal concern and respect is provided by that system, whatever it is, that improves the average welfare of all citizens counting the welfare of each on the same scale. A fourth might argue, in the name of this fundamental equality, for the priority of liberty, and for the other apparent inequalities of Rawls's two principles.

The right to equal concern and respect, then, is more abstract than the standard conceptions of equality that distinguish different political theories. It permits arguments that this more basic right requires one or another of these conceptions as a derivative right or goal.

Judicial Reasoning

23. THE COMMON LAW TRADITION

FRANCIS BACON
Essays[1]
(1628)

OF JUDICATURE

Judges ought to remember, that their Office is Jus dicere, and not Jus Dare; To Interpret Law, and not to Make Law, or Give Law ...

The Parts of a Judge in Hearing and Foure: To direct the Evidence; To Moderate Length, Repetition, or Impertinency of Speech; To Recapitulate, Select, and Collate, the Material Points of that, which hath beene said; And to Give the Rule or Sentence. Whatsoever is above these, is too much ...

For that which may concerne the Soveraigne and Estate. Judges ought above all to remember the Conclusion of the Roman Twelve Tables; Salus Populi Suprema Lex; And to know, that Lawes, except they bee in Order to that End, are but Things Captious, and Oracles not well Inspired. Therefore it is an Happie Thing in a State, when Kings and States doe often Consult with Judges; And againe, when Judges doe often Consult with the King and State: ... And let no Man weakly conceive, that Just Laws, and True Policie, have any Antipathie: For they are like the Spirits, and Sinewes, that One moves with the Other.

A L GOODHART
The Ratio Decidendi of a Case [2]
(1930)

Having, as a first step, determined all the facts of the case as seen by the judge, it is then necessary to discover which of these facts he has found material for his judgment. This is far more difficult than the first step, for the judge may fail to lable his facts. It is only the strong judge, one who is clear in his own mind as to

---

[1] Bacon, Francis (1628) *Essays*. Reprinted (1928) Oxford University Press, Oxford.
[2] From *Essays in Jurisprudence and the Common Law* (1931) p1. Reprinted from (1930) 40 *Yale Law Journal* 161.

the grounds for this decision,[3] who invariably says, 'on facts A and B and on them alone I reach conclusion X.' Too often the cautious judge will include in his opinion facts which are not essential to his judgment, leaving it for future generations to determine whether or not these facts constitute a part of the ratio decidendi. The following guides may, however, be followed in distinguishing between material and immaterial facts.

(1) As was stated above in discussing the principle of a case in which there is no opinion, the facts of person, time, place, kind and amount are presumably immaterial. This is true to an even greater extent when there is an opinion, for if these facts are held to be material particular emphasis will naturally be placed upon them.

(2) All facts which the court specifically states are immaterial must be considered immaterial. In *People* v *Vandewater*[4] the defendant, who was charged with maintaining a public nuisance, kept an illicit drinking place. There was proof that the house was actually disorderly as persons became intoxicated on the premises and left them in that condition. The majority of the New York Court of Appeals, speaking by Lehman J, held that the fact that acts of annoyance and disturbance had occurred was immaterial. The learned judge said[5]:

> It is the disorderly *character* of the illicit drinking place which constitutes the offense to the public decency. That offense arises from the nature of the acts habitually done upon the premises and the injury to the morals and health of the community which must naturally flow therefrom, apart from the annoyance or disturbance of those persons who might be in the neighbourhood.

This case strikingly illustrates the distinction between the view that a case is authority for a proposition based on all its facts, and the view that it is authority for a proposition based on those facts only which were seen by the court as material. If we adopt the first view, then the majority judgment is only a dictum, not binding in any future case in which the facts do not show actual disorder. Under the second view the court has specifically stated that the fact of disorder is immaterial. The case is, therefore, a binding precedent in all future cases in which either orderly or disorderly illicit drinking places are kept. The case can be analysed as follows:

FACTS OF THE CASE

Fact I. D maintained an illicit drinking place.

Fact II. This illicit place was noisy and disorderly.

Conclusion. D is guilty of maintaining a nuisance.

---

[3] It was Jessel, MR who said, 'I may be wrong, but I never have any doubts'. An astounding example of an uncertain judgment is Lord Hatherley's opinion in *River Wear Commissioners* v *Adamson* (1877) 2 App Cas 743, 752. Of this Atkin LJ said, in *The Mostyn* [1927] p25, that he was unable to determine whether Lord Hatherley 'was concurring in the appeal being allowed, or the appeal being dismissed, or whether he was concurring in the opinion given by Lord Cairns'.

[4] 250 NY 83.

[5] At p96. Italics mine.

Material facts as seen by the court

Fact I. D maintained an illicit drinking place.

Conclusion. D is guilty of maintaining a nuisance.

By specifically holding that fact II was immaterial, the court succeeded in creating a broad principle instead of a narrow one.

(3) All facts which the court impliedly treats as immaterial must be considered immaterial. The difficulty in these cases is to determine whether a court has or has not considered the fact immaterial. Evidence of this implication is found when the court, after having stated the facts generally, then proceeds to choose a smaller number of facts on which it bases its conclusion. The omitted facts are presumably held to be immaterial. In *Rylands* v *Fletcher*[6] the defendant employed an independent contractor to make a reservoir on his land. Owing to the contractor's negligence in not filling up some disused mining shafts, the water escaped and flooded the plaintiff's mine. The defendant was held liable. Is it the principle of the case that a man who builds a reservoir on his land is liable for the negligence of an independent contractor? Why then is the case invariably cited as laying down the broader doctrine of 'absolute liability'? The answer is found in the opinions. After stating the facts as above, the judges thereafter ignored the fact of the contractor's negligence, and based their conclusions on the fact that an artificial reservoir had been constructed. The negligence of the contractor was, therefore, impliedly held to be an immaterial fact. The case can be analysed as follows:

FACTS OF THE CASE

Fact I. D had a reservoir built on his land.

Fact II. The contractor who built it was negligent.

Fact III. Water escaped and injured P.

Conclusion. D is liable to P.

Material facts as seen by the court

Fact I. D had a reservoir built on his land.

Fact III. Water escaped and injured P.

Conclusion. D is liable to P.

By the omission of fact II, the doctrine of 'absolute liability' was established.

It is obvious from the above cases that it is essential to determine what facts have been held to be immaterial, for the principle of a case depends as much on exclusion as it does on inclusion. It is under these circumstances that the reasons given by the judge in his opinion, or his statement of the rule of law which he is following, are of peculiar importance, for they may furnish us with a guide for determining which facts he considered material and which immaterial. His reason may be incorrect and his statement of the law too wide, but they will indicate to us on what facts he reached his conclusion.

[6] (1868) LR 3 HL 330.

(4) All facts which are specifically stated to be material must be considered material. Such specific statements are usually found in cases in which the judges are afraid of laying down too broad a principle. Thus in *Heaven* v *Pender*[7] the plaintiff, a workman employed to paint a ship, was injured owing to a defective staging supplied by the defendant dock owner to the shipowner. Brett, MR, held that the defendant was liable on the grounds that,[8]

Whenever one person is by circumstances placed in such a position with regard to another that every one of ordinary sense who did think would at once recognise that if he did not use ordinary care and skill in his own conduct with regard to those circumstances he would cause danger of injury to the person or property of the other, a duty arises to use ordinary care and skill to avoid such danger.

Cotton and Bowen LJJ, agreed with the Master of the Rolls that the defendant was liable, but the material facts on which they based their judgment were[9] that (a) the plaintiff was on the staging for business in which the dock owner was interested, and (b) he 'must be considered as invited by the dock owner to use the dock and all appliances provided by the dock owner as incident to the use of the dock'. The principle of the case cannot, therefore, be extended beyond the limitation of these material facts.

(5) If the opinion does not distinguish between material and immaterial facts, then all the facts set forth in the opinion must be considered material with the exception of those that on their face are immaterial. There is a presumption against wide principles of law, and the smaller the number of material facts in a case the wider will the principle be. Thus if a case like *Hambrook* v *Stokes Bros*,[10] in which a mother died owing to shock at seeing a motor accident which threatened her child, is decided on the fact that a bystander may recover for injury due to shock, we have a broad principle of law.[11] If the additional fact that the bystander was a mother is held to be material we then get a narrow principle of law.[12] Therefore, unless a fact is expressly or impliedly held to be immaterial it must be considered material.

(6) Thus far we have been discussing the method of determining the principle of a case in which there is only a single opinion, or in which all the opinions are in agreement. How do we determine the principle of a case in which there are several opinions which agree as to the result but differ in the material facts on which they are based? In such an event the principle of the case is limited to the sum of all the facts held to be material by the various judges. A case involves facts A, B and C, and the defendant is held liable. The first judge finds that fact A is the only material fact, the second that B is material, the third that C is material. The principle of the case is, therefore, that on the material facts A, B and C the defendant is liable. If, however, two of the three judges had been in agreement that

[7] (1883) 11 QBD 503.
[8] At p509.
[9] At p515.
[10] [1925] 1 KB 141.
[11] See the judgment of Atkin LJ at p152.
[12] See the judgment of Bankes LJ at p146.

fact A was the only material one, and that the others were immaterial, then the case would be a precedent on this point, even though the third judge had held that facts B and C were the material ones. The method of determining the principle of a case in which there are several opinions is thus the same as that used when there is only one. Care must be taken by the student, however, to see that the material facts of each opinion are stated and analysed accurately, for sometimes judges think that they are in agreement on the facts when they only concur in the result.[13]

Having established the material and the immaterial facts of the case as seen by the court, we can then proceed to state the principles of the case. It is found in the conclusion reached by the judges on the basis of the material facts and on the exclusion of the immaterial ones. In a certain case the court finds that facts A, B and C exist. It then excludes fact A as immaterial, and on facts B and C it reaches conclusion X. What is the ratio decidendi of this case? There are two principles: (a) in any future case in which the facts are A, B and C, the court must reach conclusion X, and (b) in any future case in which the facts are B and C the court must reach conclusion X. In the second case the absence of fact A does not affect the result, for fact A has been held to be immaterial. The court, therefore, creates a principle when it determines which are the material and which are the immaterial facts on which it bases its decision.

It follows that a conclusion based on a fact, the existence of which has not been determined by the court, cannot establish a principle. We then have what is called a dictum. If, therefore, a judge in the course of his opinion suggests a hypothetical fact, and then states what conclusion he would reach if that fact existed, he is to creating a principle. The difficulty which is sometimes found in determining whether a statement is a dictum or not, is due to uncertainty as to whether the judge is treating a fact as hypothetical or real. When a judge says, 'In this case as the facts are so and so I reach conclusion X', this is not a dictum, even though the judge has been incorrect in his statement of the facts. But if the judge says, 'If the facts in this case were so and so then I reach conclusion X', this is a dictum, even though the facts are as given. The second point frequently arises when a case involves two different sets of facts. Having determined the first set of facts and reached a conclusion on them, the judge may not desire to take up the time necessarily involved in determining the second set. Any views he may express as to the undetermined second set are therefore dicta. If, however, the judge does determine both sets, as he is at liberty to do, and reaches a conclusion on both, then the case creates two principles and neither is a dictum. Thus the famous case of *National Sailors' and Firemen's Union* v *Reed*[14] in which Astbury J declared the General Strike of 1926 to be illegal, involved two sets of facts, and the learned judge reached a conclusion on each.[15] It is submitted that it is incorrect to say that either

[13] Cf the various judgments in *Great Western Ry Co* v *Owners of SS Mostyn* [1928] AC 57. See notes in (1928) 44 LQR 138 on this point.

[14] [1926] 1 Ch 536.

[15] The first set of facts included the fact of the General Strike. The second set excluded the General Strike, but included the fact that the internal rules of the union were violated.

one of the conclusions involved a dictum because the one preceded the other or because the one was based on broad grounds and the other on narrow ones.[16] On the other hand, if in a case the judge holds that a certain fact prevents a cause of action from arising, then his further finding that there would have been a cause of action except for this fact is an obiter dictum. By excluding the preventive fact the situation becomes hypothetical, and the conclusion based on such hypothetical facts can only be a dictum.[17]

Having established the principle of a case, and excluded all dicta, the final step is to determine whether or not it is a binding precedent for some succeeding case in which the facts are prima facie similar. This involves a double analysis. We must first state the material facts in the precedent case and then attempt to find the material ones in the second one. If these are identical, then the first case is a binding precedent for the second, and the court must reach the same conclusion as it did in the first one. If the first case lacks any material fact or contains any additional ones not found in the second, then it is not a direct precedent.[18] Thus in *Nichols v Marsland*[19] the material facts were similar to those in *Rylands v Fletcher*[20] except for the additional fact that the water escaped owing to a violent storm. If the court had found that this additional fact was not a material one, then the rule in *Rylands v Fletcher* would have applied. As it found, however, that it was a material one, it was able to reach a different conclusion.

Before summarising the rules suggested above, two possible criticisms must be considered. It may be said that a doctrine which finds the principle of a case in its material facts leaves us with hardly any general legal principles, for facts are infinitely various. It is true that facts are infinitely various, but the material facts which are usually found in a particular legal relationship are strictly limited. Thus the fact that there must be consideration in a simple contract is a single material fact although the kinds of consideration are unlimited. Again, if A builds a reservoir on Blackacre and B builds one on Whiteacre, the owners, builders, reservoirs and fields are different. But the material fact that a person has built a reservoir on his land is in each case the same. Of course a court can always avoid a precedent by finding that an additional fact is material, but if it does so without reason the result leads to

[16] For conflicting views on this point see note by a learned writer in (1926) 42 *Law Quarterley Review* 289, and also note in 42 *Law Quarterley Review* 296.

[17] In *Lynn v Bamber* [1930] 2 KB 72, McCardie J held that unconcealed fraud was a good reply to a plea of the Statutes of Limitation. As, however, he found that there was no fraud in the case before him, it is submitted that his statement as to the Statutes of Limitation was a dictum. On this point see note in (1930) 46 *Law Quarterley Review* 261.

[18] It may, however, carry great weight as analogy. Thus if it has been held in a case that a legatee who has murdered his testator cannot take under the will, this will be an analogy of some weight in a future case in which the legatee has committed manslaughter. It is important to note that when a case is used merely as an analogy, and not as a direct binding precedent, the reasoning of the court by which it reached its judgment carries greater weight than the conclusion itself. The second court, being free to reach its own conclusion, will only adopt the reasoning of the first court if it considers it to be correct and desirable. In such analogous precedents the ratio decidendi of the case can with some truth be described as the reason of the case.

[19] (1875) LR 10 Ex 255.

[20] (1868) LR 3 HL 330.

confusion in the law. Such an argument assumes, moreover, that courts are disingenuous and arbitrary. Whatever may have been true in the past, it is clear that at the present day English courts do not attempt to circumvent the law in this way.

The second criticism can be stated as follows: If we are bound by the facts as seen by the judge, may not this enable him deliberately or by inadvertence to decide a case which was not before him by basing his decision upon facts stated by him to be real and material but actually non-existent? Can this conclusion in such a case be anything more than a dictum? Can a judge, by making a mistake, give himself authority to decide what is in effect a hypothetical case? The answer to this interesting question is that the whole doctrine of precedent is based on the theory that as a general rule judges do not make mistakes either of fact or of law. In an exceptional case a judge may in error base his conclusion on a non-existent fact, but it is better to suffer this mistake, which may prove of benefit to the law as a whole, however painful its results may have been to the individual litigant, than to throw doubt on every precedent on which our law is based.

Conclusion

The rules for finding the principle of a case can, therefore, be summarised as follows:

(1)   The principle of a case is not found in the reasons given in the opinion.

(2)   The principle is not found in the rule of law set forth in the opinion.

(3)   The principle is not necessarily found by a consideration of all the ascertainable facts of the case, and the judge's decision.

(4)   The principle of the case is found by taking account (a) of the facts treated by the judge as material, and (b) his decision as based on them.

(5)   In finding the principle it is also necessary to establish what facts were held to be immaterial by the judge, for the principle may depend as much on exclusion as it does on inclusion.

LORD DENNING
The Family Story [21]
(1981)

It is in the Court of Appeal that a Judge has the chief opportunity of influencing the law – always supposing that he can get his two colleagues (or at any rate one of them) to agree with him. Many of the cases raise a point of law of some kind or other. The decision of the Court settles it. Very few cases go to the Lords.

Not many of the Judges – even of the Court of Appeal – have any conscious philosophy of the law: but subconsciously each develops his own philosophy. During

[21] Denning (1981) *The Family Story*. Butterworths, London, pp172-174, 182-183.

my term as a Lord Justice of Appeal – from 1948 to 1957 – I found myself evolving a philosophy of my own. I applied it in the cases that came before us. You will find them in the Law Reports. I also gave expression to it in lectures and addresses. These are not readily available for you. So please bear with me if I tell you of them. My philosophy can be summarised under three headings: (i) Let justice be done; (ii) Freedom under the law; (iii) Put your trust in God. I will take them in order.

In my coat of arms, I took as my motto, Fiat justitia – Let justice be done – believing it to have a respectable origin. I have since discovered that it was first used to excuse the most outrageous injustice. It comes from a story told by Seneca.[22] Piso sentenced a soldier to death for the murder of Gaius. He ordered a centurion to execute the sentence. When the soldier was about to be executed, Gaius came forward himself alive and well. The centurion reported it to Piso. He sentenced all three to death. The soldier because he had already been sentenced. The centurion for disobeying orders. And Gaius for being the cause of the death of two innocent men. Piso excused it by the plea, Fiat justitia, ruat coelum – Let justice be done, though the heavens should fall.

Afterwards Lord Mansfield used the same phrase in the celebrated case of John Wilkes: but he did it also with his tongue in his cheek. John Wilkes had published, so it was said, a seditous libel in a paper called *The North Briton*. He had fled abroad and been outlawed. He returned and himself asked for the outlawry to be reversed, but he was cast into prison meanwhile. He was a popular hero and many supported him and urged his release. Numerous crowds thronged in and about Westminster Hall. Pamphlets were issued in the name of the people, dictating to the Judges the way they should decide. Reasons of policy were urged emphasising the danger to the kingdom by commotions and general confusion. This is how Lord Mansfield answered them when he came to give judgment:

Give me leave to take the opportunity of this great and respectable audience, to let the whole world know, all such attempts are vain. Unless we have been able to find an error which will bear us out, to reverse the outlawry, it must be affirmed. The Constitution does not allow reasons of State to influence our judgments: God forbid it should! We must not regard political consequences, howsoever formidable they might be: if rebellion were the certain consequence, we are bound to say 'Fiat justitia, ruat coelum'. The Constitution trusts the King with reasons of State and policy: he may stop prosecutions: he may pardon offences: it is his, to judge whether the law or the criminal shall yield. We have no election ... We are to say, what we take the law to be: if we do not speak our real opinions, we prevaricate with God and our own consciences ... Once for all, let it be understood, that no endeavours of this kind will influence any man who at present sits here.

These are fine words but I ought, perhaps, to add that Lord Mansfield went on to find a flaw on which he could and did reverse the outlawry. It was a most technical point. The sheriff had in the formal document referred to 'my country

[22] Dialogues, III, 18.

court' without adding words 'of Middlesex' as he ought to have done – and for want of those two words the outlawry was held bad and John Wilkes was released. It would be lese-majesté to suggest that Lord Mansfield was influenced by the public clamour. But his audience knew not which to admire the more – the eloquence by which he silenced the people – or the subtlety by which he set their hero free. For myself I prefer to take the first part – 'Fiat justitia' – and discard the 'ruat coelum'. If justice is done, the heavens should not fall. They should rejoice.

My root belief is that the proper role of a judge is to do justice between the parties before him. If there is any rule of law which impairs the doing of justice, then it is the province of the judge to do all he legitimately can to avoid that rule – or even to change it – so as to do justice in the instant case before him. He need not wait for the legislature to intervene: because that can never be of any help in the instant case. I would emphasise, however, the word 'legitimately': the judge is himself subject to the law and must abide by it. ...

When William Temple on one occasion went to address a gathering of lawyers at the Inns of Court he opened his remarks by saying, 'I can't say that I know much about the law, having been far more interested in justice'. That was a piece of delicate irony directed at the lawyers then present. His hearers had been brought up in the philosophy of John Austin. That drew a clear and absolute line between law and morals. Law was simply a series of commands issued by a sovereign telling the people what to do or what not to do. Judges and advocates were not concerned with the morality of the law, but only with the interpretation of it and with its enforcement. This supposed division between law on the one hand and morals on the other has been a great mistake.

So is the supposed division between law and religion. I know that a great number of people today think that law and religion have nothing in common. The law, they say, governs our dealings with our fellows. It lays down rigid rules which must be obeyed without questioning whether they are right or wrong. But religion, they say, concerns our dealings with God: it is concerned with the things of the next world, not with the things of this world in which we are living.

That was the philosophy of law in which I was brought up. It is a philosophy which still governs many of the lawyers of my generation. But it is a false philosophy. The truth is that although religion, law and morals can be separated, they are nevertheless very dependent on one another. Without religion there can be no morality: and without morality there can be no law. ...

And speaking of the part of ordinary men, may I just say how wrong it is to apply the Austinian philosophy to them. The people of England do not obey the law because they are commanded to do so; nor because they are afraid of sanctions or of being punished. They obey the law because they know it is a thing they *ought* to do. There are of course some wicked persons who do not recognise it to be their duty to obey the law: and for them sanctions and punishment must be inflicted. But this does not alter the fact that the great majority of the people obey the law simply because they recognise it to be obligatory on them. They recognise that they are under a moral obligation to obey it. For this reason, it is most important that the law should be just. People will respect rules of law which are intrinsically right and just, and will expect their neighbours to obey them, as well of course as obeying the rules themselves: but they will not feel the same about rules which are unrighteous or unjust. If people are to feel a sense of obligation to the law, then the law must correspond, as near as may be, with justice.

So I ask you to accept with me that law is concerned with justice and that religion is concerned with justice. And thence I ask the question – What is justice? That question has been asked by many men far wiser than you or I and no one has yet found a satisfactory answer. All I would suggest is that justice is not something you can see. It is not temporal but eternal. How does man know what is justice? It is not the product of his intellect but of his spirit. Religion concerns the spirit in man whereby he is able to recognise what is justice: whereas law is only the application, however imperfectly, of justice in our everyday affairs. If religion perishes in the land, truth and justice will also. We have already strayed too far from the faith of our fathers. Let us return to it, for it is the only thing that can save us.

I was a Lord Justice of Appeal for nine years. It was a most rewarding time. Usually we were agreed, but sometimes I found myself in a minority. I was reluctant to dissent. But in the last resort I did so. It was for my own peace of mind. So long as I did what I thought was just, I was content. I could sleep at night. But if I did what was unjust, I stayed awake worrying. Afterwards, when I spoke to students I made fun about it. I used to tell them: 'When I was a Judge of first instance, sitting alone, I could and did do justice. But when I went to the Court of Appeal of three, I found that the chances of doing justice were two to one against! That was quite untrue. In the great majority of cases, we were all agreed. It was only in a very few that I dissented – and then I did so only for conscience sake – because I could not bring myself to agree.

24. DWORKIN'S LAW
AS INTEGRITY

RONALD DWORKIN
Law's Empire [1]
(1986)

I

After the American Civil War the victorious North amended the Constitution to end slavery and many of its incidents and consequences. One of these amendments, the Fourteenth, declared that no state might deny any person the 'equal protection of the laws'. After Reconstruction the southern states, once more in control of their own politics, segregated many public facilities by race. Blacks had to ride in the back of the bus and were allowed to attend only segregated schools with other blacks. In the famous case of *Plessy* v *Ferguson* the defendant argued, ultimately before the Supreme Court, that these practices of segregation automatically violated the equal protection clause. The Court rejected their claim; it said that the demands of that clause were satisfied if the states provided separate but equal facilities and that the fact of segregation alone did not make facilities automatically unequal.

In 1954 a group of black schoolchildren in Topeka, Kansas, raised the question again. A great deal had happened to the United States in the meantime – a great many blacks had died for that country in a recent war, for example – and segregation seemed more deeply wrong to more people than it had when *Plessy* was decided. Nevertheless, the states that practiced segregation resisted integration fiercely, particularly in the schools. Their lawyers argued that since *Plessy* was a decision by the Supreme Court, that precedent had to be respected. This time the Court decided for the black plaintiffs. Its decision was unexpectedly unanimous, though the unanimity was purchased by an opinion, written by Chief Justice Earl Warren, that was in many ways a compromise. He did not reject the 'separate but equal' formula outright; instead he relied on controversial sociological evidence to show that racially segregated schools could not be equal, for that reason alone. Nor did he say flatly that the Court was now overruling *Plessy*. He said only that *if* the present decision was inconsistent with *Plessy*, then that earlier decision was being overruled. The most important compromise, for practical purposes, was in the

[1] Dworkin, Ronald (1986) *Law's Empire*. Fontana Press, London, pp29–30, 33–35, 220–221, 255–258.

design of the remedy the opinion awarded the plaintiffs. It did not order the schools of the southern states to be desegregated immediately, but only, in a phrase that became an emblem of hypocrisy and delay, 'with all deliberate speed'.

The decision was very controversial, the process of integration that followed was slow, and significant progress required many more legal, political, and even physical battles. Critics said that segregation, however deplorable as a matter of political morality, is not unconstitutional. They pointed out that the phrase 'equal protection' does not in itself decide whether segregation is forbidden or not, that the particular congressmen and state officials who drafted, enacted, and ratified the Fourteenth Amendment were well aware of segregated education and apparently thought their amendment left it perfectly legal, and that the Court's decision in *Plessy* was an important precedent of almost ancient lineage and ought not lightly be overturned. These were arguments about the proper grounds of constitutional law, not arguments of morality or repair: many who made them agreed that segregation was immoral and that the Constitution would be a better document if it had forbidden it. Nor were the arguments of those who agreed with the Court arguments of morality or repair. If the Constitution did not as a matter of law prohibit official racial segregation, then the decision in *Brown* was an illicit constitutional amendment, and few who supported the decision thought they were supporting that. This case, like our other sample cases, was fought over the question of law. Or so it seems from the opinion, and so it seemed to those who fought it.

LEGAL POSITIVISM

Semantic theories suppose that lawyers and judges use mainly the same criteria (though these are hidden and unrecognised) in deciding when propositions of law are true or false; they suppose that lawyers actually agree about the grounds of law. These theories disagree about which criteria lawyers do share and which grounds these criteria do stipulate. Law students are taught to classify semantic theories according to the following rough scheme. The semantic theories that have been most influential hold that the shared criteria make the truth of propositions of law turn on certain specified historical events. These positivist theories, as they are called, support the plain-fact view of law, that genuine disagreement about what the law is must be empirical disagreement about the history of legal institutions. Positivist theories differ from one another about which historical facts are crucial, however, and two versions have been particularly important in British jurisprudence.

John Austin, a nineteenth-century English lawyer and lecturer, said that a proposition of law is true within a particular political society if it correctly reports the past command of some person or group occupying the position of sovereign in that society. He defined a sovereign as some person or group whose commands are habitually obeyed and who is not in the habit of obeying anyone else. This theory became the object of intense, and often scholastic, debate. Legal philosophers argued about whether certain obviously true propositions of law – propositions about the number of signatures necessary to make a will legally valid, for example – could really be said to be true in virtue of anyone's *command*. (After all, no one has commanded you or me to make any will at all, let alone to make a valid will.) They also debated whether any group could be said to be an Austinian sovereign in a democracy, like the United States, in which the people as a whole retain the power to alter the form of government radically by amending the constitution. But though Austin's theory was found defective in various matters of detail, and many repairs and improvements were suggested, his main idea, that law is a matter of historical decisions by people in positions of political power, has never wholly lost its grip on jurisprudence.

The most important and fundamental restatement of that idea is H L A Hart's book, *The Concept of Law*, first published in 1961. Hart rejected Austin's account of legal authority as a brute fact of habitual command and obedience. He said that the true grounds of law lie in the acceptance by the community as a whole of a fundamental master rule (he called this a 'rule of recognition') that assigns to particular people or groups the authority to make law. So propositions of law are true not just in virtue of the commands of people who are habitually obeyed, but more fundamentally in virtue of social conventions that represent the community's acceptance of a scheme of rules empowering such people or groups to create valid law. For Austin the proposition that the speed limit in California is 55 is true just because the legislators who enacted that rule happen to be in control there; for Hart it is true because the people of California have accepted, and continue to accept, the scheme of authority deployed in the state and national constitutions. For Austin the proposition that careless drivers are required to compensate mothers who suffer emotional injury at the scene of an accident is true in Britain because people with political power have made the judges their lieutenants and tacitly adopt their commands as their own. For Hart that proposition is true because the rule of recognition accepted by the British people makes judges' declarations law subject to the powers of other officials – legislators – to repeal that law if they wish.

Hart's theory, like Austin's, has generated a good deal of debate among those who are drawn to its basic idea. What does the 'acceptance' of a rule of recognition consist in? Many officials of Nazi Germany obeyed Hitler's commands as law, but only out of fear. Does that mean they accepted a rule of recognition entitling him to make law? If so, then the difference between Hart's theory and Austin's becomes elusive, because there would then be no difference between a group of people accepting a rule of recognition and simply falling into a self-conscious pattern of obedience out of fear. If not, if acceptance requires more than mere obedience, then it seems to follow that there was no law in Nazi Germany, that no propositions of law were true or in many other places where most people would say there is law, though bad or unpopular law. And then Hart's theory would not, after all, capture how all lawyers use the word 'law'. Scholars have worried about this and other aspects of Hart's theory, but once again his root idea, that the truth of propositions of law is in some important way dependent upon conventional patterns of recognizing law, has attracted wide support. ...

Consider, for example, the Supreme Court's decision in *Brown*. A pragmatist justice of a general utilitarian cast of mind would have asked himself whether a decision for the plaintiff schoolchildren, based on the illegality of all official segregation in schools, was really best for the future, all things considered. He might well have considered that it was, but he would have had to consider strong practical arguments to the contrary. It was perfectly sensible to think that such a dramatic change in the social structure of a large part of the country, ordered by a court that is not responsible to any electorate, would produce a backlash that would damage rather than advance racial equality and make education more difficult for everyone for a generation. It was also sensible to think that the Court's order would never be fully obeyed, and that its failure would impair the power of the Court to protect minorities and enforce constitutional rights in the future.

Even if a pragmatist decided in the end that the decision the Court actually reached was the best, all things considered, he might well have paused before extending that decision in the dramatic way the Supreme Court did in subsequent years. The practical arguments against busing black children to white schools, and vice versa, were and remain very powerful, as the menace and hatred in several northern cities continue to make plain. A conception of law built on the interpretive principle of integrity provides much less room for practical arguments of that sort in establishing substantive constitutional rights. It is therefore more demanding and much more radical in circumstances like those of *Brown*, when the plaintiff succeeds in showing that an important part of what has been thought to be law is inconsistent with more fundamental principles necessary to justify law as a whole. ... Judges who accept the interpretive ideal of integrity decide hard cases by trying to find, in some coherent set of principles about people's rights and duties, the best constructive interpretation of the political structure and legal doctrine of their community. They try to make that complex structure and record the best these can be. It is analytically useful to distinguish different dimensions or aspects of any working theory. It will include convictions about both fit and justification. Convictions about fit will provide a rough threshold requirement that an interpretation of some part of the law must meet if it is to be eligible at all. Any plausible working theory would disqualify an interpretation of our own law that denied legislative competence or supremacy outright or that claimed a general principle of private law requiring the rich to share their wealth with the poor. That threshold will eliminate interpretations that some judges would otherwise prefer, so the brute facts of legal history will in this way limit the role any judge's personal convictions of justice can play in his decisions. Different judges will set this threshold differently. But anyone who accepts law as integrity must accept that the actual political history of his community will sometimes check his other political convictions in his overall interpretative judgment. If he does not – if his threshold of fit is wholly derivative from and adjustable to his convictions of justice, so that the latter automatically provide an eligible interpretation – then he cannot claim in good faith to be interpreting his legal practice at all. Like the chain novelist whose judgments of fit automatically adjusted in his substantive literary opinions, he is acting from bad faith or self-deception.

Hard cases arise, for any judge, when his threshold test does not discriminate between two or more interpretations of some statute or line of cases. Then he must choose between eligible interpretations by asking which shows the community's structure of institutions and decisions – its public standards as a whole – in a better light from the standpoint of political morality. His own moral and political convictions are now directly engaged. But the political judgment he must make is itself complex and will sometimes set one department of his political morality against another: his decision will reflect not only his opinions about justice and fairness but his higher-order convictions about how these ideals should be compromised when they compete. Questions of fit arise at this stage of interpretation as well, because even when an interpretation survives the threshold requirement, any infelicities of fit will count against it, in the ways we noticed, in the general balance of political virtues. Different judges will disagree about each of these issues and will accordingly take different views of what the law of their community, properly understood, really is.

Any judge will develop, in the course of his training and experience, a fairly individualised working conception of law on which he will rely, perhaps unthinkingly, in making these various judgments and decisions, and the judgments will then be, for him, a matter of feel or instinct rather than analysis. Even so, we as critics can impose structure on his working theory by teasing out its rules of thumb about fit – about the relative importance of consistency with past rhetoric and popular opinion, for example – and its more substantive opinions or learnings about justice and fairness. Most judges will be like other people in their community, and fairness and justice will therefore not often compete for them. But judges whose political opinions are more eccentric or radical will find that the two ideals conflict in particular cases, and they will have to decide which resolution of that conflict would show the community's record in the best light. Their working conceptions will accordingly include higher-order principles that have proved necessary to that further decision. A particular judge may think or assume, for example, that political decisions should mainly respect majority opinion, and yet believe that this requirement relaxes and even disappears when serious constitutional rights are in question.

We should now recall two general observations we made in constructing the chain-novel model, because they apply here as well. First, the different aspects or dimensions of a judge's working approach – the dimensions of fit and substance, and of different aspects of substance – are in the last analysis all responsive to his political judgment. His convictions about fit, as these appear either in his working threshold requirement or analytically later in competition with substance, are political not mechanical. They express his commitment to integrity: he believes that an interpretation that falls below his threshold of fit shows the record of the community in an irredeemably bad light, because proposing that interpretation suggests that the community has characteristically dishonoured its own principles. When an interpretation meets the threshold, remaining defects of fit may be compensated, in his overall judgment, if the principles of that interpretation are particularly attractive, because then he sets off the community's infrequent lapses in respecting these principles against its virtue in generally observing them. The constraint fit imposes on substance, in any working theory, is therefore the constraint of one type of political conviction on another in the overall judgment which interpretation makes a political record the best it can be overall, everything taken into account. Second, the mode of this constraint is the mode we identified in the chain novel. It is not the constraint of external hard fact or of interpersonal consensus. But rather the structural constraint of different kinds of principle within a system of principle, and it is none the less genuine for that.

No mortal judge can or should try to articulate his instinctive working theory so far, or make that theory so concrete and detailed, that no further thought will be necessary case by case. He must treat any general principles or rules of thumb he has followed in the past as provisional and stand ready to abandon these in favour of more sophisticated and searching analysis when the occasion demands. These will be moments of special difficulty for any judge, calling for fresh political judgments that may be hard to make. It will be absurd to suppose that he will always have at hand the necessary background convictions of political morality for such occasions. Very hard cases will force him to develop his conception of law and his political morality together in a mutually supporting way. But it is nevertheless possible for any judge to confront fresh and challenging issues as a matter of principle, and this is what law as integrity demands of him. He must accept that in finally choosing one interpretation over another of a much contested line of precedents, perhaps after demanding thought and shifting conviction, he is developing his working conception of law in one rather than another direction. This must seem to him the right direction as a matter of political principle, not just appealing for the moment because it recommends an attractive decision in the immediate case. There is, in this counsel, much room for deception, including self-deception. But on most occasions it will be possible for judges to recognise when they have submitted an issue to the discipline it describes. And also to recognise when some other judge has not. ...

D PANNICK
A Note on Dworkin and Precedent [2]
(1980)

I

A theory of adjudication remains one of the more elusive goals of modern jurisprudence. Who should resolve a legal dispute and how should they resolve it? In *Taking Rights Seriously*,[3] Ronald Dworkin attacks the positivist thesis of H L A

[2] Pannick, D (1980) 'A Note on Dworkin and Precedent' 43 *Modern Law Review* 36-39.
[3] *Taking Rights Seriously* (Duckworth, 1977. New impression with an appendix, 'A Reply to Critics', 1978). Henceforth cited as 'Dworkin'.

Hart[4] that in hard cases judges exercise a quasi-legislative discretion for one party or the other. Dworkin rejects this as descriptively false. He also finds it normatively unsatisfactory because undemocratic (since it involves lawmaking by judges) and unfair (because those laws are applied ex post facto in the litigants).

Dworkin's theory of adjudication is that in all cases judges weigh and apply competing rights. Even in hard cases, one party has a right to win. His theory of adjudication is tied to a theory of what law is. For Dworkin, law embraces moral and political as well as strictly legal rights.[5] Dworkin develops a third theory of law. Law is neither merely the rights and duties created by legislation, custom and precedent; nor is law merely the edicts of natural law or morality. Rather, law is the body of rights given expression to in legislation, custom and precedent, plus the political and moral rights that are implied by the political theory that best explains and justifies the existing legislation, custom and precedent. The task of a super-human judge, Hercules, is to construct a political and moral theory that best explains and justifies the existing legal material, that ruling theory being the best guide to the rights Hercules must apply to reach the correct decision[6] in a hard case. Dworkin has produced a sophisticated version of the 'Open Sesame'[7] theory of adjudication.

Dworkin argues that his theory is not defeated by complaints about judicial law-making or retroactivity. Hercules decides hard common law cases on grounds of principle (weighing rights) not policy. Hence he is not a quasi-legislator, and the principles are not applied ex post facto.[8]

My concern is with Dworkin's claim that the rights thesis 'provides a more satisfactory explanation of how judges use precedent in hard cases than the explanation provided by any theory that gives a more prominent place to policy.'[9] He asserts a link between principled adjudication and the doctrine of precedent.

[4] *The Concept of Law* (Oxford, 1961).

[5] Dworkin, Introduction pxii: '... individuals may have legal rights other than those created by explicit decision or practice; that is, they may have rights to specific adjudicative decisions even in hard cases when no explicit decision or practice requires a decision either way.'
In deciding hard cases, judges rely on principles as well as rules. Dworkin's contention is that these principles are part of 'law', and not something extra-legal which a judge has a discretion when and how to apply. Dworkin therefore redefines these principles as legal rights.

[6] In Dworkin's jurisprudence, to every hard case there is an uniquely correct solution. If judges fail to weigh rights correctly it is not because of any ambiguity in the question posed and not because of any incompatibility between the rights. There are only practical difficulties: failures to understand the question, defects in moral reasoning powers. Dworkin has reintroduced into jurisprudence the errors of a monist vision so powerfully and persistently exposed in other areas of life by Isaiah Berlin. Sir Isaiah's writings develop the central theme that values and experience cannot be accommodated within a consistent framework without the loss of much that is thought valuable. The very notion of harmony and unity denigrates man by denying the heterogeneous quality of human life. This is as powerful a critique of a legal philosophy as it is of a political philosophy. Hercules cannot claim immunity from the painful dilemmas of choice felt by all other men.

[7] Lord Reid 'The Judge as Lawmaker', 12 *Journal of the Society of Public Teachers of Law* 22. 'There was a time when it was thought almost indecent to suggest that judges make law – they only declare it. Those with a taste for fairy tales seem to have thought that in some Aladdin's cave there is hidden the common law in all its splendour and that on a judge's appointment there descends on him knowledge of the magic words Open Sesame. Bad decisions are given when a judge muddles the pass word and the wrong door opens. But we do not believe in fairy tales any more.'

[8] Dworkin, p85.

[9] Dworkin, p87.

'An argument of principle can supply a justification for a particular decision, under the doctrine of responsibility, only if the principle cited can be shown to be consistent with earlier decisions not recanted, and with decisions that the institution is prepared to make in the hypothetical circumstances. That is hardly surprising, but the argument would not hold if judges based their decisions on arguments of policy. They would be free to say that some policy might be adequately served by serving it in the case at bar, providing, for example, just the right subsidy to some troubled industry, so that neither earlier decisions nor hypothetical future decisions need be understood as serving the same policy.'[10]

Dworkin explains that the doctrine of precedent gives a judicial decision two types of force. It has enactment force (its effect on future cases covered by its exact words) and gravitational force (its influence on later cases that fall outside the language of its opinion).[11] The language of a judicial decision does not explain its gravitational force. Nor do arguments of reliance, convenience, or accumulated wisdom. Gravitational force is justified by 'the fairness of treating like cases alike'.[12]

Because precedent is based on fairness, a judicial decision has gravitational force only if it was decided on grounds of principle. If an earlier decision is seen as justified by an argument of policy, then it only has enactment force.[13]

II

The doctrine of precedent is difficult to reconcile with a theory of adjudication based on the entitlement of the litigants to the correct decision (reached by weighing their competing rights). A judge striving to reach the right answer in a hard case has no need for rules of precedent obliging him to give gravitational or enactment force to past decisions. If the judge believes an earlier decision was correct, he will apply its reasoning and its conclusion to the present case without being forced to do so by rules of precedent. He already has an obligation to reach the right decision. If precedent is to add something to the fundamental duty of the judge to weigh rights, it can only be a role that challenges the very roots of the rights thesis. Precedent demands that a judge must give consideration to an earlier decision not because he thinks the decision was a correct one, but, rather, even though he thinks it was (legally) incorrect. Stare decisis is only of importance in so far as it ensures respect for authorities that would otherwise be ignored.[14] Precedent, far from being explained and justified by fairness, is opposed to fairness, if fairness means deciding cases according to rights.

[10] Dworkin, p88.
[11] Dworkin, p111.
[12] Dworkin, p113 (and pp318–319 in 'A Reply to Critics').
[13] Dworkin, p113.
[14] Radin, 33 *Columbia Law Review* 199. The fact that precedent is redundant if it compels respect only for correct decisions explains the contempt in which precedent is often held.
See Bentham's outburst (in his *Constitutional Code*, Book 2, Art 49): precedent 'is acting without reason, to the declared exclusion of reason, and thereby in declared opposition to reason' (cited in Goodhart, 50 *Law Quarterly Review* 40, 46).
Similarly, in Shakespeare's *The Merchant of Venice* (Act IV, Scene I) Portia declares: ' 'Twill be recorded for a precedent, And many an error by the same example Will rush into the state. It cannot be.'

Hercules is, it is true, obliged to develop a theory of mistakes to enable him to avoid giving gravitation force (and, perhaps, also enactment force) to at least some wrong decisions.[15] It is doubtful whether he can avoid giving force to all wrong decisions. But, even if he can, he has merely anaesthetised the role of precedent; stare decisis would become redundant in the right thesis, since that thesis already demands that the judge decides each case by weighing and applying competing rights.

'Fairness' cannot be the justification for the repetition of wrong decisions.[16]

<h1 style="text-align:center">III</h1>

Can Dworkin escape from the arguments that precedent is redundant in the rights thesis, and that whenever precedent is given a role it conflicts with fairness?

We can reject two weak defences of precedent as fairness in the right thesis. Precedent could serve a secretarial role, the past decision being a guide to the present judge on how to weigh precedents and statutes.[17] The difficulty here is to explain why a balancing of entitlements done 50, 100 or 200 years ago should bind today's judge, particularly as new statutes have been enacted, and the ruling political theory thereby changed. The second weak justification argues that the judge in the earlier case was better qualified, and so more likely to develop correctly the political theory than is the judge in the present case. This explanation of precedent as fairness is, at best, only acceptable when the earlier decision emanated from a superior court (and the explanation does not allow for changes in the ruling political theory that have occurred since the decision of the earlier court).

The only strong defence open to Dworkin is to argue that precedent is required by the rights thesis, and is based on fairness in giving the litigants their entitlements, because the earlier decision developed the law in some way. Without the earlier decision the law would be different in content. The past decision is thus itself an entitlement, one that judges would be in danger of ignoring but for the doctrine of precedent.[18]

The acceptance of judicial decisions as entitlements seems essential if Dworkin is to allow for the development of the common law. The insistence that the common

---

[15] Dworkin, pp119-122

[16] Swift (in *Gulliver's Travels* – 'A Voyage to the Houyhnhnms', Ch. 5) explains: 'It is a maxim among these lawyers that whatever has been done before may legally be done again, and therefore they take special care to record all the decisions formerly made against common justice and the general reason of mankind. These, under the name of precedents, they produce as authorities to justify the most iniquitous opinions, and the judges never fail of decreeing accordingly.'
However, Joseph Raz, in 'Professor Dworkin's Theory of Rights' (1978) 26 *Political Studies* 123, 135 argues that sometimes there are good reasons to perpetuate a decision that should not, in the first place, have been made.

[17] Cardozo *The Nature of the Judicial Process* (p149): '... the labour of judges would be increased almost to the breaking point if every past decision could be re-opened in every case.'

[18] Dworkin hints at this interpretation. He says, at p113: 'A precedent is the report of an earlier political decision; the very fact of that decision, as a piece of political history, provides some reason for deciding other cases in a similar way in the future.' The earlier decision has a force independent of that possessed by the rights weighed in it.

law evolves can be termed the 'Galileo' theory of adjudication.[19] Without it, *Donoghue* v *Stevenson*[20] would have been similarly decided in 1922, 1832 or 1632 (if an analogy can be found for ginger-beer and glass bottles). Other judicial decisions would not influence the correct result in *Donoghue* v *Stevenson*, whenever litigated, if those decisions are merely the correct weighings of existing entitlements. The common law develops because wrong judicial decisions (ie ones in which rights are defectively weighed) create new rights.[21]

---

[19] In *Lister* v *Romford Ice and Cold Storage Co* [1957] AC 555, 591-592, Lord Radcliffe said: 'No one really doubts that the common law is a body of law which develops in process of time in response to the development of the society in which it rules. Its movement may not be perceptible at any distinct point in time, nor can we always say how it gets from one point to another; but I do not think that, for all that, we need abandon the conviction of Galileo that somehow, by some means, there is a movement that takes place.'

[20] [1932] AC 652.

[21] We can only avoid the conclusion that judicial decisions are entitlements by arguing that entitlements created by statute have a gravitational force of their own and so affect common law decisions in which they are not directly applied. Statutory entitlements will also cause a change in the ruling political theory.

Legal Concepts

25. THE ANALYSIS OF RIGHTS

W N HOHFELD
Fundamental Legal Conceptions as
Applied in Judicial Reasoning [1]
(1923)

One of the greatest hindrances to the clear understanding, the incisive statement, and the true solution of legal problems frequently arises from the express or tacit assumption that all legal relations may be reduced to 'rights' and 'duties', and that these latter categories are therefore adequate for the purpose of analysing even the most complex legal interests, such as trusts, options, escrows, 'future' interests, corporate interests, etc. Even if the difficulty related merely to inadequacy and ambiguity of terminology, its seriousness would nevertheless be worthy of definite recognition and persistent effort toward improvement; for in any closely reasoned problem, whether legal or non-legal, chameleon-hued words are a peril both to clear thought and to lucid expression. As a matter of fact, however, the above mentioned inadequacy and ambiguity of terms unfortunately reflect, all too often, corresponding paucity and confusion as regards actual legal conceptions. That this is so may appear in some measure from the discussion to follow.

The strictly fundamental legal relations are, after all, sui generis; and thus it is that attempts at formal definition are always unsatisfactory, if not altogether useless. Accordingly, the most promising line of procedure seems to consist in exhibiting all of the various relations in a scheme of 'opposites' and 'correlatives', and then proceeding to exemplify their individual scope and application in concrete cases. An effort will be made to pursue this method:

Opposites	right	privilege	power	immunity
	no-right	duty	disability	liability
Correlatives	right	privilege	power	immunity
	duty	no-right	liability	disability

---

[1] Hohfeld, W N (1923) *Fundamental Legal Conceptions as Applied in Judicial Reasoning.* Ed W W Cook. Yale Univesity Press, London.

RIGHTS AND DUTIES

As already intimated, the term 'rights' tends to be used indiscriminately to cover what in a given case may be a privilege, a power, or an immunity, rather than a right in the strictest sense. ...

Recognising, as we must, the very broad and indiscriminate use of the term 'right', what clue do we find, in ordinary legal discourse, towards limiting the word in question to a definite and appropriate meaning? That clue lies in the correlative 'duty', for it is certain that even those who use the word and the conception 'right' in the broadest possible way are accustomed to thinking of 'duty' as the invariable correlative. As said in *Lake Shore & MSR Co v Kurtz*:[2]

> 'A duty or a legal obligation is that which one ought or ought not to do. "Duty" and "right" are correlative terms. When a right is invaded, a duty is violated.'

In other words, if X has a right against Y that he shall stay off the former's land, the correlative (and equivalent) is that Y is under a duty toward X to stay off the place. If, as seems desirable, we should seek a synonym for the term 'right' in this limited and proper meaning, perhaps the word 'claim' would prove the best. The latter has the advantage of being a monosyllable. ...

PRIVILEGES AND 'NO-RIGHTS'

As indicated in the above scheme of jural relations, a privilege is the opposite of a duty, and the correlative of a 'no-right'. In the example last put, whereas X has a *right* or *claim* that Y, the other man, should stay off the land, he himself has the *privilege* of entering on the land; or, in equivalent words, X does not have a duty to stay off. The privilege of entering is the negation of a duty to stay off. As indicated by this case, some caution is necessary at this point; for, always when it is said that a given privilege is the mere negation of a *duty*, what is meant, of course, is a duty having a content or tenor precisely *opposite* to that of the privilege in question. Thus, if, for some special reason, X has contracted with Y to go on the former's own land, it is obvious that X has, as regards Y, both the privilege of entering and the *duty of entering*. The privilege is perfectly consistent with this sort of duty – for the latter is of the *same* content or tenor as the privilege; – but it still holds good that, as regards Y, X's privilege if entering is the precise negation of a duty *to stay off*. Similarly, if A has not contracted with B to perform certain work for the latter, A's privilege of *not* doing so is the very negation of a duty of *doing* so. Here again the duty contrasted is of a content or tenor exactly opposite to that of the privilege.

Passing now to the question of 'correlatives', it will be remembered, of course, that a duty is the invariable correlative of that legal relation which is most properly called a right or claim. That being so, if further evidence be needed as to the fundamental and important difference between a right (or claim) and a privilege, surely it is found in the fact that the correlative of the latter relation is a 'no-right',

---

[2] (1894) 10 Ind App 60.

there being no single term available to express the latter conception. Thus, the correlative of X's right that Y shall not enter on the land is Y's duty not to enter; but the correlative of X's privilege of entering himself is manifestly Y's 'no-right' that X shall not enter.

In view of the considerations thus far emphasised, the importance of keeping the conception of a right (or claim) and the conception of a privilege quite distinct from each other seems evident; and, more than that, it is equally clear that there should be a separate term to represent the latter relation. No doubt, as already indicated, it is very common to use the term 'right' indiscriminately, even when the relation designated is really that of privilege; and only too often this identity of terms has involved for the particular speaker or writer a confusion or blurring of ideas. ...

... On grounds already emphasised, it would seem that the line of reasoning pursued by Lord Lindley in the great case of *Quinn* v *Leathem*[3] is deserving of comment:

> 'The plaintiff had the ordinary *rights* of the British subject. He was *at liberty* to earn his living in his own way, provided he did not violate some special law prohibiting him from so doing, and provided he did not infringe the rights of other people. *This liberty* involved *the liberty* to deal with other persons who were willing to deal with him. *This liberty* is a *right* recognised by law; its *correlative* is the general *duty* of every one not to prevent the free exercise of this *liberty* except so far as his own liberty of action may justify him in so doing. But a person's *liberty* or *right* to deal with others is nugatory unless they are at liberty to deal with him if they choose to do so. Any interference with their liberty to deal with him affects him.'

A 'liberty' considered as a legal relation (or 'right' in the loose and generic sense of that term) must mean, if it have any definite content at all, precisely the same thing as *privilege*; and certainly that is the fair connotation of the term as used the first three times in the passage quoted. It is equally clear, as already indicated, that such a privilege or liberty to deal with others at will might very conceivably exist without any peculiar concomitant rights against 'third parties' as regards certain kinds of interference.[4] Whether there should be such concomitant rights (or claims) is ultimately a question of justice and policy; and it should be considered, as such, on its merits. The only correlative logically implied by the privileges or liberties in question are the 'no-rights' of 'third parties'. It would therefore be a non sequitur to conclude from the mere existence of such liberties that 'third parties' are under a *duty* not to interfere, etc. Yet in the middle of the above passage from Lord Lindley's opinion there is a sudden and question-begging shift in the use of terms. First, the 'liberty' in question is transmuted into a 'right'; and then, possibly under the seductive influence of the latter word, it is assumed that the 'correlative' must be 'the general duty of every one not to prevent', etc.

Another interesting and instructive example may be taken from Lord Bowen's oft-quoted opinion in *Mogul Steamship Co* v *McGregor*.[5]

[3] [1901] AC 495, 534.
[4] Compare *Allen* v *Flood* [1898] AC 1.
[5] (1889) 23 QBD 59.

'We are presented in this case with an apparent conflict or antimony between two rights that are equally regarded by the law – the right of the plaintiffs to be protected in the legitimate exercise of their trade, and the right of the defendants to carry on their business as seems best to them, provided they commit no wrong to others.'

As the learned judge states, the conflict or antinomy is only apparent; but this fact seems to be obscured by the very indefinite and rapidly shifting meanings with which the term 'right' is used in the above quoted language. Construing the passage as a whole, it seems plain enough that by 'the right of the plaintiffs' in relation to the defendants a legal right or claim in the strict sense must be meant; whereas by 'the right of the defendants' in relation to the plaintiffs a legal privilege must be intended. That being so, the 'two rights' mentioned in the beginning of the passage, being respectively claim and privilege, could not be in conflict with each other. To the extent that the defendants have privileges the plaintiffs have no rights; and, conversely, to the extent that the plaintiffs have rights the defendants have no privileges ('no-privilege' equals duty of opposite tenor).

. . .

POWERS AND LIABILITIES

As indicated in the preliminary scheme of jural relations, a legal power (as distinguished, of course, from a mental or physical power) is the opposite of legal disability, and the correlative of legal liability. But what is the intrinsic nature of a legal power as such? Is it possible to analyse the conception represented by this constantly employed and very important term of legal discourse? Too close an analysis might seem metaphysical rather than useful; so that what is here presented is intended only as an approximate explanation, sufficient for all practical purposes.

A change in a given legal relation may result (1) from some super added fact or group of facts not under the volitional control of a human being (or human beings); or (2) from some super added fact or group of facts which are under the volitional control of one or more human beings. As regards the second class of cases, the person (or persons) whose volitional control is paramount may be said to have the (legal) power to effect the particular change of legal relations that is involved in the problem.

This second class of cases – powers in the technical sense – must now be further considered. The nearest synonym for any ordinary case seems to be (legal) 'ability', – the latter being obviously the opposite of 'inability', or 'disability'. The term 'right', so frequently and loosely used in the present connection, is an unfortunate term for the purpose, – a not unusual result being confusion of thought as well as ambiguity of expression. The term 'capacity' is equally unfortunate; for, as we have already seen, when used with discrimination, this word denotes a particular group of operative facts, and not a legal relation of any kind.

Many examples of legal powers may readily be given. Thus, X, the owner of ordinary personal property 'in a tangible object' has the power to extinguish his own legal interest (rights, powers, immunities, etc), through that totality of operative facts known as abandonment; and – simultaneously and correlatively – to create in other persons privileges and powers relating to the abandoned object – eg the power to acquire title to the latter by appropriating it. *Similarly*, X has the power to transfer his interest to Y – that is, to extinguish his own interest and concomitantly create in Y a new and corresponding interest. So also Y has the power to create contractual obligations of various kinds. Agency cases are likewise instructive. By the use of some *metaphorical* expression such as the Latin, qui facit per alium, facit per se, the true nature of agency relations is only too frequently obscured. The creation of an agency relation involves, inter alia, the grant of legal powers to the so-called agent, and the creation of correlative liabilities in the principal. That is to say, one party, P, has the power to create agency powers in another party, A, – for example, the power to convey P's property, the power to impose (so-called) contractual obligations on P, the power to discharge a debt owing to P, the power to 'receive' title to property so that it shall vest in P, and so forth. In passing, it may be well to observe that the term 'authority', so frequently used in agency cases, is very ambiguous and slippery in its connotation. Properly employed in the present connection, the word seems to be an abstract or qualitative term corresponding to the concrete 'authorisation' – the latter consisting of a particular group of operative facts taking place between the principal and the agent. All too often, however, the term in question is so used as to blend and confuse these operative facts with the powers and privileges thereby created in the agent. A careful discrimination in these particulars would, it is submitted, go far toward clearing up certain problems in the law of agency.

... Passing now to the field of contracts, suppose A mails a letter to B offering to sell the former's land, Whiteacre, to the latter for ten thousand dollars, such letter being duly received. The operative facts thus far mentioned have created a power as regards B and a correlative liability as regards A. B, by dropping a letter of acceptance in the box has the power to impose a potential or inchoate obligation ex contractu on A and himself; and, assuming that the land is worth fifteen thousand dollars, that particular legal quantity – the 'power *plus* liability' relation between A and B – seems to be worth about five thousand dollars to B. The liability of A will continue for a reasonable time unless, in exercise of his power to do so, A previously extinguishes it by that series of operative facts known as 'revocation'. These last matters are usually described by saying that A's 'offer' will 'continue' or 'remain open' for a reasonable time, or for the definite time actually specified, unless A previously 'withdraws' or 'revokes' such offer. While, no doubt, in the great majority of cases no harm results from the use of such expressions, yet these forms of statement seem to represent a blending of non-legal and legal quantities which, in any problem requiring careful reasoning, should preferably be kept distinct. An offer, considered as a series of physical and mental operative facts, has spent its force and become functus officio as soon as such series has been completed by the 'offeree's receipt'. The real question is therefore as to the *legal effect*, if any, at that moment of time. If the latter consists of B's power and A's correlative liability, manifestly it is those *legal relations* that 'continue' or 'remain open' until modified by revocation or other operative facts. What has thus far been said concerning contracts completed by mail would seem to apply, mutatis mutandis, to every type of contract. Even where the parties are in the presence of each other, the offer creates a liability against the offeror, together with a correlative power in favour of the offeree. The only distinction for present purposes would be in the fact that such power and such liability would expire within a very short period of time.

... In view of what has already been said, very little may suffice concerning a liability as such. The latter, as we have seen, is the correlative of power, and the opposite of immunity (or exemption). While no doubt the term 'liability' is often loosely used as a synonym for 'duty', or 'obligation', it is believed, from an extensive survey of judicial precedents, that the connotation already adopted as most appropriate to the word in question is fully justified.

. . .

IMMUNITIES AND DISABILITIES

As already brought out, immunity is the correlative of disability ('no-power'), and the opposite, or negation, of liability. Perhaps it will also be plain, from the preliminary outline and from the discussion down to this point, that a power bears the same general contrast to an immunity that a right does to a privilege. A right is one's affirmative claim against another, and a privilege is one's freedom from the right or claim of another. Similarly, power is one's affirmative 'control' over a given legal relation as against another; whereas an immunity is one's freedom from the legal power or 'control' of another as regards some legal relation.

A few examples may serve to make this clear. X, a landowner, has, as we have seen, power to alienate to Y or to any other ordinary party. On the other hand, X has also various immunities as against Y, and all other ordinary parties. For Y is under a disability (ie has no power) so far as shifting the legal interest either to himself or to a third party is concerned; and what is true of Y applies similarly to every one else who has not by virtue of special operative facts acquired a power to alienate X's property. If, indeed, a sheriff has been duly empowered by a writ of execution to sell X's interest, that is a very different matter: correlative to such sheriff's power would be the *liability* of X – the very opposite of immunity (or exemption). It is elementary, too, that as against the sheriff, X might be immune or exempt in relation to certain parcels of property, and be liable as to others. Similarly, if an agent has been duly appointed by X to sell a given piece of property, then, as to the latter, X has, in relation to such agent, a liability rather than an immunity.

... In the latter part of the preceding discussion, eight conceptions of the law have been analysed and compared in some detail, the purpose having been to exhibit not only their intrinsic meaning and scope, but also their relations to one another and the methods by which they are applied, in judicial reasoning, to the solution of concrete problems of litigation. Before concluding this branch of the discussion a general suggestion may be ventured as to the great practical importance of a clear appreciation of the distinctions and discriminations set forth. If a homely metaphor be permitted, these eight conceptions, – rights and duties, privileges and no-rights, powers and liabilities, immunities and disabilities, – seem to be what may be called 'the lowest common denominators of the law'. Ten fractions (1-3, 2-5, etc), may, *superficially*, seem so different from one another as to defy comparison. If, however, they are expressed in terms of their lowest common denominators, (5-15, 6-15, etc); comparison becomes easy, and fundamental similarity may be discovered. The same thing is of course true as regards the lowest generic conceptions to which any and all 'legal quantities' may be reduced.

Reverting, for example, to the subject of powers, it might be difficult at first glance to discover any essential and fundamental similarity between conditional sales of personality, escrow transactions, option agreements, agency relations, powers of appointment, etc. But if all these relations are reduced to their lowest generic terms, the conceptions of legal power and legal liability are seen to be dominantly, though not exclusively, applicable throughout the series. By such a process it becomes possible not only to discover essential similarities and illuminating analogies in the midst of what appears superficially to be infinite and hopeless variety, but also to discern common principles of justice and policy underlying the various jural problems involved. An indirect, yet very practical, consequence is that it frequently becomes feasible, by virtue of such analysis, to use as persuasive authorities judicial precedents that might otherwise seem altogether irrelevant. If this point be valid with respect to powers, it would seem to be equally so as regards all of the other basic conceptions of the law. In short, the deeper the analysis, the greater becomes one's perception of fundamental unity and harmony in the law.

RONALD DWORKIN
Taking Rights Seriously [6]
(1977)

Legal argument, in hard cases, turns on contested concepts whose nature and function are very much like the concept of the character of a game. These include several of the substantive concepts through which the law is stated, like the concepts of a contract and of property. But they also include two concepts of much greater relevance to the present argument. The first is the idea of the 'intention' or 'purpose' of a particular statute or statutory clause. This concept provides a bridge between the political justification of the general idea that statutes create rights and those hard cases that ask what rights a particular statute has created. The second is the concept

[6] Dworkin, Ronald (1977) *Taking Rights Seriously*. Gerald Duckworth, London, pp105-107.

of principles that 'underlie' or are 'embedded in' the positive rules of law. This concept provides a bridge between the political justification of the doctrine that like cases should be decided alike and those hard cases in which it is unclear what that general doctrine requires. These concepts together define legal rights as a function, though a very special function, of political rights. If a judge accepts the settled practices of his legal system – if he accepts, that is, the autonomy provided by its distinct constitutive and regulative rules – then he must – according to the doctrine of political responsibility, accept some general political theory that justifies these practices. The concepts of legislative purpose and common law principles are devices for applying that general political theory to controversial issues about legal rights.

We might therefore do well to consider how a philosophical judge might develop in appropriate cases, theories of what legislative purpose and legal principles require. We shall find that he would construct these theories in the same manner as a philosophical referee would construct the character of a game. I have invented, for this purpose, a lawyer of superhuman skill, learning, patience and acumen, whom I shall call Hercules. I suppose that Hercules is a judge in some representative American jurisdiction. I assume that he accepts the main uncontroversial constitutive and regulative rules of the law in his jurisdiction. He accepts, that is, that statutes have the general power to create and extinguish legal rights, and that judges have the general duty to follow earlier decisions of their court or higher courts whose rationale, as lawyers say, extends to the case at bar.

Suppose there is a written constitution in Hercules' jurisdiction which provides that no law shall be valid if it establishes a religion. The legislature passes a law purporting to grant free busing to children in parochial schools. Does the grant establish a religion?[7] The words of the constitutional provision might support either view. Hercules must nevertheless decide whether the child who appears before him has a right to her bus ride.

He might begin by asking why the constitution has any power at all to create or destroy rights. If citizens have a background right to salvation through an established church, as many believe they do, then this must be an important right. Why does the fact that a group of men voted otherwise several centuries ago prevent this background right from being made a legal right as well? His answer must take some form such as this. The constitution sets out a general political scheme that is sufficiently just to be taken as settled for reasons of fairness. Citizens take the benefit of living in a society whose institutions are arranged and governed in accordance with that scheme, and they must take the burdens as well, at least until a new scheme is put into force either by discrete amendment or general revolution. But Hercules must then ask just what scheme of principles has been settled. He must construct, that is, a constitutional theory; since he is Hercules we may suppose that he can develop a full political theory that justifies the constitution as a whole. It must be a scheme that fits the particular rules of this constitution, of course. It

[7] See *Everson v Board of Education*, 330 US 1 (1947).

cannot include a powerful background right to an established church. But more than one fully specified theory may fit the specific provision about religion sufficiently well. One theory might provide, for example, that it is wrong for the government to enact any legislation that will cause great social tension or disorder; so that since the establishment of a church will have that effect, it is wrong to empower the legislature to establish one. Another theory will provide a background right to religious liberty, and therefore argue that an established church is wrong, not because it will be socially disruptive, but because it violates that background right. In that case Hercules must turn to the remaining constitutional rules and settled practices under these rules to see which of these two theories provides a smoother fit with the constitutional scheme as a whole.

But the theory that is superior under this test will nevertheless be insufficiently concrete to decide some cases. Hercules decides that the establishment provision is justified by a right to religious liberty rather than any goal of social order. It remains to ask what, more precisely, religious liberty is. Does a right to religious liberty include the right not to have one's taxes used for any purpose that helps a religion to survive? Or simply not to have one's taxes used to benefit one religion at the expense of another? If the former, then the free transportation legislation violates that right, but if the latter it does not. The institutional structure of rules and practice may not be sufficiently detailed to rule out either of these two conceptions of religious liberty, or to make one a plainly superior justification of that structure. At some point in his career Hercules must therefore consider the question not just as an issue of fit between a theory and the rules of the institution, but as an issue of political philosophy as well. He must decide which conception is a more satisfactory elaboration of the general idea of religious liberty. He must decide that question because he cannot otherwise carry far enough the project he began. He cannot answer in sufficient detail the question of what political scheme the constitution establishes.

So Hercules is driven, by this project, to a process of reasoning that is much like the process of the self-conscious chess referee. He must develop a theory of the constitution, in the shape of a complex set of principles and policies that justify that scheme of government, just as the chess referee is driven to develop a theory about the character of his game. He must develop that theory by referring alternatively to political philosophy and institutional detail. He must generate possible theories justifying different aspects of the scheme and test the theories against the broader institution. When the discriminating power of that test is exhausted, he must elaborate the contested concepts that the successful theory employs.